U.S. POLITICS AND
THE GLOBAL ECONOMY

U.S. Politics and the Global Economy

Corporate Power, Conservative Shift

Ronald W. Cox
Daniel Skidmore-Hess

LYNNE
RIENNER
PUBLISHERS

BOULDER
LONDON

Published in the United States of America in 1999 by
Lynne Rienner Publishers, Inc.
1800 30th Street, Boulder, Colorado 80301

and in the United Kingdom by
Lynne Rienner Publishers, Inc.
3 Henrietta Street, Covent Garden, London WC2E 8LU

Library of Congress Cataloging-in-Publication Data
Cox, Ronald W., 1962–
   U.S. politics and the global economy : corporate power,
conservative shift / by Ronald W. Cox and Daniel Skidmore-Hess.
      p.   cm.
   Includes bibliographical references and index.
   ISBN 1-55587-771-0 (alk. paper)
   1. United States—Economic policy. 2. United States—Politics and
government—20th century. 3. Ideology—United States—History.
4. International economic integration. I. Skidmore-Hess, Daniel,
1964–   II. Title.
HC106.C73   1999
337.73—dc21   98-29595
                                                                CIP

British Cataloguing in Publication Data
A Cataloguing in Publication record for this book
is available from the British Library.

Printed and bound in the United States of America

5 4 3 2 1

P 77187

Contents

Introduction: A Critical-Historical Perspective on Globalization   1

1   The New Deal and Liberal Hegemony   17

2   The Postwar Political Economy   37

3   Business Conflict and Cold War Ideology   67

4   Liberal Globalization in the 1960s   105

5   The End of Bretton Woods   137

6   The Reagan Revolution   161

7   Conclusion: The 1990s and Beyond   203

List of Acronyms   223
Selected Bibliography   225
Index   237
About the Book   250

Introduction:
A Critical-Historical Perspective
on Globalization

Economic power has long intersected with political and ideological dimensions of power. The ability of owners of economic assets to shift production from the sovereign territory of one nation-state to another is a crucial and ever-increasing manifestation of the linkages between private economic power and political capability. The fact that more global companies are engaging in greater volumes of trade and foreign production than at any other time in history has placed enormous constraints and pressures on policymakers to compete for sources of economic wealth.[1]

The nature of the relationship between the globalization of the world's economic resources and the public policies adopted by nation-states has been the subject of considerable discussion and debate in recent academic literature. Most discussions have tended to view the march toward globalization as a product of the inherently expansionist tendencies of capitalist economic actors to search for increased markets and lower production costs in the face of increasingly sophisticated technological competition. In this view, globalization is an economic process driven by the logic of capitalist production relations, which necessitates that governments amend their domestic policies so as not to get left behind in the race for access to global capital investments. This perspective tends to see the globalization of the world economy as unidirectional: driven by the competitive pressures of the private market that then influence the policies of nation-states around the world.[2]

Our analysis focuses attention on the role of both structural economic factors *and* political coalitions in shaping the pace, direction, and scope of globalization by establishing particular global structures that provide ideological and institutional support for increased trade and investment. Because the United States has been the dominant economic, political, and ideological actor in post–World War II global politics, some of the most important and influential political coalitions behind the long-term processes

1

of globalization have been based in the United States and have long exported an ideological and political vision of the limits and possibilities of
globalization to other parts of the world.[3] For us, then, globalization is not
simply a process driven by the economic tendencies of the capitalist marketplace to expand, innovate, and invest on a global scale. Instead, globalization is a historical process led by constellations of political actors,
many of which originated in the overlapping worlds of business and politics in the United States.[4] The most aggressive and systematic efforts of
U.S.-based political coalitions to promote increased investment and trade
in Europe originated with the so-called Bretton Woods coalition of 1944,
where we begin our analysis. This coalition was established by U.S. political and business elites as a response to the destructive tariff wars of the
1930s, which in many accounts led to the carnage and devastation of
World War II. The task for Bretton Woods planners was to fashion a political and economic system that could alleviate the tendencies toward tariff
wars and facilitate global negotiation toward free trade.

We argue, in short, that the Bretton Woods coalition was a set of
global rules and regulations promoted by a political coalition of business
internationalists and political elites in the United States as a way of overcoming the "beggar-thy-neighbor" policies of the 1930s. But the Bretton
Woods system, as some have called it, was deliberately restrictive in the
limits it placed on financial capital mobility, reflecting a series of compromises among business groups, political elites, and trade unions in the
United States and Western Europe.[5] The essence of the Bretton Woods system was that trade barriers would be gradually reduced by negotiation between the major capitalist powers but that governments would be able to
defend independent monetary and fiscal policies systematically by limiting
financial capital mobility, and business nationalists would be able to negotiate exceptions to the tariff reduction tendencies of the system.

By the mid-1970s, however, the Bretton Woods system had been liberalized considerably. Business internationalists and political elites in the
United States took the lead in aggressively lobbying their domestic government and foreign governments for removal of restrictive financial capital controls. Other business groups, beset with foreign competition that
threatened erosion of market share or even bankruptcy, advocated that new
protectionist barriers be erected by their home governments to protect their
domestic U.S. industries.[6] In addition, a whole range of industries, both
nationalist and internationalist, expanded their political lobbying networks
to advance a series of concessions from the U.S. government, including
tax breaks and subsidies, to allow them to compete more aggressively with
foreign firms.[7]

The efforts of some U.S. business internationalists to weaken the Bretton Woods system of restrictions on capital mobility reflect both economic

and political trends, although many analysts treat the "collapse of Bretton Woods" as solely an economic phenomenon.[8] Our analysis recognizes that U.S. business internationalists have sought to lower their production costs and, in some cases, to overcome declining rates of profit by diversifying production overseas to acquire cheaper sources of capital and lower productive inputs. The rise of Japanese and German global economic competition has been a driving force behind the efforts of U.S.-based global companies to diversify their production lines further and expand their export markets around the world. And, most important, increased international competition among multinational banking corporations has given these businesses a vested interest in liberalizing global capital markets.[9]

However, these multinational companies, many with headquarters in the United States, have not abandoned their reliance on the U.S. nation-state, as some analysts have concluded. Instead, U.S. business internationalists have relied on U.S. political elites to enhance their global competitiveness through deregulation of capital markets, starting with the United States, extending to various European nation-states, and culminating in an aggressive ideological and political effort in the 1980s and 1990s to promote opened markets and freer capital investment in the less developed world. At the same time, the efforts to promote capital mobility in the United States have been coupled with an unprecedented lobbying campaign to roll back the country's social welfare programs and to enlist the support of the U.S. government in weakening the political and economic position of its labor unions.[10]

Thus the erosion of the so-called Bretton Woods system is both a product of intercapitalist competition, political and ideological conflict, and the articulation of class interests that have been strongly expressed in the shifting political and economic coalitions in the United States since 1950. Seen in this light, globalization is not simply a product of market trends but part of a larger political and ideological process that has involved the establishment of extensive lobbying networks created by global business elites, often led by groups based in the United States, to achieve political support from the United States and other governments in a period of increasing international economic competition.

Our analysis examines the U.S.-based political coalitions that have helped fashion global institutions from the post–World War II period to the present. These coalitions have included business organizations and blocs of political elites from the Democratic and Republican parties that have advanced particular international and domestic policy agendas based on their immediate political, economic, and ideological interests. We argue that these interests are reflected in political debates in the U.S. nation-state at the level of congressional and presidential elections and have resulted in a decline of liberalism in the United States. The decline is evidenced by the rise of conservative political coalitions in both the Democratic and Republican Parties that have advocated substantial "reform" and curtailment of the U.S. welfare state.

The "right turn" of U.S. politics and ideological discourse is expressed in an assault on a supposedly outdated liberalism. A Democratic president has opportunistically declared that "the era of big government is over," and a more committedly conservative congressional majority seems somewhat serious about actually dismantling it. Our perspective is that the great bulk of the welfare state as well as the sizable U.S. defense budget are key components of corporate hegemony in the United States. This is not because the welfare state co-opts or buys off the poor, but for the simple and direct reason that its beneficiaries are primarily middle- to upper-income groups.

Certain components of the welfare state, such as Medicaid, Aid to Families with Dependent Children (AFDC), and affirmative action, are being downsized or even eliminated because they benefit or are perceived to benefit primarily marginal social groups such as the poor or African Americans. The identity politics of the present, expressed in the reactive surge in 1994 of "angry white males" in the middle- to upper-income strata to the Republican Party, are intertwined with the fiscal and monetary crises of U.S. liberalism.[11] Our perspective is that in the wake of the collapse of the Bretton Woods system and the parallel decline in the capacity of the state to expand the welfare state in a framework of low taxes, a variety of neoliberal and neoconservative projects have vied for position. These projects began with the crisis-borne election of Richard Nixon in 1968 and continue up to the recent dueling of Bill Clinton, Bob Dole, Newt Gingrich, Pat Buchanan, and Ross Perot. What typifies all these political tendencies is their common attack on the legacy and legitimacy of "big government" as a signifier of an old and mythically overgenerous liberalism.

The level of analysis throughout this book is the intersection of international and domestic politics in the United States. The remainder of this chapter subdivides the international and domestic levels of our analysis in order to illustrate the linkages between increased globalization and domestic U.S. politics. U.S.-based political coalitions took the lead in supporting the expansionary Bretton Woods system, which fixed the dollar to gold at $35 an ounce and restricted capital movements internationally. The implications for U.S. domestic politics included the establishment of an international monetary framework that allowed for an expansionary fiscal and monetary U.S. state. The Bretton Woods environment was conducive to the Great Society programs of the 1960s, expansionary U.S. fiscal and monetary policies, and dramatic increases in military spending.

The collapse of the Bretton Woods system has been defined by the liberalization of financial markets, floating exchange rates whose values are determined by international currency speculators and financial institutions, and increased economic competition for overseas capital and market shares characterizing the period after 1973. We argue that the collapse was not solely predetermined by economic trends but was advocated by well-organized political coalitions that lobbied both internationally and domestically for a rollback of the Bretton Woods system.

With this in mind, we focus our analysis on the shifting political coalitions advocating a breakup of the Bretton Woods system and their impact on U.S. domestic politics. U.S.-based multinationals that once championed Bretton Woods found the system too restrictive by the 1960s and 1970s, when international competition increased, labor unions achieved notable gains, and the development of vast regulatory bureaucracies in the United States and Western Europe threatened to lower profit margins further.[12] These defectors from the Bretton Woods coalition have been an important political force internationally and in the realm of U.S. domestic politics. They have developed a political, economic, and ideological agenda responsible for creating the liberalized financial market structure of the post–Bretton Woods period, which has undermined expansionary fiscal and monetary policies in the United States and elsewhere, generating consistent attacks on the social welfare state in the process.

The remainder of this chapter identifies the international and domestic levels of analysis used throughout this book. We address four primary themes: (1) the role of U.S. elites in promoting Bretton Woods institutions internationally and New Deal policies domestically from the end of World War II through the 1960s, as well as business conflict over Bretton Woods and New Deal programs in the 1940s–1960s; (2) the domestic and international factors leading to the collapse of the Bretton Woods and New Deal coalitions in the mid-1970s and the implications for the social welfare state; (3) the rise of conservative coalitions within both the Democratic and Republican Parties that are increasingly funded by business coalitions advocating a right turn in U.S. social and fiscal policy; (4) the implications of such a right turn for U.S. domestic politics and how such shifts in political economy have affected elections at both the congressional and presidential levels.

THE BRETTON WOODS AND NEW DEAL COALITIONS: RESOLVING INTERBUSINESS CONFLICT

Business conflict is the key variable in our analysis of the crisis of liberalism in the United States. In our view, U.S. politics is typified by alignment politics expressed in electoral and legislative coalitions.[13] What distinguishes our perspective is the understanding that no alignment can gain significant influence without the leadership of some key segment of business. For example, as we argue elsewhere,[14] the 1993 congressional vote on the North American Free Trade Agreement (NAFTA) would not have been close were it not for the opposition of many business nationalists to the trade agreement.

Politics in the United States is best described as being dominated by the structural and ideological hegemony of business. Yet business "as a class" is internally divided along sectoral and industrial lines; key business groups and leaders diverge in their views and interests over many major issues. Further, as a constitutionally based electoral system, albeit one dominated by private campaign financiers and a systematically entrenched two-party framework, elite economic groups must gain the consent of a broader social base of voters and other supporters. These formations, which we refer to as "coalitions" or "blocs," have been subordinated, at least to this point in U.S. political history, to the interests of business, or more exactly to some particular segment of the dominant class.

The first and second chapters of this book focus on the rise of a liberal faction of business firms in the United States that promoted the New Deal in the 1930s and continued to advocate the preservation and growth of a social welfare state during the post–World War II period. These groups consisted of a bloc of capital-intensive investors concentrated in sectors of investment and commercial banking, oil, electrical machinery, agribusiness, and chemicals, as well as numerous capital-intensive manufacturing firms with considerable international investments in Western Europe.[15] For these firms, the New Deal promised regulatory and political stability that could help deter class conflict. Characterized by high productivity and profitability, considerable international investments, and a capital-intensive structure, these firms could afford the increased labor costs associated with New Deal social and regulatory policies.

Business opponents of the New Deal were concentrated in the relatively labor-intensive industries of textiles, clothing, and steel and iron production. These firms felt most threatened by the increased regulatory and social spending of the New Deal, which raised labor costs and undercut the slim profit margins of small businesses and labor-intensive manufacturing firms. This bloc of firms has been most committed to conservative political coalitions throughout the post–World War II period, especially the right wing of the Republican Party and the elevation of Barry Goldwater to the presidential nomination of 1964.[16] However, much of this right-wing business coalition was undercut by the Depression of the 1930s, which bankrupted and weakened small businesses opposed to the New Deal.[17]

In addition, the militarization of the U.S. economy during World War II provided a strong stimulus for the domestic economy, rescuing numerous manufacturing industries from bankruptcy and politically strengthening the faction of liberal, capital-intensive industries that had supported the New Deal.[18] This capital-intensive, pro–New Deal bloc of industries also joined with state elites in formulating the ideological and strategic rationale for rebuilding Western Europe in the aftermath of World War II. In Western Europe, as in the United States, this capital-intensive political coalition, often labeled business internationalists, was able to invest behind high tariff walls and accept capital controls and to tolerate the emergence of strong regulatory states and social welfare spending in exchange for political stability, which became the essence of the Bretton Woods system. The coalition also aggressively lobbied for international institutions such as the World Bank and the International Monetary Fund, which would provide resources for the creation of infrastructure and lending necessary to promote foreign investment and trade.

This group of capital-intensive foreign investors also lobbied the U.S. government for bilateral aid programs to Western Europe, including the Marshall Plan, the most extensive aid program in U.S. history, designed to facilitate the conditions for increased trade and investment in the region.[19] Debates over the Marshall Plan in the United States pitted business internationalists against their nationalist counterparts who had opposed the New Deal, had little or no stake in foreign investment, and were committed to a U.S. state that reduced its levels of social spending and foreign aid.

The ability of business internationalists to win support for extensive bilateral aid and Bretton Woods institutions hinged on couching them in terms of the imperative of U.S. national security and the start of the Cold War. The development of a vast military and security apparatus in the United States helped provide lucrative subsidies to a range of manufacturing industries that might have otherwise opposed the promotion of Bretton Woods and bilateral foreign aid programs. As we argue in Chapter 3, Cold War military spending became the U.S. version of Western European social welfare programs, providing extensive state payments to military and military-related manufacturing industries while integrating Western Europe into a military and economic partnership that would benefit business internationalists with European investments *and* business nationalists tied to the domestic U.S. market but dependent on military spending.

We also note in Chapter 3 that the role of business internationalists was important in providing political and ideological support for the strategic and economic programs that institutionalized the U.S.–Western European alliance. U.S.-based business firms with an interest in consolidating, enlarging, or beginning their foreign direct investments in Western Europe supported the European Economic Community (EEC). Business internationalists, especially those firms at the high end of the product life cycle, welcomed the opportunity to invest and trade within an expanded European market. After having passed through the stages of U.S. domestic production and trade, such multinationals had the size, resources and capital to dramatically expand their foreign direct investments.

THE COLLAPSE OF BRETTON WOODS: REVIVAL OF INTERBUSINESS CONFLICT

We argue in Chapter 4 that the mid-1960s and early 1970s saw the beginnings of what some have termed a crisis in U.S. hegemony.[20] The emergence of revived and internationally competitive German and Japanese economies meant shrinking market shares for U.S.-based multinational corporations. Relying on aggressive export strategies and strong state support for internationally competitive manufacturing and high-technology firms, the German and Japanese nation-states challenged U.S. businesses in Europe and the United States, a phenomenon that contributed to the decline in the real value of the dollar, as foreign and domestic investors were busy exchanging dollars for gold in the U.S. market.

Meanwhile the costs of U.S. hegemony were reflected in the spiraling commitments of the national security state. State spending on the Vietnam War escalated dramatically during the years 1965–1968, supported by an array of manufacturing industries buoyed by lucrative war contracts. Other business elites, however, started to question the war, largely because of its negative impact on the U.S. dollar.[21] By the late 1960s and early 1970s, business internationalists in investment and commercial banking, along with capital-intensive manufacturing industries with little or no ties to military spending, expressed opposition to the war and called for U.S. elites to de-escalate.

The increasingly competitive international climate of the late 1960s and early 1970s polarized business groups previously committed to Bretton Woods internationally and Great Society spending at home. More competitive U.S.-based oil, computer, banking, and capital-intensive manufacturing firms championed de-escalation in Vietnam, détente with the Soviet Union, and the opening of new foreign markets in Eastern Europe (and possibly the Soviet Union) as a strategy for reviving U.S. competitiveness.[22] These business internationalists further advocated expanding investment opportunities by deregulating foreign capital markets—a strategy aggressively pursued by U.S.-based multinational banks with considerable success—while maintaining U.S. efforts to reduce trade barriers with Western Europe.

Other business groups, especially business nationalists with investments concentrated in the United States and regionalists with investments concentrated in North America, and less competitive business internationalists, opposed efforts to liberalize trade and foreign capital markets.

Joined by military contractors dependent on high levels of Cold War spending, these interests opposed efforts to promote détente and wanted to abandon the Bretton Woods commitment to lower trade barriers. The most hawkish elements of this group provided a strong base for the rise of "new right" conservatism in the Republican Party with the founding of the Committee on the Present Danger, a high-powered lobbying organization that warned of the dangers of détente and opposed efforts to promote arms control.[23]

The economic contradictions of high military spending, vast foreign commitments, and the emergence of highly competitive foreign economies led to a growing trade imbalance and increasing budget deficits. The Nixon administration, pressured by U.S. export industries that were hurt by the overvalued dollar (still pegged at $35 an ounce by the Bretton Woods agreements) and domestic business interests facing increased competition for the U.S. market, signaled the formal end of Bretton Woods by unilaterally suspending the dollar's convertibility to gold and imposing a 10 percent surcharge on all foreign imports. Although business internationalists and foreign governments were able to persuade the Nixon administration to abandon the surcharge, through the famous Smithsonian Agreements of 1973–1974, the so-called Nixon shocks paved the way for floating exchange rates that ended the Bretton Woods system.

The remainder of the decade saw a number of developments that have been labeled by some observers as indicative of a right turn in U.S. foreign policy. First, business internationalists failed in their efforts to promote détente, and many joined their conservative counterparts in calling for higher rates of military spending in 1979 after the success of several revolutionary movements in the less developed world (especially the Middle East) threatened the investments of U.S.-based multinationals. Second, business internationalists, previously willing to tolerate the increased social and regulatory spending of the New Deal and Great Society programs, began lobbying aggressively to scale back those programs dramatically. Seen as a costly burden in the competitive international environment of the 1970s, social programs, regulatory reform, and labor legislation became a battleground for class conflict during the latter part of the decade.[24]

AFTER BRETTON WOODS: BUSINESS CONFLICT AND THE GLOBAL CONTEXT OF CONSERVATIVE REALIGNMENT

The fifth and sixth chapters of this book trace the decline of liberalism in the context and aftermath of the collapse of the Bretton Woods system. Chapter 5 focuses on the 1970s and emphasizes the impact of the stagflationary economy of the period. The economic stresses of the period led to broad business support for neoconservative policies that would reverse the decline in real rates of profit by decade's end. This paved the way for the Reagan "revolution" that is addressed in Chapter 6. Chapter 7 examines the contradictions of the new conservative bloc and charts the potential for various coalitions of business and political elites through the 1990s and beyond.

Political and economic time are never entirely synchronic. In the history of liberalism in the United States, the political crisis has preceded the economic by five years. The year 1968 was one of global crisis in liberal hegemony. In the United States liberal reform was challenged by new social movements of African Americans, women, and others who saw the Great Society reforms as inadequate, neglectful of attention to the root causes of racism and poverty, or even designed to forestall necessary social change. Further, the human costs of the interventionist foreign policy of the Johnson administration in Southeast Asia evoked increasing and broad public opposition to the continuation of the war.

By the end of the 1960s increased global competition was placing greater pressure on the dollar and on U.S.-based multinational firms. The welfare-warfare spending and lowered taxes of the Johnson years also increased inflationary tendencies in the U.S. economy. The financial sector then looked to the Nixon administration to reign in those pressures with more conservative fiscal and monetary policies. Also, labor-intensive industries in the manufacturing sector, which had to a great extent remained aligned with the Republicans even through 1964, looked for favorable policies from the Nixon administration.

Nonetheless, the Nixon administration anticipated remaining within the broad Keynesian framework of the previous era. While relying on the support of core Republicans, Nixon sought to gain the approval of those business interests in the international and financial markets that generally had been aligned with the Democrats since the New Deal.[25] Any successful conservative at the time would have certainly had to adapt as well to the strong popular support for key elements of the expanded welfare state.

In mass politics, the early 1970s remain an underappreciated era of labor militancy in which low levels of unemployment combined with new social currents that challenged traditional labor-management relationships.[26] At the institutional level, organized labor remained generally moderate (even abandoning the Democratic Party in 1972!) and populist politicians such as George Wallace sought the support of more socially conservative members of the lower middle to working class. Yet even with unimaginative leadership, wage earnings continued to improve and the Nixon administration supported a degree of enhanced regulatory protection of worker safety. The onset of inflation led to a new convergence of interests between financial and labor-intensive industrial capital as corporate interests emphasized the "wage push" element of inflation and the use of wage/price controls was openly portrayed as an effort to limit the power of organized labor.[27]

After 1974 the Bretton Woods system was a thing of the past, and the oil shock had made the new global dependency of the U.S. economy obvious. In a context of higher unemployment and the emergence of the "rust belt," the position of organized labor was in precipitous decline. Domestic sources of resistance to market liberalization were severely weakened, just as new business coalitions were emerging. On the surface, Watergate appeared to have put conservative forces in retreat and heightened public critical awareness of the influence of moneyed interests in politics. Nonetheless, post-Watergate reforms in such areas as campaign finance ultimately became new conduits for business investment in the political process.[28]

The new subaltern status of labor in U.S. politics was perhaps best illustrated by the failure of moderate labor law reform during the Carter administration. In the late 1970s, labor sought federal redress for so-called open shop laws that had been passed at the state level. In the face of rejuvenated business antiunionism, this attempt to strengthen the National Labor Relations Act failed. As Domhoff suggests, the renewed business-labor conflict revealed the collapse of the liberal-labor coalition that had been able to forward its agenda and increase both real and social wages within the Bretton Woods system.[29]

In our analysis the Carter years were an initial effort at a neoliberalism based upon the old New Deal electoral coalition. The failure to successfully navigate business conflict; especially in the areas of energy policy and federal subsidies to western agricultural interests, led to the defeat of this effort in the Congress, the bureaucracy, and the electorate. Central to this problem was the reaction of key sectors—the aforementioned western interests and even more decisively the defense industries—to the austerity of Carter's neoliberalism.

The Reagan revolution presents itself to us, then, as a coalesced business response to declining profits. Consider the broad range of business interests that are satisfied by the Reaganite "big tent" with its peculiar combination of military Keynesianism and monetarist restraint. Across the board, the costs of capital in the forms of labor, regulation, taxes, and energy were decreased or at least held in check while the subsidization of the defense industries was increased. Here, then, was a neoconservative bloc that even included a subaltern popular component appealing to a broad range of social conservatives, who at the end of the day had little to show for their support for the New Right. But this was a bloc too easily put together in the unifying context of a second Cold War. Its contradictions were most manifest in growing fiscal deficits and the continued stagnation of real wages.

As the Reagan revolution proceeded, sectors of capital split over such crucial issues as the levels of military spending and trade policy. Commercial and investment bankers, joined by computer and data-processing firms with considerable investments in Western Europe, openly criticized Reagan's high rates of military spending and unilateral foreign policy initiatives as interfering with U.S. trade and investment opportunities in Western Europe. By the early to mid-1980s, these firms were financing many of the foundations most critical of Reagan's security policies. However, firms dependent on military spending and on labor-intensive foreign investment, as well as investors in troubled spots of the world economy such as the Middle East, championed high rates of military spending.

Beset by the increased internationalization of the U.S. economy, nationalist firms fought for increased protectionism in trade. Firms that we label regionalists, especially the auto and electronics sectors, pushed for regionally based investment guarantees that promoted the low-cost relocation of U.S. production to the Caribbean Basin (Caribbean Basin Initiative) and Mexico (North American Free Trade Agreement). Meanwhile capital-intensive and globally competitive firms, highly dependent on exports, imports, and foreign direct investment for their profitability, championed multilateral initiatives through the Uruguay Round of General Agreement on Tariffs and Trade (GATT).

The fiscal crisis of the liberal capitalist state reached a peak as the 1990s began. The four years of the Bush administration (1989–1993) saw government deficits reach in excess of $300 billion, levels considered unimaginable in the headiest days of the Keynesian vogue. To be sure, the peak deficits of the Bush years had an efficient cause in the savings and loan crisis/bailout that was rooted in the deregulation of capital markets, the same process of capital market transformation underscored in the globalization and post-Fordism literature.[30] Yet these deficits had, and have, underlying causes that are part and parcel of the crisis of liberalism in U.S. politics.

In 1973 James O'Connor[31] diagnosed the contradiction between the accumulation and legitimation functions of the state. The capitalist state must necessarily facilitate capital accumulation by maintaining a good business climate. This includes a stable currency, interest rates, and the banking system (not to mention the social reproduction of the labor force). This function can be facilitated through deficit spending in a slump, but long-term deficits also appear to disrupt—some would say distort—capital markets. The legitimation function of the Keynesian welfare state had been to facilitate hegemonic consent by providing subordinate social groups with a safety net. The long-term deficit problem is likely insoluble with entitlement reform, a euphemism for rolling back the welfare state, particularly its stronger components that primarily benefit the middle-wage and salary-earning strata.

For present purposes it is not necessary to decide if the deficit is indeed a problem that must be solved. An analysis that is quite sound within a capitalist logic would be that what is more crucial is the long-run ratio of debt to GDP. A permanent debt is perfectly normal, even requisite, in any large-scale corporate enterprise (so too, then, the state in a market economy!). What matters economically is that the debt grow in pace with the economy, not faster. What is significant politically is how the deficit intersects with business conflict and how it can be used symbolically to delegitimate the welfare state.

The Bush administration was caught in the tensions of its own electoral bloc. On the one hand, the capital market sectors demanded that the deficit be brought under control, even if that meant a tax increase (so long, of course, as this increase would fall on wage and salary earners or, better yet, consumers). On the other hand, the industrial sectors, especially those that were attracted to the supply-side ethos, and Bush's mass base among upper-middle-income voters required, as the price of their support, that he keep his pledge of "no new taxes." The budget settlement of 1991 brought these tensions to the surface and fragmented the Reagan coalition in the run-up to the 1992 election.

Additional sources of business conflict in trade policy were illustrated by Pat Buchanan's emergence and the significant opposition to NAFTA within the Republican coalition. While the structural crises of the U.S. economy post–Bretton Woods had taken liberalism out of power, they had also undercut the ability of conservatism to maintain and consolidate power.

This book concludes by mapping out the ideological and sectoral business conflicts of the 1990s. We look at the Republican Party and the efforts of its leaders to create a new hegemonic neoconservative bloc. Also significant from our perspective is the ongoing neoliberal efforts to combine austerity with some of the socially inclusive rhetoric of the old liberalism. Clinton's effort to build a new Democratic bloc relies on the combination of free trade with further cuts in the social welfare state, completing the dismantling of key features of the liberal state from the New Deal through the Great Society. In the Clinton administration's second term, virtually all the social welfare elements of the federal New Deal targeted to the poor are being dismantled in favor of a devolution of welfare policies to the state governments. In addition, the administration has institutionalized much of the Reagan military buildup, maintaining rates of military spending that, in real dollars, are close to the average rates of spending during the Cold War.

Organized labor, seeing Clinton as the last hope for retaining some elements of a state commitment to defending the interests of unions, has remained embedded within the Democratic Party. However, on virtually

every important union issue, from NAFTA to the use of replacement workers in strikes, labor has suffered defeats that have been coauthored by both
the Clinton White House and a newly elected Republican Congress. In
fact, the labor liberals of the Democratic Party are very much a minority in
a two-party system increasingly dominated by corporate investments designed to further roll back the regulatory and social welfare bureaucracy
established during the New Deal.

Just when labor has been counted for dead, however, recent victories,
combined with the most sustained organizing drive in decades, have
helped to produce growing confidence within organized labor. Perhaps the
most impressive economic victory is the triumph of the United Parcel Service workers, who were able to resist concessions by management and win
improvements in wages and benefits for both full-time and part-time workers. In addition, labor relied on its allies in the Democratic Party and on a
frustrated nationalist business sector, to derail efforts by the Clinton White
House and the Republican congressional leadership to pass fast-track legislation through Congress.

The fault lines between labor and business are easy to discern and
promise to bring more urgency and dissenting voices to the political debate
in future years. While Clinton triumphs his "economic recovery," ordinary
working-class Americans are barely better off than they were during the
last deep recession. Furthermore, the effects of steadily declining real
wages since 1973 have generated a potential for new labor militancy that
could shift the direction of the political debate. A key question that we
pose in the last chapter is the prospects for U.S. politics to shift from a primarily intraelite affair to a greater expression of class conflict.

NOTES

1. For empirical evidence of the increased volume of trade since 1972, see Timothy McKeowan, "A Liberal Trade Order? The Long-Run Pattern of Imports to the
Advanced Capitalist States," *International Studies Quarterly* 35 (1991): 151–172. On
production trends in the 1970s and 1980s, see Robert Ross and Kent Trachte, *Global
Capitalism: The New Leviathan* (Albany: State University of New York Press, 1990).

2. For an example of such a view, see Robert Reich, *Work of Nations* (New
York: Vintage Press, 1992).

3. For a good account of U.S. efforts to promote global cooperation after
World War II, see Gabriel Kolko and Joyce Kolko, *The Limits of Power* (New
York: Harper and Row, 1972). For a recent account of U.S. efforts to promote lib-
eralization of capital markets in the 1960s and 1970s, see Eric Helleiner, *States and
the Reemergence of Global Finance: From Bretton Woods to the 1990s* (Ithaca,
NY: Cornell University Press, 1994).

4. In examining the relationship between business elites and the intersection
between foreign and domestic policy, this work is part of a growing tradition in

political science labeled the "business conflict" approach. Examples include Thomas Ferguson, "From Normalcy to New Deal: Industrial Structure, Party Competition, and American Public Policy in the Great Depression," *International Organization 33* (Winter 1984): 41–93; David Gibbs, *The Political Economy of Third World Intervention* (Chicago: University of Chicago Press, 1991); Ronald W. Cox, *Power and Profits: U.S. Policy in Central America* (Lexington: University of Kentucky Press, 1994); Gregory P. Nowell, *Mercantile States and the World Oil Cartel, 1900–1939* (Ithaca, NY: Cornell University Press, 1994); Benjamin Fordham; *Building the Cold War Consensus* (Ann Arbor: University of Michigan Press, 1998); and Peter Trubowitz, *Defining the National Interest* (Chicago: University of Chicago Press, 1998).

5. For a classic discussion of the restrictive nature of Bretton Woods, see John Ruggie, "International Regimes, Transactions and Change: Embedded Liberalism in the Postwar Economic Order," *International Organization* 36, 2 (Spring 1982).

6. For a good discussion of this conflict, see Helen Milner, *Resisting Protectionism* (Princeton, NJ: Princeton University Press, 1988).

7. On the ability of business groups to win numerous concessions from the U.S. and Western European governments during the 1970s and 1980s, see Joyce Kolko, *Restructuring the World Economy* (New York: Pantheon Press, 1988).

8. A classic example of such an approach is Richard Rosecrance, *The Rise of the Trading State: Commerce and Conquest in the Modern World* (New York: Basic Books, 1986).

9. For background, see Barbara Stallings, *Banker to the World* (Berkeley: University of California Press, 1987).

10. For a good account of this, see Thomas Ferguson and Joel Rogers, *Right Turn: The Decline of the Democrats and the Future of American Politics* (New York: Hill and Wang, 1986).

11. The 1994 electoral shift was very marginal; the national Republican congressional vote rose by 4 percent. However, it was a national trend that manifested itself most strongly among white men (11 percent swing). *New York Times*, November 13, 1994.

12. A good overview of this period is Philip Armstrong, Andrew Glyn, and John Harrison, *Capitalism Since World War II: The Making and the Breakup of the Great Boom* (London: Fontana Press, 1984).

13. Walter Dean Burnham, *Critical Elections and the Mainspring of American Electoral Politics* (New York: W. W. Norton, 1970).

14. Ronald W. Cox and Daniel Skidmore-Hess, "The Politics of the 1993 NAFTA Vote," *Current Politics and Economics of the U.S.*, 1, 2/3 (1995).

15. For an overview of this business coalition and a history of its commitment to the New Deal, see Thomas Ferguson, *Golden Rule: The Investment Theory of Party Competition and the Logic of Money-Driven Political Systems* (Chicago: University of Chicago Press, 1995).

16. For an overview of business groups and a history of their ties to prominent political officials, see Philip Burch, *Elites in American History*, Vol. II (New York: Holmes and Meier, 1981).

17. Jeffrey Frieden, "Sectoral Conflict and U.S. Foreign Economic Policy," in John Ikenberry, David Lake, and Michael Mastanduno, ed. *The State and American Foreign Economic Policy* (Ithaca, NY: Cornell University Press, 1989).

18. For a good discussion of the importance of these firms to the decision to increase military spending dramatically in the post–World War II period, see Fred Block, *The Origins of International Economic Disorder* (Berkeley: University of California Press, 1977).

19. Michael Hogan, "American Marshall Planners and the Search for a European Neocapitalism," *American Historical Review* 90 (February 1985): 44–72.

20. One of the most sophisticated accounts of this hegemonic crisis is Robert Cox, *Production, Power and World Order: Social Forces in the Making of History* (New York: Columbia University Press, 1987).

21. For a good account of this conflict, see Eric Devereux, "Industrial Structure, Internationalism and the Collapse of the Cold War Consensus," in Ronald W. Cox, ed., *Business and the State in International Politics* (Boulder, CO: Westview Press, 1996).

22. See Jerri-Lynn Scofield, "The Business of Strategy: The Political Economy of U.S. Trade Policy Toward the U.S.S.R., 1945–1975," in Ronald W. Cox, ed., *Business and the State in International Relations* (Boulder, CO: Westview Press, 1996).

23. Jerry Sanders, *Peddlers of Crisis: The Committee on the Present Danger and the Politics of Containment* (Boston: South End Press, 1983).

24. On the origins of these efforts, see Joel Rogers and Thomas Ferguson, eds., *The Hidden Election* (New York: Pantheon Press, 1981).

25. Herbert Stein, *Presidential Economics* (Washington, DC: American Enterprise Institute, 1988). At p. 135 Stein remarks that Nixon "was certainly in tune with conventional wisdom that the country valued continuous high employment above price stability"—this as of 1969, of course. The collapse of the Bretton Woods arrangement would change this political calculus and give key business elites an opportunity to redirect policy toward containing inflation.

26. The new militancy of that era is documented in Stanley Aronowitz, *False Promises* (New York: McGraw-Hill, 1974).

27. For the business mobilization against organized labor in the early to mid-1970s and its relation to the rightward shift, see Thomas Edsall, *The New Politics of Inequality* (New York: W. W. Norton, 1984).

28. Barry Bluestone and Bennett Harrison, *The Great U-Turn* (New York: Basic Books, 1988), refer to the association between the rise of unemployment and the movement of manufacturing to low-wage regions. For campaign finance, see Frank Sorauf, *Inside Campaign Finance: Myths and Realities* (New Haven, CT: Yale University Press, 1992).

29. William Domhoff, *The Power Elite and the State: How Policy Is Made in America* (New York: Aldine de Gruyter, 1990).

30. Michel Aglietta, *A Theory of Capitalist Regulation: The U.S. Experience* (London: New Left Books, 1979).

31. James O'Connor, *The Fiscal Crisis of the State* (New York: St. Martin's Press, 1973).

1

The New Deal
and Liberal Hegemony

BUSINESS CONFLICT AND U.S. FOREIGN POLICY

The most fundamental and enduring conflict in U.S. foreign policy in the twentieth century is between internationalists and nationalists. Internationalists, including political and business elites driven by ideology and economic interests, have supported global institutions committed to lowering trade barriers and facilitating international trade and investment through multilateral lending arrangements. Nationalists, also driven by ideology and economic interests, have supported high tariff barriers and opposed U.S. involvement in global institutions. Internationalists have included business firms with the most extensive ties to foreign markets through exports and foreign direct investments. In contrast, nationalist business interests have been tied to the U.S. domestic market and historically dependent on tariffs or other forms of trade protection to secure a profitable niche in the U.S. market.[1]

Although these labels are useful starting points for students of foreign policy making, they need to be modified to account for the historical patterns of business involvement in the dominant foreign policy coalitions of the twentieth century. Business internationalists are themselves divided on foreign policy issues based on the regional (or global) location of their investments and the competitiveness of their firms in the international marketplace. Historically, the most globally competitive and capital-intensive business internationalists have been the leading champions of what some have called "liberal internationalism."[2] As an important historical economic and ideological force in U.S. foreign policy, liberal internationalists posit a relationship between domestic economic prosperity and access to foreign markets.[3] In addition, they have been the most ardent supporters of free trade, bilateral foreign assistance, and multilateral institutions of all U.S. foreign policy interest groups.

In the 1930s, liberal internationalists and their political allies in the Roosevelt White House and State Department joined to form a New Deal coalition committed to increased federal regulation at home. By the end of the 1930s, these same internationalists formed a Bretton Woods coalition committed to U.S. political leadership abroad. This business coalition was distinguished from other U.S.-based business groups by its extensive investments in Western Europe, its oligopolistic position within the U.S. market, and the relative capital-intensive nature of its investments at home and abroad.[4]

Liberal internationalism was represented by such business organizations as the Committee for Economic Development (CED), the Business Advisory Council (BAC), the Council on Foreign Relations (CFR), and a host of industry-government committees linked to the State Department that pursued postwar economic planning. This liberal internationalist coalition would soon constitute part of a global hegemonic bloc committed to the postwar revitalization of Western Europe. In U.S. politics these organizations would provide what one scholar of the Council on Foreign Relations has termed "an important function in a corporatist strategy to devise the foreign policy of the United States" that "provided a well-organized, yet informal link" between elites and the state and public opinion.[5]

Owing to the lack of legal formalization of the interconnections in the United States between organized interests and government, we do not use the term "corporatist" to describe corporate political blocs. Instead, what we find is a pattern of business-government alliances that revolves around the factors of industrial structure (labor versus capital intensive, nationalist versus internationalist) that are described here. These alliances can shift, especially so in times of crisis, leaving party/political leaders such as FDR in a broker's role of finding suitable coalition partners; and like any broker the politician must find sufficient investors to stay in business.

During the 1920s and much of the 1930s, business nationalists were able to defeat many of the proposals advanced by business internationalists in U.S. foreign policy. Nationalists, represented by the National Association of Manufacturers and local chambers of commerce and trade associations, as well as an influential lobbying group called the American Tariff League, had successfully lobbied Congress to raise tariff barriers to all-time highs, from the Fordney-McCumber tariff of 1922 to the Smoot-Hawley tariff of 1930.[6] In addition, business nationalists and their political allies in the Republican Party had led the opposition to U.S. involvement in the League of Nations while opposing any efforts by the U.S. government to cancel or reduce allied war debts from World War I. In contrast, business internationalists advocated membership in the league, cancellation or reduction of allied war debts, and an extension of U.S. governmental loans to European allies.

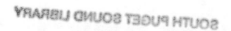

In the aftermath of repeated political failures at home, business internationalists with extensive investments in Western Europe led the effort
to promote a favorable European investment climate by extending considerable loans to Weimar Germany and rescheduling Germany's war debts.
Because of nationalist dominance in Congress and the concerns of the executive branch about catering to a strong isolationist mood at home, business internationalists worked closely with the executive branch to advance
their global agenda. Business groups often took the lead in developing a
foreign policy that would promote European recovery and provide the pre-
requisites for increased U.S. trade and investment in the region.[7] The Republican White House, however, was timid about involving itself too heavily in these efforts on account of the Republican Party's dependence on a
nationalist bloc of U.S. manufacturers committed to high tariffs and opposed to foreign loans or reduction of foreign debts.

Toward the end of the global depression of the 1930s, business internationalists were more aggressive and successful in pursuing their domestic and foreign policy agendas. First, business internationalists worked
with political allies in the Roosevelt State Department in lobbying for the
Reciprocal Trade Agreements Act of 1934. The act strengthened the hand
of the White House in foreign economic policy making by shifting tariff
authority from Congress to the president. Although this act was primarily
used during the 1930s to increase trade regionally with Latin American
countries, it provided the institutional building block for post–World War
II efforts to lower trade barriers globally. Second, business internationalists, especially those with capital-intensive investments, worked to promote many of the most important acts of the New Deal. Seeking standardized federal regulation to avoid the bureaucratic difficulties of dealing
with a maze of diverse state business laws, these capital-intensive firms
supported such New Deal programs as the Social Security Act. In addition,
some of these firms, faced with growing labor unrest and radicalization,
had long developed strategies of corporate-labor cooperation designed to
strengthen company unions, moderate labor militancy, and defeat successful unionization efforts.

As much research has shown, most internationalists and virtually all
nationalist factions of business opposed collective bargaining and the
Wagner Act of 1935. However, internationalists within the farm export
sector of the Democratic Party agreed to support the Wagner Act provided
that it exclude farm workers from collective bargaining provisions.[8] Business internationalists also continued to work within the Democratic Party
based on its commitment, most evident by the mid to late 1930s, to work toward expanded trade and investment to ease the impact of the global depression. These business leaders saw foreign trade and investment and the
establishment of U.S. leadership in global financial and political institutions

as central to pulling the U.S. economy out of the depression. They also saw foreign trade and investment as an important solution to growing labor militancy at home and as an antidote to governmental proposals to regulate production and trade further.[9]

In contrast, just as their internationalist counterparts were shifting their resources to the Democratic Party, nationalist business factions and labor-intensive internationalists stayed within the Republican Party and expressed strong and consistent opposition to New Deal reform measures. Leading the charge was the National Association of Manufacturers and local trade associations comprising small- to medium-size firms relatively dependent on the domestic market or tied to regional markets in Latin America.[10] Having little or no European investments and characterized by their labor-intensive production structure (with a relatively high percentage of wages as value added in production), these business groups were the most ardent opponents of the New Deal. They also gave heavily to the ultra–right wing faction of the Republican Party, including the well-known Liberty League, which characterized the New Deal as a communist-led plot to take over the United States.[11] This chapter is primarily concerned with the historical background necessary for understanding the triumph of liberal internationalists as a hegemonic interest in U.S. foreign policy making after World War II. We argue that the foundation of that triumph was the formation of the New Deal coalition of the 1930s, which was extended to a Bretton Woods coalition of the 1940s. These coalitions supported the interests of capital-intensive foreign investors and exporters with close ties to European markets. Both coalitions sought to regulate capitalism domestically through the New Deal and globally through the creation of such multilateral institutions as the International Monetary Fund (IMF) and the World Bank and the General Agreement on Tariffs and Trade (GATT). In addition, the Bretton Woods coalition supported extensive U.S. bilateral aid to Europe in the form of the British loan and the Marshall Plan.

THE NEW DEAL COALITION

A wealth of academic writing has explored the New Deal from a variety of competing theoretical perspectives.[12] Our analysis focuses on the foreign policies of a liberal internationalist business-state coalition that supported increased governmental regulation and, more reluctantly, an expanded social welfare state in the context of increasing class conflict. Most accounts of the New Deal have ignored or minimized the role of business internationalists in formulating and supporting aspects of the New Deal. We draw on recent archival research to draw a different conclusion: that internationalist business groups were central players in developing the New Deal. During the 1930s this New Deal coalition formulated the global economic and strategic policies adopted in the post–World War II period, especially the Bretton Woods system. After a brief examination of the emergence of the liberal internationalist business coalition, we trace its influence on foreign economic policies during and after the New Deal.

The political and economic power of internationalist business groups grew during the 1920s and 1930s. Numerous analysts have written about the growth of the John D. Rockefeller banking and oil empire and its rivalry with J. P. Morgan's investment and commercial banking empire; the oligopolistic concentration of wealth, profits, and market position within the auto, steel, machine tool, and rubber industries; and the steady expansion of the top Fortune 500 business firms into foreign markets in both Latin America and Europe.[13] What is missing from most analyses, however, is a sectorally specific evaluation of the domestic and foreign policy behavior of these internationalist firms. Particularly, what needs to be explained is the political rivalry between capital-intensive business internationalists who supported various aspects of the New Deal and contributed heavily to the Democratic Party and their labor-intensive counterparts who were ardent opponents of the New Deal.

The ascendancy of a liberal internationalist bloc of U.S.-based multinational firms has its roots in the expansion of U.S. investments in Western Europe during the 1920s. The United States emerged from World War I as a creditor nation, and U.S. commercial and investment banking interests were eager to take the lead in lending money to Germany and other European countries to facilitate increased U.S. investment and trade. Led by the House of Morgan and Rockefeller commercial banks and joined by capital-intensive investors including Westinghouse and General Electric, U.S. multinationals pushed for a U.S. foreign policy that would reduce tariffs, scale back European debts, and actively involve the U.S. government in promoting the conditions for stable trade with and investments in Europe.

At home, these same capital-intensive business interests, led by Rockefeller firms, worked to develop a program called Industrial Relations Counselors, Inc. (IRC), as a response to the labor militancy of the immediate post–World War I period. The IRC promoted labor practices referred to as "welfare capitalism," including company pensions, employee stock ownership plans, company unions (erroneously dubbed "labor-management bargaining teams"), and, in some cases, the provision of life and health insurance plans. These practices later provided the industrial model for the New Deal.[14] Promoted by the leaders of some of the most capital-intensive firms in the United States, especially oil and banking enterprises, the IRC was an attempt to weaken the development of independent unions and maintain stability and high profits during the 1920s.

Labor-intensive firms in steel and textiles and chemical firms that were undercut by growing international competition adopted a more conventional response to organized labor and class conflict. Dubbed the "American Plan," and adopted by U.S. steel and other labor-intensive firms as a concerted antiunion strategy, this approach relied on hiring company spies to weed out union organizers and private security forces to physically repress workers with ties to independent unions and to silence those who complained about unsafe working conditions, wages, or lack of benefits. The latter method of responding to labor conflict was far more common throughout U.S. history than the IRC approach, but both strategies had the same goal: to prevent the establishment of independent unions and genuine collective bargaining in favor of management control.

The differences in the relationship with labor between the liberal internationalists who would later join the New Deal coalition and their conservative counterparts who would stick with the Republican Party can be explained by looking at a key statistical variable. The backers of the New Deal tended to be capital-intensive firms whose overriding distinction was that wages represented a lower percentage of their value added in production than their labor-intensive counterparts.[15] Therefore, the efforts of these liberal internationalists to offer some company benefits in exchange for management control over production decisions and shop floor relations made sense given the capital-intensive nature of their production.

For their part, manufacturing firms faced with wage costs that constituted a high percentage of value added in production tended to advocate traditional methods of repression in dealing with labor. There were other ideological differences between these competing business interests. Labor-intensive industrialists opposed any effort to develop a national regulatory apparatus that would institutionalize social security and assistance programs. Fearful that such efforts would only increase labor costs and push them out of business, leading representatives of labor-intensive firms relied on the National Association of Manufacturers, local chambers of commerce, and trade associations to oppose the New Deal.

It must be pointed out that despite these differences between capital- and labor-intensive investors, even the capital-intensive investors would have opposed the New Deal if the level of class struggle and fears of the social consequences of the Great Depression had not reached a crisis point in the mid-1930s. In fact, there is strong evidence that capital-intensive foreign investors were concerned about the rising militancy of labor in the United States and Western Europe. In both domestic and foreign policy, business leaders of the New Deal developed programs designed to dampen further expressions of class militancy. They also developed programs designed to regulate capitalism nationally and internationally to avoid a continuation or a repetition of the Great Depression in future years.

The New Deal can be conveniently divided into two periods. The early New Deal (1933–1935) was an ad hoc attempt by the Roosevelt administration to bring together a network of business interests and conservative labor leaders to regulate capitalism. The high point of this period was the short-lived National Industrial Recovery Act (NIRA), which attempted to please both oligopolistic industries and small- and medium sized firms by its varied provisions. First, the federal government suspended antitrust laws for two years, which increased the already high concentration of wealth and profits in several industrial sectors. Second, the NIRA allowed for the imposition of price controls, which were often determined by the representatives of oligopolistic industries that dominated the boards of the National Recovery Administration (NRA), the agency in charge of administering the act. Finally, the federal government ostensibly allowed for collective bargaining under provision 7a of the congressional legislation authorizing the NIRA. But in reality the boards that determined whether collective bargaining was justified were dominated by corporate representatives. Labor was essentially frozen out of the implementation of the NIRA.[16]

In order to please small- and medium-sized businesses and labor-intensive factions of capital, the NIRA also included a wealth of contradictory provisions involving a commitment on the part of regulators to promote "fair competition" and to guard against price fixing by large oligopolies. However, the large oligopolies grew stronger during the Depression years, in both size and profitability. And representatives of oligopolistic, capital-intensive industries were far more prevalent on NRA boards than were smaller and medium-size firms. At the very time that the NIRA was disintegrating under its own bureaucratic contradictions, labor-intensive firms and small businesses accused the Roosevelt administration of openly siding with monopolies at the expense of competitive enterprise.[17]

At the same time, labor activists seized on provision 7a of the NIRA to press for the right to unionize. The early defensive struggles waged by labor to protect wages and, in many cases, jobs gave way to a wave of offensive efforts to unionize. Beginning with the strike wave of 1934, which included the Minneapolis truckers' strike, the San Francisco longshoremen's strike, the Electric Auto-Lite strike, and the East Coast textile strike, workers challenged companies to bargain with independent unions.[18] Union leaders hoped to take advantage of the perceived benefits of clause 7a of the NIRA. One enduring legacy of the strike wave of 1934 is the Wagner Act of 1935, which legalized collective bargaining with independent unions based on majority support for such unions by workers on the shop floor.

The Wagner Act went beyond what many capital-intensive employers had been promoting to deal with labor problems. Its passage in 1935 heralded the second phase of the New Deal period, in which the most extensive and enduring legislation was enacted, including the Social Security Act. It was during this phase of the New Deal that capital-intensive investors, threatened by the urgency of class conflict and supporting a regulated capitalism designed to restore stability to capital-labor relations, shifted in droves to the Democratic Party. For if the post-1935 system of national labor relations went beyond welfare capitalism in promoting independent unions, it also helped limit and segment the potential power of organized labor.

The New Deal bloc was led by the ideology and interest of liberal internationalism and other key elements, including commercial farmers who benefited from the planning and subsidies initiated in the early New Deal (Agricultural Adjustment Administration),[19] southern and western regional business interests dependent on federal projects (Tennessee Valley Authority, Rural Electrification Administration), and organized labor. In the agricultural sector, New Deal policy favored larger commercial farmers, whereas benefits were frequently denied to tenant farmers.[20] In industrial labor, the NIRA had provided a window of opportunity intended primarily for the more conservative craft unions of the American Federation of Labor (AFL). The longtime practice of segmenting U.S. workers along racial lines was continued; under NIRA codes "African Americans frequently received lower minimum wages than whites."[21] Also, as noted earlier, the Wagner Act was sectoral in application, leaving the agricultural worker outside of its protections. Thus the New Deal coalition did not include tenant farmers in Arkansas and farm laborers in California whose attempts to organize in the 1930s were repressed. Further, organized labor never became more than a regional junior partner to the Democratic coalition because U.S. federalism allowed for the subsequent proliferation of antiunion shop laws that effectively undermined the congressionally mandated collective bargaining right in many southern and western states.

All in all, the New Deal remains best typified as liberal reform that accomplished conservative ends.[22] The liberal corporate supporters were such business leaders as Gerard Swope, president of General Electric, and Henry Harriman of the New England Power Company and president of the U.S. Chamber of Commerce, both of whom were influential in formulating the Social Security Act of 1935. Along with the Wagner Act, Social Security heralded the beginning of the second phase of the New Deal. Working within the Commerce Department's Business Advisory Council, these business leaders were joined by the heads of IBM, Chase Manhattan Bank, Mead Paper company, and a huge bloc of retailers and other corporations in drafting the outlines of the Social Security Act.[23] Capital-intensive firms recognized the advantages of a national social security act that could overcome the disparities of state legislation and stabilize costs for national firms. Furthermore, oligopolists such as Swope and Harriman, along with their allies in the Business Advisory Council, resigned themselves to the fact that there would be some form of social insurance and that they should "concentrate their efforts upon getting it into acceptable form."[24]

Capital-intensive investors helped ensure that the final piece of legislation offered little fundamental change in income redistribution; in fact, it levied a highly regressive tax on payrolls. The final act also protected the sanctity of the wage-labor market by ensuring that benefit levels would never be higher than minimum-wage levels, that contributory provisions tied old age security to labor force participation, and, finally, that welfare benefits were defined in terms of age, not need. According to Quadagno, this last provision helped ensure that the agenda for future policy debates would be established around "intergenerational conflict rather than class."[25]

Labor-intensive firms and those domestic manufacturers who faced intense price competition were opposed to the Social Security Act and lobbied against its passage. Associations such as the National Metal Trades Association, the Illinois Manufacturing Association, the Connecticut Manufacturers' Association, and the Ohio Chamber of Commerce exerted pressure on congressional representatives to ensure limitations on federal control and more authority for the individual states over the provisions and implementation of the act. The fact that these manufacturers' associations represented highly influential local, state, and regional interests meant that their political pressure was extremely influential with congressional representatives. In contrast, the capital-intensive firms, represented by Swope, Harriman, and organizations such as the Business Advisory Council, relied on their growing ties to the Roosevelt administration to shape the provisions of the act.

The labor-intensive firms within the manufacturers' associations were able to shift some control from the federal government to the states. For example, the Old Age Assistance provision involved channeling federal funds to the states for old age pensions to needy persons over the age of sixty-five on a 50-50 matching basis up to a maximum contribution of $15 per month. Each state was then "allowed to set its own standards for eligibility, and many states incorporated traditional poor-law criteria such as means tests, familial responsibility clauses and residency requirements."[26] At the same time capital-intensive investors within the Business Advisory Council used their influence with the national bureaucracy and the executive branch to secure opposition to alternative welfare proposals. These included the more "radical" Lundeen bill, which called for "compensation equal to average local wages for all unemployed workers, for supplementary benefits to part-time workers unable to secure full-time employment and for payments to all workers unable to work because of sickness or old age, the source of funds being the general treasury of the United States."[27] Capital-intensive investors criticized the bill as redistributive and socialistic in its policy aims, thereby helping to isolate its congressional and public supporters. Meanwhile, the AFL's national leadership, contrary to the wishes of many locals, came out against the bill, another important factor leading to its defeat.

The active involvement of capital-intensive investors in promoting a national social security act reflected their increasing influence within the Democratic Party. In the 1936 presidential campaign, liberal internationalists contributed heavily to the Democratic Party, far eclipsing the monetary donations of any other interest group supporting the Democrats. For example, the Bank of America and New Orleans banker Rudolph Hecht, formerly president of the American Bankers Association, bulwarked the Good Neighbor League, a Roosevelt campaign vehicle. Joining Hecht were other Fortune 500 banking elites, including Averell Harriman of Brown Brothers Harriman; James Forrestal of Dillon, Read; and John Milton Hancock of Lehman Brothers. They were joined by top executives of Standard Oil of California and Standard Oil of New Jersey; Reynolds Tobacco; American Tobacco; Coca-Cola; International Harvester; Johnson and Johnson; General Electric; Zenith; IBM; Sears Roebuck; ITT; United Fruit; Pan Am; and Manufacturers Trust. Under the encouragement of banker George Foster Peabody, the *New York Times* supported Roosevelt, as did the Scripps-Howard papers. Thomas Ferguson explains the flurry of activity by capital-intensive investors leading to the 1936 election:

> In the final days of the campaign, as [Alfred] Landon furiously attacked social security, Teagle of Standard Oil of New Jersey, Swope of GE, the Pennsylvania Retailers Association, the American Retail Federation, and the Lorillard tobacco company, among others, spoke out in defense of the program. Last, if scarcely least, the firm that would incarnate the next thirty years of multinational oil and banking, the Chase National Bank, loaned the Democratic National Committee $100,000.[28]

Labor-intensive firms, led by U.S. Steel, and textiles and chemical firms facing tough international competition (Du Pont being the most important) stayed with the Republican Party and levied consistent attacks against the New Deal program. These interests opposed the regulatory reforms of the New Deal and the (increasingly) free trade posture of the Roosevelt administration. The next battlefield for these firms would be foreign policy making, where capital-intensive firms working within the Committee for Economic Development and the Council on Foreign Relations began developing an ambitious Bretton Woods program that promised to greatly expand the U.S. leadership role in the post–World War II period.

THE BRETTON WOODS COALITION

The movement of capital-intensive investors to the Democratic Party helped shape both phases of the New Deal. In the second phase (1935–1938), these business internationalists connected their domestic policy recommendations to three major concerns about the future of global capitalism. The first concern was the lack of global leadership to stabilize trade and investment conditions in Western Europe, by far the most lucrative market for capital-intensive investors during the 1920s and early 1930s. Business internationalists working inside the Committee for Economic Development and the Council on Foreign Relations joined with State, Commerce, and Treasury officials under the Roosevelt administration to propose a political leadership role for the United States in world affairs. Meeting shortly before the outset of World War II and preparing a series of planning documents during the early war years, these businessmen and political officials agreed that the United States must lead in the creation of global financial institutions following World War II.

The collaborative wartime planning committees, labeled "Studies of American Interests in the War and the Peace," formed five study groups: Economic; Financial; Security and Armaments; Territorial; and Future World Organizations. The first two were soon collapsed into one Economic-Financial group, and the Future World Organizations group became the Political group. The study groups developed the political and economic rationale for what became known as the post–World War II Bretton Woods system. The term refers narrowly to the creation of the World Bank and International Monetary Fund and more generally to the set of financial rules and regulations that governed the relationship between the United States and Western Europe in the post–World War II period. The Bretton Woods financial regime allowed governments to maintain capital controls to protect national currencies. In doing so, the regime provided many of the structural financial preconditions for the expansion of trade and investment between the United States and Europe during the postwar period.

U.S. corporate and political elites conceived of the Bretton Woods system as a transition from British global hegemony to U.S. global hegemony. As a hegemonic power, the United States would be forced to respond strategically, and not simply to maximize economic interests, in directing the establishment of multilateral global institutions. The lack of global leadership was identified as a central factor in the deterioration of the global economy during the depression of the 1930s. Specifically, capital-intensive investors and high-level officials in the Roosevelt administration wanted to avoid the "beggar-thy-neighbor" policies of the interwar period. This meant developing both multilateral and bilateral programs to counter the formation of trading blocs of the type that emerged during the interwar years.

The second concern of capital-intensive investors and political elites, closely related to the first, was the construction of a stable alliance system capable of rebuilding war-torn Europe and reducing trade barriers between the United States and Europe. U.S. planners saw Great Britain as a crucial partner in building such alliance systems and in promoting freer postwar trade. Britain and the United States alone participated in over 50 percent of world trade. During the interwar years, the British had raised the tariff barriers around their colonial empire to protect their manufacturing trade and stabilize the pound sterling. U.S. business internationalists and political elites insisted that a domestic postwar recovery hinged on reducing these British trade barriers. The wartime policy of the United States, even before it formally entered World War II, was to exchange U.S. lend-lease aid to Great Britain for a British pledge to break up its Imperial Preference System after the war.

In addition, business internationalists involved in drafting the economic-financial reports of the wartime study groups tied the postwar recovery to cooperation among four blocs involved in the "location, production, and trade of key commodities and manufacturers on a world-wide basis."[29] These four blocs were: (1) the Western Hemisphere; (2) Continental Europe and the Mediterranean Basin (excluding the Soviet Union); (3) the Pacific area and the Far East; and (4) the British Empire. Early U.S. planning documents (1939–1942) emphasized the importance of revitalizing U.S.–Western European trade as a top priority. The importance of Latin America and the Far East was largely due to their complementary supply of raw materials to the United States and Western Europe, respectively. In addition, capital-intensive planners anticipated that the increased production and sales of U.S. and European manufactured goods after the war would depend on the viability and accessibility of the Latin American and Asian markets.

Planners identified Germany and Britain as central to the long-term revival of the European economies. Twenty of the leading Fortune 500 U.S. firms had extensive investments in Germany during the 1920s and 1930s. In the 1930s, U.S. capital-intensive investors worked closely with the State Department in developing an appeasement policy toward the Nazi regime of Adolf Hitler. The aim was to steer Hitler away from a series of preferential bilateral trading agreements that had systematically reduced U.S. trade and investment in Germany during the 1930s. Specifically, a major concern of U.S. policymakers was the use of newly created aski marks, a German currency created in the 1930s that could be used only to purchase German goods. The German government lent the aski mark to a number of Latin American countries, including Brazil, Argentina, Chile, and Uruguay. As a result, German exports to Latin America doubled during the years 1934–1936. Meanwhile, the Nazi exchange control program, combined with discriminatory preferential trade agreements, systematically reduced U.S. exports to Germany from 8.4 percent of U.S. total exports in 1933 to 3.7 percent in 1937.[30]

Despite the trade tensions with Germany during the 1930s, expressed in disputes between the German Foreign Ministry and the U.S. State Department, the U.S. continued to pursue an appeasement policy, which entailed maintaining trade relations. The reasons involved the same concerns that motivated internationalists after the war: Germany had been and would remain a lucrative trade and investment market for the most capital-intensive U.S. firms. During the 1930s, IBM, Eastman Kodak, Standard Oil, General Motors, and Union Carbide all worked closely and sometimes secretly with Nazi German firms until the late 1930s. Ford and General Motors produced half of Hitler's tanks at one point in the 1930s.[31]

The shift from an appeasement strategy toward a war strategy with Nazi Germany came only after the German invasion of Poland made it clear that Germany would not respond to U.S. appeals to loosen its trade restrictions. As those restrictions increased and as Germany sought to consolidate what some internationalists called a "closed trading bloc" through military aggression, the United States shifted from appeasement to war preparation. Using the Reciprocal Trade Agreements Act, the Roosevelt administration secured trade deals with Latin America that weakened Germany's position in the Western Hemisphere. Globally, between 1934 and 1945, twenty-nine Reciprocal Trade Agreements treaties were made between the United States and various Latin American countries. In the five years after the act was passed in 1934, U.S. exports rose more than $1 billion, and the nation's trade balance soared from half a billion dollars to nearly twice that amount.[32]

Meanwhile, capital-intensive planners and State Department officials agreed on the central importance of both Britain and Germany to postwar U.S. planning. A healthy German economy was deemed necessary, indeed essential, to revitalize Europe as a whole. A healthy British economy, absent an Imperial Preference System, would provide an important avenue for acquisition of raw materials from the British Empire to Western Europe and would also be an important market for manufactured goods. U.S. firms, able and willing to invest in Western Europe, would look toward opportunities to renew ties with German industrialists after the war.

The third and final factor that made the construction of a Bretton Woods system necessary to U.S. planners was the likely ascendancy of leftist and nationalist groups in Western Europe from the devastation of World War II. Wartime planning documents warned of the class struggle likely to ensue in the aftermath of the war. Business internationalists insisted that the United States must be prepared to defuse politically the threat to the emergence of private enterprise, trade, and investment in the all-important region of Western Europe. It is to this crucial issue of labor-capital conflict that helped shape Bretton Woods that we turn to in the next section of this chapter.

CLASS CONFLICT AND BRETTON WOODS

The greatest threat to the interests of U.S. liberal internationalists in the postwar period and a primary reason for the final shape of the Bretton Woods system was the rise of powerful trade union movements in the United States and sections of Western Europe and the possible collapse of Western European currencies: especially the British pound sterling. The wartime boom had consolidated the potential economic and political strength of the working class, especially in the United States, Great Britain, Italy, and France. At the same time, the relative weakness of European currencies threatened the construction of a multilateral trading system.

There is substantial evidence that labor enjoyed a structural power during and after World War II reflected in economic and social trends. In the United States, for example, "days occupied in strikes rose from around 1 million a month during the later months of the war to 7–8 million in the last three months of 1945 to 20 million in January 1946 and 23 million in February when 175,000 electrical workers and 800,000 steel workers joined the 225,000 General Motors workers and nearly a million others out on strike."[33] The Bureau of Labor Statistics wrote that "it was the most concentrated strike wave in the country's history."[34] A key battle took place at General Motors when the union insisted that the company open the books to "justify its assertion that it could not pay the '30 percent claim—the 40 hour work week at 48 hours pay.'" The strikers eventually secured half their wage goal and fought off GM's attempt to secure union guarantees of no opposition to speedups and no strikes. However, Ford Motor Company soon set the pattern, "gaining the unrestricted right to hire and fire, promote and demote, fix production schedules, and discipline strikers and others charged with violating company rules."[35]

Yet this structural power of organized labor did not manifest itself in federal policy of the late 1940s and 1950s. The Fair Deal extensions of the New Deal into such areas as health care and civil rights failed to make headway in Congress. Labor and other core Democratic constituencies such as African Americans found themselves in the familiar position of gaining few benefits for their electoral loyalty. For their part, the conservative nationalist coalition around Robert Taft and the Republican right wing were generally stymied in their efforts to roll back the New Deal. Yet they did succeed in passing the Taft-Hartley Act to counterattack the labor militancy of the postwar era and eviscerate labor's ability to use the strike as a weapon of militant action. In more recent decades, unions have turned to the strike as a defensive weapon often of last resort and only infrequently as part of drives to organize the unorganized.

The labor unrest in the United States affected the political and economic strategies of capitalists at the international level. However, capitalists were hardly united in their policy positions. As Thomas Ferguson and Bruce Cumings have noted, there were significant differences between capital-intensive foreign investors and labor-intensive investors tied to the U.S. market. The rise of the New Deal coalition in the 1930s was a product of the ascendancy of the former group, concentrated in sectors of commercial and investment banking, oil, electrical machinery, agribusiness, and some chemical firms. Their labor-intensive counterparts were concentrated in textiles, clothing, steel, and iron industries. As we have shown, capital-intensive industrialists generally favored the state spending associated with the New Deal, and their labor-intensive counterparts opposed state intervention because of labor market constraints.[36]

Within these sectoral categories, there were further divisions among firms based on their global competitiveness and international investments. Firms that were most competitive internationally and relatively dependent on foreign investments tended to advocate liberal international policies promoted in the Bretton Woods agreements, especially the liberalization of trade. Firms that were labor-intensive and tied to the U.S. domestic market tended to oppose liberal internationalism, especially in trade.[37] However, the latter firms, especially those tied to the military-industrial complex, often supported increased military spending at home and abroad. This was especially true for aircraft and machine tool industries, which lobbied aggressively for increased military spending at home to counter cyclical downturns in the U.S. domestic economy, including the U.S. recession of 1948 and 1949.

If there had been no labor unrest during the postwar period, liberal internationalists probably would have succeeded in their push for more aggressive efforts to promote the elimination of trade barriers, currency controls, and capital controls in Western Europe, which for international bankers was the preferred policy package of Bretton Woods. However, the full employment boom of the war years gave labor a structural power in Western Europe that affected the position of the liberal internationalists. The foremost objective of liberal internationalists was to check the ascendancy of militant labor movements and the left in Western Europe.[38] By agreeing to a postwar compromise that allowed European nation-states to maintain currency controls through the first decade of the Bretton Woods system, rising social wages and profits could be protected from the ravages of devaluation and inflation.

Furthermore, Bretton Woods also allowed nation-states to protect their domestic currencies and their domestic investors by controlling the flow of capital funds across borders. This system allowed nation-states to control their exchange rates by limiting financial transactions that might weaken their domestic currencies and prevent the adoption of social welfare and full employment policies demanded by a politicized working class. Although the Bretton Woods system was a compromise between capitalists and workers, it was also a compromise between internationalist and nationalist capitalists, allowing the latter to benefit from national capital controls to protect themselves against foreign competition.

It is interesting to note that both national and international industrialists with fixed investments in plants and machines tended to support capital controls and leading international commercial banks dependent on liquid assets tended to oppose them. Commercial bankers, such as Winston Aldrich of Chase National, feared the potentially inflationary impact of currency management by states pursuing Keynesian demand stimulation. Alternatively, the international commercial banking sector favored allowing market forces to establish exchange rates through the Bank of International Settlements for reasons that are at once ideological and economic; after all, this industry experienced fixed exchange rates and currency controls as a direct limit on their freedom of operation.[39] By contrast, industries seeking markets in Europe, such as manufacturing and banks with loans to productive industries, would benefit from the leeway the Bretton Woods currency system would give to the Europeans to practice Keynesian stimulus.

In the final analysis, U.S. business internationalists and their nationalist counterparts were concerned that full currency convertibility would result in the financial collapse of Western European currencies as financial investors sought to maximize their returns on investments by converting pounds, francs, marks, and liras into dollars. Consequently, Western European countries would be unable to buy U.S. goods. Both U.S. State Department officials and business internationalists worried that such an outcome would have an adverse effect on U.S. capitalism, perhaps resulting in a return to the depression conditions of the 1930s, which were overcome only by the full employment economy and productivity boom of World War II. In the aftermath of the war, trade with Western Europe had fallen off dramatically. State Department officials worried that trade would continue to deteriorate unless steps were taken to stabilize key foreign currencies, especially the British pound. According to a leading State Department official, "The British financial problem is admittedly the greatest present barrier to rapid progress towards free multilateral payments and relaxation of barriers to trade. It threatens not only delay, but indeed the ultimate success of our economic foreign program."[40]

In 1946, liberal internationalists pressed the U.S. government for a loan to Britain of over $3 billion in an effort to stem the tide of that nation's financial collapse. It seems clear that the loan policy embodied the compromises of Bretton Woods in light of the fact that the United States was never able to force Britain to abide by the stated terms of the loan: (1) the elimination of the sterling area dollar pool, (2) the introduction of free currency convertibility, and (3) the substantial reduction of empire trade preferences. Britain adopted these conditions only in the late 1950s, a decade after the U.S. loan had been secured. While U.S. bankers pushed for full convertibility and the elimination of the dollar pool, other liberal internationalists, especially capital-intensive industrialists, insisted that the primary goal of the loan should be to ensure that the British currency did not collapse, a fate that would have surely increased the radical strains within the British labor movement.

The compromise of Bretton Woods, specifically the maintenance of capital controls, was in part a reflection of the strength of organized labor in Great Britain, France, and Italy at the end of World War II. During World War II, union membership in Great Britain rose by approximately one-third to eight million workers, some 45 percent of the workforce. The political strength of the working class was evident in the landslide victory of the Labor Party in 1945. Laborites advanced an eleven-point program that advocated a series of nationalization measures and increased government spending to maintain a full-employment, high-wage economy in the aftermath of World War II. Faced with these demands, the British government was incapable politically of pressing for currency convertibility and the removal of capital controls.

Thus capital-labor relations after World War II provide a partial explanation of the compromises of the Bretton Woods system. However, a more complete understanding of the Bretton Woods financial regime requires a detailed analysis of the interaction among business coalitions in the construction of that regime. In the next chapter, we examine the role of business and political elites in the construction of Bretton Woods and develop an overview of the defining features of what we describe as a Bretton Woods financial regime. The role of business and political elites in the construction and unraveling of such a financial regime is the thread that ties the remaining chapters together.

NOTES

1. For further discussion of the historical patterns of these divisions, see Jeffrey Frieden, *Banking on the World: The Politics of American International Finance* (New York: Harper and Row, 1987).

2. For an account of the relationship of U.S. liberal internationalists to the global economy, see Robert Cox, *Production, Power and World Order: Social Forces in the Making of History* (New York: Columbia University Press, 1987).

3. For an elegant theoretical and historical elaboration of the perspective of liberal internationalists, see N. Gordon Levin, Jr., *Woodrow Wilson and World Politics* (New York: Columbia University Press, 1968).

4. This may be measured by the magnitude of wages as a percentage of value added in production. In measuring the capital- and labor-intensive characteristics of firms, this study follows the statistical analysis of Thomas Ferguson, "From Normalcy to New Deal: Industrial Structure, Party Competition, and American Public Policy in the Great Depression," *International Organization* 38 (Winter 1984), pp. 41–94.

5. For a good history of the role of the Council on Foreign Relations in U.S. foreign policy, see Lawrence Shoup and William Minter, *Imperial Brain Trust* (New York: Monthly Review Press, 1977). For a discussion of its "corporatist strategy," see Michael Wala, *The Council on Foreign Relations and American Foreign Policy in the Early Cold War Era* (Providence, RI: Berghahn Books, 1994), p. 243.

6. For a useful overview of this period, see Michael Hogan, *Informal Entente: The Private Structure of Cooperation in Anglo-American Economic Diplomacy, 1918–1928* (Columbia: University of Missouri Press, 1977).

7. On this period, see Carl Parrini's excellent study *Heir to Empire: United States Economic Diplomacy* (Pittsburgh: University of Pittsburgh Press, 1969).

8. William Domhoff, *The Power Elite and the State: How Policy is Made in America* (New York: Aldine de Gruyter, 1990), pp. 91–104.

9. For the best recent account of this period, drawing extensively on private archival documents, see Patrick Hearden, *Roosevelt Confronts Hitler* (DeKalb: Northern Illinois University Press, 1987).

10. For a good history of the National Association of Manufacturers during this period, see Philip H. Burch, "The NAM as Interest Group," *Politics and Society* (Fall 1973).

11. Thomas Ferguson, "Industrial Conflict and the Coming of the New Deal: The Triumph of Multinational Liberalism in America," in Steve Fraser and Gary Gerstle, eds., *The Rise and Fall of the New Deal Order* (Princeton: Princeton University Press, 1989), pp. 3–31.

12. Essentially there are two broad perspectives regarding the New Deal. The first can be loosely grouped under the label "statist" approach, which argues that government bureaucrats and middle-class technocrats acted autonomously in promoting the New Deal. A representative work is Theda Skocpol and John Ikenberry, "The Political Formation of the American Welfare State in Historical and Comparative Perspective," in Richard F. Tomasson, ed., *Comparative Social Research* (Greenwich, CT: JAI, 1983). Other works, closer to the tradition supported by our research, can be labeled societal-based approaches and include Jill Quadagno, *The Transformation of Old Age Security* (Chicago: University of Chicago Press, 1988). We also draw on class-based approaches to the welfare state, including the recent work by Rhonda Levine, *Class Struggle and the New Deal: Industrial Labor, Capital and the State* (Lawrence: University Press of Kansas, 1988).

13. For an excellent overview, see Robert Sobel, *The Age of Giant Corporations: A Microeconomic History of American Business, 1914–1970* (Westport, CT: Greenwood Press, 1972).

14. Barbara Brents, "Class Power and the Control of Knowledge: Policy Reform Groups and the Social Security Act," Paper presented to the meeting of the American Sociological Association, San Francisco, 1989, cited in Domhoff, *The Power Elite and the State.* For "welfare capitalism," see David Brody, *Workers in Industrial America* (New York: Oxford University Press, 1980).

15. To determine the labor- and capital-intensive distinctions among firms, we have relied on the 1929 Census of Manufacturers and subsequent primary research by Ferguson, "From Normalcy to New Deal."

16. Levine, *Class Struggle and the New Deal,* pp. 64–91.

17. Ibid.

18. Jeremy Brecher, *Strike!* (San Francisco: Straight Arrow Books, 1972).

19. Kenneth Finegold and Theda Skocpol, *State and Party in America's New Deal* (Madison: The University of Wisconsin Press, 1995), contrast the political success of the AAA with the failure of the NIRA in terms of their concept of "state capacity," pp. 66–115.

20. Ibid., p. 19.

21. John Hope Franklin and Alfred A. Moss, Jr., *From Slavery to Freedom* (New York: Alfred A. Knopf, 1994), p. 395, also write that "few African Americans lamented the fact that the Supreme Court in 1935 declared the NIRA unconstitutional."

22. Barton J. Bernstein, "The New Deal: The Conservative Achievement of Liberal Reform," in Barton Bernstein, ed., *Towards a New Past: Dissenting Essays in American History* (New York: Pantheon Books, 1968), pp. 263–288.

23. Edward Berkowitz and Kim McQuaid, *Creating the Welfare State* (New York: Praeger, 1980), pp. 96–116.

24. Jill Quadagno, "Welfare Capitalism and the Social Security Act of 1935," *American Sociological Review* 49: 640.

25. Ibid., 634.

26. Ibid., 634.

27. Ibid.

28. Thomas Ferguson, "Industrial Conflict and the Coming of the New Deal," p. 23.

29. Domhoff, *The Power Elite and the State,* p. 122.

30. Hearden, *Roosevelt Confronts Hitler,* p. 68.

31. Walter LaFeber, *The American Age: U.S. Foreign Policy at Home and Abroad,* Vol. 2 (New York: Norton, 1994), p. 383.

32. Ibid., p. 375.

33. Armstrong, Philip, Andrew Glyn, and John Harrison, *Capitalism Since World War II: The Making and the Breakup of the Great Boom* (London: Fontana, 1984), p. 12.

34. Ibid.

35. Ibid.

36. See the essay by Bruce Cumings in his edited volume *Child of Conflict* (Seattle: University of Washington Press, 1983) for an overview of the competing interests of sections of capital during the post–World War II period.

37. See Frieden, *Banking on the World.*

38. The prestige and rise of the left in Western Europe as an immediate consequence of its role in the war against Hitler is emphasized by Eric Hobsbawm, *The Age of Extremes* (New York: Pantheon, 1995).

39. Eric Helleiner, *States and the Reemergence of Global Finance: From Bretton Woods to the 1990s* (Ithaca, NY: Cornell University Press), pp. 39–41.

40. A memo from a State Department official to the White House, quoted in Gabriel and Joyce Kolko, *The Limits of Power* (New York: Harper and Row, 1972).

2

The Postwar Political Economy

In this book we advance a business conflict approach to understand the dynamics of U.S. foreign policy in the post–World War II period. The approach builds upon a scholarly tradition that has emphasized the interplay between global and domestic business interests and the U.S. government in the construction of international institutions during the postwar period. In order to explain key transitions in U.S. foreign policy, we develop an alternative terminology that differs from traditional conceptual models used in international relations and political science. We argue that the use of terms such as "state," "national interest," and "interest group" have tended to obscure the relationship between competing business interests and U.S. foreign policy officials.[1]

We offer a conceptual approach that borrows from a venerable tradition of political economy to shed light on the interaction of private and public actors in the international arena. Our contribution is to extend the approach of a business conflict model to an extensive study of major transitions in U.S. foreign policy, including the construction of a Bretton Woods financial regime, which provided the structural foundations for the postwar relations between the United States and Western Europe. The construction of this regime was closely linked to trade and national security policy during the early years of its formulation. Most important, the interaction between competing business groups and U.S. policymakers shaped the development of the Bretton Woods financial regime in such a manner that it cannot be adequately conveyed by previous theories of the evolution of that regime.[2] It is this pattern of interaction that we label "business conflict."

To convey the links between business actors and political institutions, at both the U.S. nation-state and global levels, we have supplemented the traditional use of "state" and "interest group" with "interest blocs," defined as the interlocking relationships between policymakers and business elites in the construction of a global financial and trade regime during the

37

postwar period.[3] The competition among interest blocs in U.S. foreign policy helps explain the domestic and international political battles resulting in the construction of a Bretton Woods financial regime at the end of World War II. In addition, various interest blocs also participated in the dismantling of key aspects of that regime by the mid to late 1970s.

Interest blocs cut across traditional categories of international politics. Such blocs are not confined to the interaction between business elites and national political institutions but involve cooperation and conflict among public and private actors within global institutions.[4] Classical economic theory, especially the development of the product life cycle, provides the structural economic preconditions for the development of interest blocs at the global level. Applications of the product life cycle theory hold that private firms expand their range of investments in response to market competition, from trade to foreign direct investment to integrated global supply networks that link one subsidiary with another. As firms expand their market operations globally, they develop corresponding political structures that link them with various political bureaucracies throughout the world.[5]

The business conflict model argues that such economic expansion has long intersected with political expansion, especially the construction of global institutions necessary for the accumulation of wealth through increased trade and foreign direct investment. After World War II, U.S. political and business internationalists joined Western European internationalists to construct a Bretton Woods financial regime that provided the preconditions for a rapid expansion of trade and investment during the 1950s and 1960s.[6] This financial regime began with the establishment of the World Bank and the International Monetary Fund (IMF) and continued with U.S. bilateral aid programs such as the Marshall Plan and the dramatic increases in military assistance to the North Atlantic Treaty Organization alliance. Although most analysts separate these post–World War II assistance programs, we argue that an internationalist bloc led by the White House, the U.S. State Department, and a group of competitive, capital-intensive international firms supported and developed these measures as a response to political and economic conditions in Europe and the United States. Thus we propose an understanding of global politics that links international and strategic considerations with domestic conflict among business interests and political officials grouped within interest blocs.

In the case of the United States or any other nation-state within the broader constellation of "interest bloc" competition, institutional dynamics—the laws and procedures regulating the cooperation and conflict among competing bureaucracies—affect the way in which interest blocs advance their competing agendas. The federal structure of the United

States has long given business groups at the low end of the product life cycle, or nationalist firms, the ability to advance their agenda through interest blocs tied to political representatives in the U.S. House and Senate.[7] As we will show in this study, the political economy of particular congressional districts often provides important structural clues as to the relative influence of business nationalists or internationalists within Congress. Nationalist interest blocs tied to important congressional committees can have important effects on the construction of global political institutions.[8]

Similarly, internationalist business groups at the high end of the product life cycle can make their influence felt in interest bloc formation at a variety of levels. The distinguishing feature of internationalist firms is their ability to engage in foreign direct investment and extensive foreign trade. By being located at the crossroads of foreign policy making, these internationalists are often able to contribute to interest bloc formation at the global and national levels. For example, U.S.-based multinationals participated in an interest bloc with internationalists in Britain, France, Germany, and the White House and State Department to further an internationalist agenda toward Western Europe during and at the end of World War II.[9] This included the construction of the Bretton Woods financial regime, which includes the IMF and the World Bank and which was stabilized by the Marshall Plan, and the ambitious military spending program outlined by National Security Council document 68 (NSC 68).

Nationalist firms worked with congressional committees in interest blocs opposed to the Bretton Woods system and the Marshall Plan. However, nationalist business groups with strong ties to investments and/or imports of raw materials from the less developed world supported U.S. military expansion in Asia, including the efforts to roll back communism during the Korean War.[10] The coalition between the nationalist and internationalist foreign policy blocs was forged by mutual support for the directives of National Security Council document 68, which satisfied internationalists by increasing economic assistance to Europe and nationalists by extending U.S. military commitments to Asia.

This chapter will show how the interest bloc approach is linked to the product life cycle, national security policy, institutional structure, and class structure in U.S. foreign policy making. At the same time, we will apply the approach to four important foreign policy transitions in the postwar period: the creation of the World Bank and IMF as the pillars of the Bretton Woods financial regime, the development of the Marshall Plan as an extension of this financial regime, the rapid expansion of military spending authorized by NSC 68 as part of an effort to rescue the financial regime, and the important linkage between the rise of military spending and the demise of key aspects of the Fair Deal during the Truman administration.

BUSINESS CONFLICT AND THE PRODUCT LIFE CYCLE

Classical political economy has furnished us the tools to understand how market competition and state regulation combine to influence trade and investment decisions by global corporations. Less attention has been focused on the important role of long-term state and corporate planning in providing the preconditions for foreign trade and investment. Most economists simply assume that corporations will follow the market and ask for state assistance only to protect or enhance the profitability of existing investments.[11] Most political scientists have separated the national interests of state actors from the market interests of private firms. This statist framework assumes that policymakers secure the support of private corporations to promote broader national security goals.[12]

The business conflict model argues that firms at the high end of the product life cycle, defined as capital-intensive firms dependent on foreign direct investment for at least 30 percent of their global profits, are more likely to engage in long-term political planning with high-level executive branch actors. In the United States, these multinationals do not simply lobby the government for resolution of conflicts over foreign investment and trade opportunities. Instead, at key conjunctures in U.S. post–World War II foreign policy, they have engaged in long-term planning to promote the preconditions for a dramatic expansion of foreign investment and trade.

Business internationalists are often able to influence foreign policy making at the highest levels of the executive branch bureaucracy, especially given the fact that the White House and the leading foreign policy advisers are overwhelmingly recruited from the ranks of capital-intensive, Fortune 500 multinational firms. In addition, located at the crossroads of U.S. foreign policy and in charge of formulating the outlines of a broad foreign policy agenda, the president and his immediate advisers often rely on foreign investors for political and economic information regarding countries of strategic and economic importance. A mutual interdependence has long characterized the relationship between the top foreign policy officialdom and the White House, exemplified by a post–World War II commitment by Democratic and Republican presidents to the goals of expanding trade and investment globally and defining U.S. influence by the extent to which a foreign country opens its borders to U.S. foreign direct investment and trade. The entire anti-communist ideology of U.S. foreign policy in the post–World War II period quickly loses meaning unless these goals are appreciated.

However, there is nothing automatic about the particular institutional mechanism that business internationalists use to influence important cabinet officials. As we will demonstrate in our study, administrations are distinctive in the organization of their foreign policy bureaucracy. The hierarchy of cabinet officials relied on to develop foreign policy agendas changes within and between particular administrations. Whether foreign policy is relatively centralized and subject to influence by a few designated officials or more broadly dispersed, highly contested, and subject to debate among numerous competing and conflicting interests can influence the extent to which business internationalists or nationalists are effective or ineffective in promoting particular interests. In addition, the business interests that constitute the core of a party's fund-raising and constituency base also help determine the extent to which nationalists or internationalists can gain influence on foreign policy decisions. As we will show, changes in the international political economy and the competitive positions of particular business firms can result in shifts from one interest bloc to another, indicating the extent to which the formation of interest blocs is dependent on particular structural economic and political factors.

Indeed, no generalization can be made regarding the precise mechanism that business internationalists use to influence and participate in the direction of government policy other than the fact that leading White House foreign policy advisers, and most often high-level foreign policy officials in the State, Treasury, and Commerce Departments, are recruited from the top internationalist business firms in the United States. Their ties to these firms influence their worldview and predispose them toward an internationalist orientation in U.S. foreign policy. But administrations are often conflicted, choosing to rely on a wide range of voices, both internationalist and nationalist (ideologically and economically motivated), to guide them in foreign policy deliberation. Also, administrations recognize the political necessity of negotiating compromises between internationalist and nationalist business sectors, especially when both sectors are influential in Congress and can threaten to block or obstruct foreign policy goals.

Despite its traditional ties to varied business interests, the White House remains concerned with promoting a set of policies that establish the overall framework for foreign investment and trade rather than the particular interests of individual firms. In so doing, it relies on designated officials—formal White House advisers, cabinet officials drawn from designated departments, or leading business internationalists appointed to commissions—to devise strategies to promote the creation of global regimes that provide an institutional framework to increase trade and investment. As we explained in the previous chapter, capital-intensive firms with extensive foreign investments have joined with State Department and White House officials to design the most enduring of the post–World War II regimes, the Bretton Woods financial system.

This financial system was most compatible with the interests of U.S. firms at the high end of the product life cycle, especially commercial banks with European investments and electrical equipment, aeronautics, electronics, petroleum, automobile, and chemical firms.[13] These industries were not monolithic, and among firms within particular industries there were significant nationalist and internationalist divisions based on the firms' levels of foreign investment. Nonetheless, particular firms with a combination of trade and foreign direct investment interests in Europe, as well as prospective direct investors, participated in extensive discussions, research, and planning for a post–World War II Bretton Woods financial regime capable of enhancing investment opportunities in the region.

The Political Economy of Bretton Woods

The outlines of the Bretton Woods regime include the following elements. First, the establishment of a World Bank that would complement, but not compete with, private capital in establishing financing for the infrastructure and exports necessary to attract increased investment to Western Europe. Second, the establishment of the International Monetary Fund, which would provide short-term financing for countries facing balance-of-payments difficulties that inhibited their participation in trade with the United States. Third, an adherence on the part of these multilateral institutions to provide financing for states in exchange for a transitional commitment to currency convertibility. Such convertibility was viewed as essential for the growth of trade and investment between the United States and Western Europe. Finally, an allowance for European governments to maintain capital controls as a way to promote stable exchange rates and to allow for domestic monetary expansion required to fuel increased production.

Overall, the Bretton Woods regime satisfied U.S. foreign direct investors who were able to take advantage of both multilateral and bilateral spending programs to expand their foreign direct investments in Western Europe, especially during the 1950s and 1960s. The lag time between extensive U.S. direct investment in Europe and the construction of the Bretton Woods regime has led most observers to conclude that business interests played little or no role in the development of these postwar institutional arrangements. Such analyses miss the fact that a particular group of firms, namely those at the high end of the product life cycle, participated in the construction of both the Bretton Woods financial regime and bilateral aid programs such as the Marshall Plan with the intention of promoting the preconditions for a rapid expansion of U.S. foreign direct investment during the 1950s.

In a planning document drafted during World War II, the Council on Foreign Relations and the State Department distinguished between firms that would be most supportive of the Bretton Woods regime and bilateral lending and those that would be either ambivalent or opposed. The document, released as part of the *Studies of American Interests in the War and the Peace*, captured the essence of the relevance of the product life cycle and business conflict by distinguishing among three types of firms.[14] The first group of firms were capital-intensive firms that had passed through the first two stages of the product life cycle, domestic production and foreign trade, to enter the third stage characterized by foreign direct investment. This group of firms, according to the document, was most supportive of an aggressive U.S. foreign economic program that provided bilateral and multilateral lending to expand foreign investment opportunities.

These firms, capable of relocating branch plants within regional common markets, were less concerned about dramatic reductions in trade barriers between the United States and Western Europe than were U.S. export-dependent firms. U.S. foreign direct investors supported the creation of a European common market in which investors could expand their European operations through intra-European trade and investment linkages. Although these investors also favored reducing trade barriers between Western Europe and the United States, their priority was to expand investment opportunities within the European market. In documents drafted during World War II, the Council on Foreign Relations, representing these firms, advocated a corporatist coalition among capital-intensive U.S. and European investors, high-level U.S. and European policymakers, and labor unions tied to these sectors in constructing European regional institutions that would provide the preconditions for an expansion of trade and investment in Western Europe.[15]

The second group of firms identified in the planning document were export-dependent U.S. firms that had moved into the second phase of the product life cycle but had few foreign direct investments. These firms, which had close ties to the Commerce Department and various regional ties to the House and the Senate, were committed to lowering European tariff barriers. They hoped to use the General Agreement on Tariffs and Trade (GATT) and multilateral and bilateral lending arrangements as forums and bargaining chips to press European governments to reduce trade barriers. Both exporters and U.S. foreign direct investors tended to support the expansion of multilateral and bilateral lending to Western Europe but on different terms, a disagreement that generated tensions among U.S. interest blocs over the nature of the Bretton Woods financial regime.

At the institutional level, U.S. foreign direct investors worked with State Department officials in an interest bloc committed to establishing European regional institutions that would expand investment and trade opportunities within Western Europe. This bloc remained ambivalent about the conditionality of lower tariff barriers sought by U.S. exporters in exchange for U.S. and multilateral loan guarantees. Foreign direct investors felt that such conditionality was a potential obstacle to the promotion of foreign investment opportunities in Western Europe. They were willing to tolerate high tariff barriers with the United States in favor of a breakdown in European bilateral trade agreements. In addition, both foreign direct investors and exporters to Western Europe expressed support for a key pillar of the Bretton Woods financial regime: capital controls.

Under the terms of Bretton Woods, Western European governments could employ capital controls to limit cross-border financial transactions, thereby protecting their currencies from rapid and uncontrolled devaluation. Such limits on capital mobility were supported by U.S. foreign direct investors and by commercial bankers with loans to European governments or to U.S. and European investors.[16] It was believed that the controls would allow Western European governments to stabilize their domestic currencies and prevent wildly fluctuating exchange rates, thereby encouraging a better environment for foreign investors. For exporters, capital controls were beneficial because they helped check a further run on European currencies in international financial markets, stabilizing the value of European currencies to allow for more favorable conditions for the exportation of U.S. products.[17]

There were significant divisions, however, among sectors of U.S.-based multinational capital over the allowance of capital controls in Western Europe. Investment and commercial bankers without major investments in Western Europe and with close ties to the Treasury Department and the International Monetary Fund tended to oppose capital controls because of their long-standing opposition to unorthodox financial policies.[18] With a few exceptions, U.S.-based multinational financial interests aggressively lobbied against capital controls and used their connections with the Treasury Department and the International Monetary Fund to attempt to impose conditional agreements with Western European loan recipients that entailed the eventual removal of capital controls.[19]

By 1947, however, a competing interest bloc centered on capital-intensive U.S. foreign direct investors, U.S. exporters, banks with loans to U.S. firms with European investments, the State Department, and the Economic Cooperation Administration succeeded in promoting European regional integration schemes that allowed for capital controls.[20] U.S. foreign direct investors, like State Department officials, took a long-term view of European political economy that recognized a linkage between future investment opportunities and political stability within the region. Concerned about the national security threat posed by the strength of Communist parties in France and Italy, these investors felt that capital controls would help maintain economic stability necessary for the promotion of further lending and investment opportunities. U.S. exporters supported capital controls as a vehicle to increase U.S. trade with Western Europe by stabilizing the value of European currencies. Particular international events between 1947 and 1949 bolstered the position of this interest bloc against its opponents in the Treasury Department and the IMF.

By 1947, State Department officials and U.S. foreign direct investors spoke of the urgency of stabilizing the European political economies against the twin threats of a "dollar gap" and a political crisis centered on the revival of class struggle that threatened to promote nationalistic solutions to European economic problems.[21] For both State Department officials committed to providing a broad policy framework for the long-term accumulation of capital in Western Europe and U.S. foreign direct investors concerned about prospects for future large-scale European regional operations, the necessity for a dramatic expansion of U.S. bilateral lending programs was becoming obvious. For such an expansion to occur, however, this interest bloc would need the cooperation of a third group of firms, close to congressional Republicans and midwestern Democrats, that had little or no interest in the Western European market.

As early as the 1940s, the Council on Foreign Relations expressed concern that a third group of U.S. firms, business nationalists, would attempt to block foreign lending programs to Europe (and elsewhere) because of their relative dependence on either the U.S. market or, in some cases, the U.S. market and less developed markets in Latin America and Asia. Nationalist firms, compared with their counterparts that depended on trade and investments in Western Europe, were more interested in protecting their position in the U.S. market and, in some cases, their access to raw materials exports and investments in the less developed world. They had little interest in, and expressed much opposition to, U.S. foreign aid packages destined for business competitors in Western Europe.[22]

However, in the area of national security, business nationalists could often be persuaded to support aid packages explicitly billed as anticommunist in purpose. Business internationalists, tied to the White House and State Department, sought to take advantage of a changing international environment to promote dramatic shifts in the direction of U.S. policy: first via the Marshall Plan and second via the proposed increases in military spending that solidified U.S.-European alliances by dramatically increasing U.S. military aid to European economies. The national security context of such bilateral lending is crucial for understanding the ways in which internationalists promoted lending programs to appeal to nationalist interest blocs in Congress that were otherwise hostile to an expansion of foreign aid.

As the following sections illustrate, interest blocs formed around the key pillars of post–World War II economic assistance to Western Europe. An internationalist interest bloc involving the White House, the State Department, foreign direct investors, and exporters often used national security rhetoric to attempt to win support for important aid programs. This bloc championed the creation of Bretton Woods multilateral institutions, bilateral aid programs such as the Marshall Plan, and, finally, dramatic increases in U.S. military spending outlined in National Security Council document 68. Institutionally, this internationalist interest bloc extended to congressional representatives in districts characterized by commercial ties to Western Europe, whether through bank loans or through foreign direct investments in the region. As we demonstrate later, congressional representatives from such districts tended to consistently support U.S. aid programs. This bloc also received organizational support from internationalist business firms within the Council on Foreign Relations, the Committee for Economic Development, the Business Advisory Council, and the leadership of the American Federation of Labor and Congress of Industrial Organizations (AFL-CIO), all of whom worked with White House and State Department officials and, in some cases, European political and business officials from the Economic Cooperation Administration in planning and implementing the post–World War II aid regime.

As discussed earlier, both U.S. foreign direct investors and exporters to Western Europe largely supported developmental assistance after World War II. However, they were divided in their preferences for implementation of the various forms of assistance. U.S. exporters with ties to the Commerce Department pushed for aid on the conditionality of immediate reductions in trade barriers between the United States and Western European countries. Some investment and commercial bankers pushed for an end to capital controls that inhibited financial speculation in the region. In fact, a number of leading investment bankers criticized the International Monetary Fund precisely because the institution did not pressure Western European governments to remove capital controls.

In opposition to the agenda of this internationalist interest bloc, a business nationalist bloc formed around congressional districts with little or no ties to Western Europe. These districts were dominated by two types of firms: nationalist firms tied to the U.S. market and expansionist firms with a stake in exports or foreign direct investments in the Latin American or Asian markets. The expansionist firms could be counted on to support aid programs designed to oppose communism and protect U.S. investments in the less developed world, especially Asian investments. However, both nationalists and expansionists were consistently opposed to U.S. aid programs to Europe. The organizations most active in building opposition to the European aid programs included the National Association of Manufacturers (NAM), local chambers of commerce with a base in nationalist congressional districts, and various local trade associations.

The divisions between internationalist and nationalist interest blocs can be seen most clearly by a careful examination of the institutional fault lines that divided the two blocs in Congress, which we explore in a later section of this chapter. First, however, we examine the particular divisions between these blocs in the context of the Bretton Woods financial regime and the Marshall Plan. Then we explore the interrelationship between the institutional conflicts among the various business sectors and the growth of a political coalition advocating dramatic increases in military spending proposed by National Security Council document 68. It is here that we link the domestic politics of the United States, including the fate of the Truman administration's Fair Deal, with the administration's effort to lead an interest bloc committed to massive increases in U.S. military spending, which served as an extension of the multilateral and bilateral aid programs sought by the United States beginning with the construction of a Bretton Woods financial regime.

BUSINESS CONFLICT AND BRETTON WOODS

An internationalist bloc of firms, led by the Council on Foreign Relations and the Committee for Economic Development, worked with the State Department to draft the outlines of the Bretton Woods Monetary Agreements during World War II. The council and the committee represented a group of capital-intensive investors who either had a stake in the Western European markets or hoped to expand their investments in the region. These internationalist business interests included Standard Oil, General Motors, General Electric, ITT, Pan American Airlines, Westinghouse, the National City Bank of New York, General Mills, American President Lines, Bristol-Myers, Hilton Hotels, and Chase National Bank.[23] They championed a Bretton Woods agreement that would complement but not compete with private capital in establishing the preconditions for an influx of new loans and foreign direct investment into Western Europe.

Internationalists overwhelmingly agreed on the need for the World Bank and worked to establish the parameters within which the organization would operate. Industrialists within the internationalist bloc secured guarantees from the State and Treasury Departments that the World Bank would not displace private investors in their funding of long-term, low-interest projects. U.S. commercial and investment bankers were concerned about the potential inflationary aspects of such lending but were reassured by the fact that leaders of the bank would be drawn from the U.S. banking establishment. State Department officials assured the New York investment banking establishment, a leading force behind the American Bankers Association, an early critic of capital controls and the potential expansionary impact of the Bretton Woods Monetary Agreements, that the World Bank would work closely with Wall Street in making securities and bonds available for purchase by private investors.

Foreign direct investors and exporters benefited from World Bank loans to Western Europe, especially during the 1945 to 1947 period, prior to the approval and implementation of the Marshall Plan. The first article of the Articles of Agreement that established the guidelines for bank lending indicated that a major purpose of the bank was to "promote private foreign investment by means of guarantees or participation in loans and other investments made by private investors; and when private capital is not available on reasonable terms, to supplement private investment by providing, on suitable conditions, finance for productive purposes out of its own capital funds raised by it and its other resources."[24] In addition, World Bank loans to Western Europe benefited U.S. exporters because these program loans financed imports in many different sectors of the European economy rather than specific projects, which was more typical of the bank's loans to low-income countries.

The first World Bank loan was a $250 million package to France in 1946. France was obligated to use the loan to overhaul and rebuild its steel industry and to import a wide variety of industrial goods, equipment, and raw materials. This program loan allowed U.S. producers of commercial airplanes, oil, semifinished steel products, and other industrial raw materials to export to France under the terms of the agreement. The French government was obligated to deliver receipts for purchases of all of these items to the World Bank. In addition, the French government guaranteed that no other foreign loans would have priority over the bank's loan.[25] The World Bank loan to France established the pattern for further bank assistance to European countries, including a 1947 loan to Denmark that financed the import of agricultural and textile machinery, machine tools, trucks, steel products, textiles, and chemicals.[26]

Internationalists expressed unanimous support for the World Bank, whose loans served to benefit U.S. foreign direct investors, exporters, and private bankers whose purchase of bonds financed much of the Bank's early operations. However, much has been made of the opposition of some international commercial and investment banks to the International Monetary Fund, especially in Fred Block's influential study of the period and in Eric Helleiner's more recent study. Block greatly emphasizes the influence of Treasury Department officials such as Harry Dexter White in the original planning of the International Monetary Fund during World War II. It is true that White's plans went well beyond what the U.S.-based international financial community would accept. Early criticism of the fund by U.S. bankers pointed to the potential inflationary aspect of the fund's lending programs (as drafted by White). Bankers felt that loans were going to be too easy to obtain, thereby generating inflationary pressures throughout Europe. The American Bankers Association objected to the lack of U.S. veto power over dollar loans made by the fund (in contrast to those made by the World Bank). They also objected to the broad terms of IMF lending, which, as initially drafted, could be used for general stabilization purposes for countries facing difficulties in maintaining the value of their currencies.

Reflecting this opposition, the House Banking and Currency Committee initially blocked the Bretton Woods Monetary Agreements with an alliance between internationalist New York bankers and nationalist House Republicans. The nationalist Republicans were close to domestic interests opposed to foreign multilateral aid commitments. Representative Howard Buffett, a Nebraska Republican, joined with leaders of the National Association of Manufacturers in a nationalist bloc opposed to the bill. The NAM testified against the World Bank and the IMF, arguing that the agreement violated the spirit of free enterprise by substituting government assistance for private market initiative. Internationalist New York bankers joined in opposing the IMF, fearing that it would be "wrongly used by needy countries to provide themselves with short-term reconstruction and transition loans under the excuse of monetary adjustments."[27]

Responding to the previous concerns, the pro–Bretton Woods internationalist bloc greatly circumscribed the role of the IMF in order to convert the bankers. Working with the State and Commerce Departments during World War II, the business internationalist Committee for Economic Development, whose membership consisted of both foreign direct investors and exporters to Western Europe, as well as international commercial bankers, reduced the broad discretionary lending of the IMF in favor of short-term loans to alleviate specified balance-of-payments deficits. The eventual fund agreement, which regulated the lending patterns of the institution, required that the fund limit its loans "to countries in deficit, out of its holdings of gold and currencies arising from subscriptions (to the Fund) by its members in relation to their 'quotas' (to be determined according to each member's size in the world economy)."[28] But the fund was not allowed to lend to finance outflows of capital (a provision insisted on by the United States). The amendments largely satisfied commercial bankers, especially the New York faction of the internationalist bloc, which eventually, if somewhat reluctantly, supported the Bretton Woods accords through its most influential lobbying group, the American Bankers Association.

Having consolidated support among internationally oriented firms, the following people testified before the House Committee on Banking and Currency on behalf of the Bretton Woods Monetary Agreements: Randolph Burgess of National City Bank of New York; W. L. Hemingway of the American Bankers Association; Charles Dewey of Chase National Bank; William McC. Martin, chairman of the Export-Import Bank; Leon Fraser, president of First National Bank of New York; Leonard Ayres, vice-president of Cleveland Trust Co.; and Carl M. Wynne, president of the

Chicago Exports Managers Club. In addition, over 100 firms with a stake in exports or foreign direct investments in Western Europe formed the Business and Industry Committee for Bretton Woods. The shift of the American Bankers Association in favor of the agreements was enough to generate a remarkable turnaround on the House Banking and Currency Committee, which agreed to release the bill to a floor vote. The measure was approved by wide margins in both the House and the Senate.[29]

However, divisions persisted during the implementation of the Bretton Woods financial regime in Western Europe. Foreign direct investors and exporters tended to support a Bretton Woods regime that encouraged a liberal multilateral lending policy that facilitated increased production and investment opportunities. This internationalist bloc formed links between U.S. investors, exporters, and White House and State Department officials who opted for a "productionist approach" to European lending. This approach supported the maintenance of capital controls, advocated low levels of conditionality in exchange for multilateral (and bilateral) loans, and sought to liberalize the availability of assistance from the World Bank and the International Monetary Fund.

Internationalists within the Treasury Department, along with IMF officials, however, typically emphasized a "monetarist approach" in multilateral lending arrangements. This approach, advocated by some investment and commercial bankers (most notably the American Bankers Association), emphasized high levels of conditionality in multilateral lending programs. Specifically, bankers tended to prefer guarantees from Western European borrowers that efforts would be made to reduce and eliminate capital controls as a condition for borrowing money from the International Monetary Fund. In addition, bankers close to the Treasury Department and the IMF advocated stricter terms for borrowers than their counterparts in the White House, State Department, and Commerce Department. Investment bankers, in particular, wanted specified efforts to stabilize currencies through adjustments of government budgets as a precondition for assistance in addition to the removal of capital controls. Bureaucratic conflicts thus emerged within the internationalist interest bloc committed to Bretton Woods, causing some amount of confusion in the implementation of the Bretton Woods financial regime.

Ultimately, the limitations and bureaucratic conflict surrounding the World Bank and the International Monetary Fund posed problems for an internationalist bloc concerned about a growing dollar gap in Western Europe. The fact that European economies were experiencing an economic crisis in 1947, complete with the emergence of Communist Party coalition governments in France and Italy, led State Department planners and their allies in the business world to push for a bilateral assistance program to supplement existing multilateral aid programs. In addition, State Department officials recognized that the Treasury Department and the International Monetary Fund had some institutional power to limit multilateral financing. The close relationship among investment bankers, the Treasury Department, and the IMF prevented State Department officials from dramatically increasing the availability of multilateral assistance. However, bilateral aid programs could overcome these limitations by placing their implementation under the control of a productionist bloc of internationalists including the State Department and U.S. foreign direct investors.

BUSINESS CONFLICT AND THE MARSHALL PLAN

The financial regime outlined in the Bretton Woods Monetary Agreements failed to satisfy a U.S.-based internationalist bloc intent on closing the European dollar gap and expanding U.S. trade and investment in Western Europe. Bureaucratic conflicts emerged between a productionist bloc centered on U.S. foreign direct investors, U.S. exporters, the White House, and the State Department and a monetarist bloc linking commercial and investment bankers, the Treasury Department, and the International Monetary Fund. By 1947 the productionist bloc communicated extensively regarding the limitations (and ultimate failure) of the multilateral loans to help generate the conditions for European recovery. Whereas the productionist bloc wanted to extend the availability of multilateral assistance, the monetarist bloc wanted any assistance packages, especially those from the IMF, conditioned by monetary and fiscal adjustments in the recipient countries, especially the convertibility of currencies and the removal of capital controls.

Despite the availability of multilateral assistance and some U.S. bilateral aid, the foreign exchange reserves of Europe and Japan were being rapidly depleted. In 1946–1947, the rest of the world used about $6 billion to finance its deficit with the United States. The gold and dollar reserves of Europe fell by one-fourth in this period. State Department officials, led by Undersecretary of State Dean Acheson and Undersecretary of State for Economic Affairs William Clayton, connected the fate of the European economies with the long-term growth needs of the U.S. economy. Acheson felt that the United States needed to sustain the $14 billion in exports that helped it pull out of the Depression during World War II. White House and State Department officials argued that the economic crisis in Europe would soon lead to the rise of leftist nationalist solutions unless immediate steps were taken to raise production.

Within this context, Secretary of State George Marshall delivered his Marshall Plan address in June 1947. At the same time, William Clayton began assembling a group of private sector internationalists, exporters, and foreign direct investors to enlist support for the broad outlines of the most ambitious U.S. aid package in history. The formulation of the aid package involved U.S. firms at the highest end of the product life cycle, which either had or were planning foreign direct investments in Western Europe. U.S. exporters to Europe also supported the Marshall Plan, with its promises of increased European production leading to increased exports, but were less involved in the formulation and implementation of Marshall Plan directives.

The productionist bloc linked the State Department, high-level White House officials, and U.S. investors with European ministers, senior officials, and industrialists to guide the implementation of the Marshall Plan. This arrangement led to the close involvement of U.S. officials in the economic policies of the recipient countries. In each country the United States established a mission headed by a director with ambassadorial rank and staffed with business and government experts on industry, trade, and finance. The corporatist makeup of the Marshall Plan involved close cooperation between governments and U.S. and European business and labor groups with interests in expanding production opportunities throughout the European market. The final outlines of the Marshall Plan agreements indicate that it was geared toward increased production and trade within the European market but allowed European governments to continue to protect their domestic industry with tariffs and capital controls.

The framework of the Marshall Plan achieved some of the broad objectives of the U.S. productionist bloc in securing easier terms of assistance for Western European governments than had been possible through multilateral lending. The bilateral character of the Marshall Plan ensured that the State Department negotiated the terms of the U.S. loan packages with European aid recipients through such entities as the European Recovery Administration and the Organization for European Economic Cooperation (OEEC). The result was that the monetarist bloc in the Treasury Department and the IMF was now unable to substantially affect the terms of the loans. As a result, the Marshall Plan, with its allowance of capital controls and its agreements to delay currency convertibility, focused on providing assistance to increase production and trade opportunities throughout Western Europe. This productionist approach benefited some U.S. firms exporting to the region, especially those that could "jump over" the European wide tariff barriers, and provided the preconditions necessary for a dramatic expansion of U.S. foreign direct investment during the 1950s.

In brief, the Marshall Plan continued, on productionist terms, the financial aid regime that the U.S.-based internationalist bloc had begun with the establishment of the World Bank and the International Monetary Fund. The precise terms of Marshall Plan lending included three important characteristics:

1. Marshall Plan loans were exchanged for efforts by European countries to liberalize trade among themselves while maintaining restrictions on imports from dollar areas. The United States sponsored the creation of the European Payments Union to facilitate the liberalization and expansion of multilateral intra-European trade and payments while enabling European countries to conserve their scarce dollar reserves.

2. The United States encouraged aid recipients to expand their exports to the dollar area, and European governments devalued their currencies by about 30 percent in 1949 to comply with this effort. Multilateral assistance had been unable to accomplish such a devaluation, but Marshall Planners had succeeded in bargaining for it.

3. To appease international bankers, governments receiving Marshall Plan assistance were encouraged not to spend it all for imports but to hold a portion of the dollars so as to rebuild their depleted reserves. Pursuit of balance-of-payments surpluses was established as a laudable objective.[30]

The terms of the Marshall Plan reflected several converging interests that united to develop the outlines of the plan. These interests included European ministries favoring some levels of protection against U.S. exports, European investors hoping to take advantage of opportunities to expand their investments throughout the region, and capital-intensive U.S. investors hoping to establish the preconditions for increased U.S. foreign direct investment throughout the region. The State Department and the White House guided this global interest bloc committed to breaking down intra-European tariff barriers but maintaining import restrictions and capital controls. Other U.S. interests, specifically the American Bankers Association, were largely shut out of the implementation of the Marshall Plan. Having advocated a monetarist approach to multilateral and bilateral lending, and joined by bureaucratic allies in the Treasury Department and the International Monetary Fund, these bankers criticized the implementation of the plan because it maintained capital controls. However, bankers with extensive loans to Europe had been strong supporters of the Marshall Plan in Congressional hearings, though they played a small role in the implementation of the Plan.[31]

U.S. exporters, many of whom had been strong supporters of the Marshall Plan in Congress, also criticized the implementation of the plan. Exporters felt that the plan did not go far enough in guaranteeing eventual progress in reducing U.S.-European trade barriers. Still, U.S. production advantages were so great at the outset of the implementation of the Marshall Plan that most exporters chose to maintain solid backing for the plan, despite some misgivings. In congressional hearings, U.S. exporters joined with a wide range of international investors in supporting the plan against nationalist critics. The inability of U.S. export interests to secure their

objectives from the Marshall Plan reflected the fact that European governments were simply unwilling to cooperate in guaranteeing substantial reductions in tariff barriers with the United States but were willing to expand
trading opportunities on a regional basis within Western Europe.

On the other side of the interest bloc divide, nationalists relied on
leaders from the National Association of Manufacturers and congressional
representatives from the West and Midwest to oppose the Marshall Plan.
These interests, led by businessmen Curtis Calder (NAM) and Arnold Wilson (Illinois NAM) and Senator Burke Hickenlooper (Iowa Republican),
argued that the Marshall Plan was a form of state planning that threatened
the principles of the free enterprise system. They criticized the plan as
"undermining the American economy through taxes and inflation and post-
poning the inevitable day of reckoning for profligate European planners
and politicians."[32] This nationalist bloc wanted three guarantees from Europe in exchange for U.S. assistance:

1. a provision that guaranteed the United States access to strategic
   materials and air bases, especially in European colonies or former
   colonies in Asia;
2. a stronger anticommunist and anti-Soviet posture on the part of
   U.S. and European governments; and
3. a willingness on the part of Europeans to cease all socialistic programs and to provide U.S. businessmen advantageous treatment in
   relation to the nationals of any other country.[33]

The nationalist bloc included an expansionist current that had extensive investments in and trade with Asia. However, the bloc had little or no
European investments. The White House and the State Department hoped
to build a bridge to these expansionist interests, especially the "Asia-
firsters," by emphasizing that the aid program would provide access to raw
materials and primary products in the underdeveloped world. In fact, State
Department planners saw a relationship between European recovery and
overseas European territories, especially in Africa and Asia. Early drafts of
the Marshall Plan argued for the importance of a revival of trade networks
that would involve increased European exports to their territories, thereby
easing their balance-of-payments problems. The territories would earn dollars to pay for those exports by selling raw materials and primary products
to the United States.[34]

The Marshall Plan included various mechanisms to increase the sales
of raw materials, strategic materials, and primary products to the United
States. The inclusion of these mechanisms satisfyied the interests of business expansionists who would be able to take advantage of Asian investments and also spoke to the interests of the internationalist bloc by taking

the steps it believed necessary to promote European recovery. First, various mechanisms for U.S. stockpiling of raw materials were built into the operating structure of the European Recovery Program. For example, the United States could use up to 5 percent of the counterpart funds its aid generated to purchase strategic materials. Second, the U.S. aid treaties negotiated with each European country included guaranteed access for U.S. investors "to the development of raw materials within participating countries on terms of treatment equivalent to those afforded to the nationals of the participating country concerned." Third, a special Marshall Plan fund was established for investments in increased production of strategic materials.[35]

The inclusion of such provisions in the Marshall Plan aid package swayed business nationalists with investments in Asia, as well as prospective U.S. mineral investors, to support the Marshall Plan. The Truman administration used a combination of national security rhetoric and investment guarantees for U.S. firms in the less developed world to win support for the bilateral program. This did not succeed, of course, in swaying ideological nationalists or those who objected to aid programs in principle. Nor did it succeed in swaying nationalists who had little or no important foreign investments in the less developed world. Still, the broad use of Marshall Plan funds suggested the institutional alliances that might be secured by internationalists hoping to expand U.S. bilateral assistance to Western Europe.

The economic limitations of the Marshall Plan were becoming clear by late 1949 and early 1950, when economic trends suggested that European recovery was not proceeding fast enough to give potential U.S. investors the confidence to increase their business inventories. Despite increases in production facilitated by the Marshall Plan, State Department officials recognized that the plan ultimately would not solve the dollar gap problem. European countries would not be able to earn enough dollars to cover its dollar trade deficit or to expand the purchase of U.S. products. The termination of Marshall Plan funding in 1952 threatened to increase the strategic and economic problems facing the U.S.-based internationalist bloc: progressive insulation of the European economies, reduced trade with the United States, and limited opportunities for increasing foreign direct investment in the region.

The logical response would have been to extend the Marshall Plan for three or four more years until Europe was able to earn more dollars through increased trade with the United States and increased foreign direct investment. Nationalists in Congress were not likely to permit such an option, however. In addition, some members of the original coalition of internationalist firms that supported the Marshall Plan, especially U.S. export interests, were becoming skeptical of its positive impact. In 1949, European ministries used the Organization for European Economic Cooperation to block moves toward liberalizing trade with the United States. U.S. Marshall planners hoped to use $150 million in the plan's appropriations to reward countries that had made the most progress in tariff reduction and were suffering from balance-of-payments problems. The OEEC blocked such a measure, antagonizing U.S. export interests that believed the Marshall Plan had not done enough to reduce tariff barriers on U.S. exports.

Meanwhile, congressional nationalists thought the Marshall Plan had not gone far enough in securing guarantees for U.S. business interests. Nationalists criticized the plan as an aid giveaway that offered little to help U.S.-based producers expand their operations in Europe. Given such strong criticism of the plan, the Truman administration felt that the chances for an extension of aid from Congress were slim.

These political circumstances were aggravated by a U.S. recession of late 1948, 1949, and early 1950. The recession has been described as an inventory recession caused by a major disinvestment in business inventories, especially among export-oriented firms with a stake in European markets. There had been a decline in business investment in capital goods of approximately $6 billion between the first quarter of 1948 and the last quarter of 1949. The decline was accompanied by concern, reflected in the business press, regarding the limitations of the Marshall Plan in significantly expanding U.S. exports to the European market. This trend was exacerbated by the fall of U.S. exports to $3.6 billion in the second half of 1949, which reversed the favorable trends in export growth at the outset of the Marshall Plan. The fluctuations in total exports and the increasing percentages of exports financed by temporary aid flows meant that export demand did not appear to be strong or stable enough to justify new additions to industrial capacity. In addition, unemployment averaged 5.9 percent in 1949 and reached a peak of 7.6 percent in February 1950.

State Department planners were concerned about the ability of the internationalist bloc to maintain levels of European assistance compatible with the amount deemed necessary to sustain the health of the U.S. domestic economy.[36] The divergent interests within the internationalist bloc, as well as nationalist opposition to European aid that was expressed in congressional hearings, led senior White House and State Department officials to look for other solutions to the ongoing dollar gap crisis in Europe. Ultimately, State Department planners decided that an increased program of military aid to Europe would solve the U.S. strategic and economic crises while allowing for the formation of a domestic political coalition firmly committed to the foreign policy strategy of the internationalist bloc.

THE MILITARIZATION OF THE FAIR DEAL

The commitment of a liberal state to war, even war on a global scale, does not suspend that nation's domestic social and political conflicts. The war mobilization of 1942–1945 introduced a degree of state intervention, bureaucratic planning, and organization of labor on an unprecedented scale. The war economy produced enormous growth for the core sectors of U.S. industry as well as the leverage of a full-employment economy for labor. Under conditions of wartime autarchy, the U.S. manufacturing sectors rebounded from the Great Depression.

In the postwar period, a resurgence of business nationalism initially supported a broad diminution of the "warfare-welfare" state created in the 1930s and 1940s. With voter turnout down, owing in part to wartime displacement of wage workers, and with higher-income voters and many businesses irritated by the restriction on consumer markets, the Republicans briefly returned to majority status in Congress after the 1946 elections with promises to "clean house" and "sweep out" the bureaucrats and New Dealers. In the context of peace, this initially meant cutting the military budget as well as the New Deal.[37]

The initiation of the Cold War would eventually change the political calculus of budgeting, but the antipathy of many business nationalists to liberal internationalism had, and still does have, material roots. However, the development of postwar capitalism would draw U.S. business nationalists away from isolationism and toward a strident anticommunism that often favored colonialist-style military intervention.

An elite coalition with strong ties to the executive branch and the national Democratic Party had developed the Bretton Woods framework. As described earlier, this framework for trade, international monetary policy, and market development served the interests of both commodity and capital exporters with a strong orientation to European reconstruction (in combination with the Marshall Plan). Liberal internationalists tended to favor, or at least allow for, a somewhat Keynesian-style resuscitation of European industry, albeit within the discipline that currency convertibility would place upon European fiscal policy. Business nationalists, in contrast, certainly had no material interest in restoring foreign manufacturing and agriculture to their prewar market positions.

The Truman administration's initially moderate reaction to the victory of the Chinese Communists and its antipathy to Chiang Kai-shek's junta on Formosa indicate the specifics of the global orientation of the liberal internationalist tendency in the late 1940s. The administration, consistent with the interests of its liberal coalition, was interested in developing a foreign aid approach as articulated in Truman's "Point Four" that would promote New Deal–style development policies as the means of competing with the communist appeal in Asia and other "emerging nations," as they were often referred to. Conservative Republicans in Congress, who had close ties to the nationalist business sectors, strongly opposed this approach on both ideological and economic grounds and were able to minimize the foreign aid spending proposed by the Truman administration.

However, as both Cumings and Frieden point out, the nationalist business sector also included interests that imported raw materials such as cloth, rubber, and minerals, and these interests were threatened by communist expansion, especially in East and Southeast Asia. In the context of the Korean War, business nationalists would, to a degree, acquiesce to the administration's spending policies.[38]

The Korean War does appear to have been the efficient cause of the rapid shift toward the militarization of the Fair Deal. However, even as military spending increased from $13.5 billion to $45 billion in less than three years (1949–1951), relatively little of this amount was actually used to finance the war in Korea. As Fordham points out, "military budgets have not since returned to the relatively low levels prevailing between 1946 and 1950." NSC 68 proposed a rapid and massive U.S. rearmament plan that would simultaneously provide for the containment of the perceived Soviet threat and provide Europeans with needed foreign exchange to finance the U.S. trade surplus and cope with the problem of the "dollar overhang."[39]

While there was a superficial foreign policy consensus in favor of Truman's intervention in Korea, there was a significant degree of stress placed on the internationalist bloc in both Congress and public opinion.[40] In the Senate, Joseph McCarthy was able to use the intensification of Cold War sentiment to forward right-wing efforts not only to deinstitutionalize what was left of the left but also to take aim at liberal internationalism more broadly. Hamby typifies the McCarthyites as neoisolationist in that they seemed more concerned with fighting domestic "subversion" and internal anticommunism than with the fate of nascent democracies elsewhere.[41]

The congressional allies of the business nationalists favored the military intervention in Korea. Indeed, many supported General Douglas MacArthur against Truman in the former's more aggressive and overtly pro-Taiwanese orientation. In the executive branch, this tendency was represented by Defense Secretary Louis Johnson, who up until the outbreak of war in Korea had been aggressively administering the cutting of the defense budget. Johnson was known as a conservative Democrat who had been an effective fund raiser for Truman in 1948; his public support of MacArthur led to his dismissal as defense chief at the same time that Truman fired MacArthur.[42] As was the case with Secretary Johnson, business nationalists in general did not support the broad buildup of military spending, particularly because, as Eden finds, it was linked to trade and aid in the right's perspective at the time.[43] This discovery is consistent with Fordham's finding that conservative Republicans in the Senate voted consistently against the Truman administration's stated positions on domestic policy and opposed increased military spending for purposes of European aid/rearmament.

Hamby portrays McCarthyism as "irrational," yet it is intriguing to note that one of its first victims was one of the very architects of the Bretton Woods arrangement, Harry Dexter White.[44] Indeed, McCarthy's own voting pattern was one consistent with the interests of business nationalism: opposing the Fair Deal and the rearmament program pursuant to NSC 68. Wisconsin industries such as meatpacking and paper milling were (and remain) protectionist (as was McCarthy) and did not contain the kind of finance capital sector or foreign direct investment interests that were elsewhere associated with liberalism or, at least, consensus internationalism.

Conservative business nationalism expressed in the form of trade protectionism and opposition to expressions of liberal internationalism such as foreign aid (military or otherwise) would remain a strong tendency, especially in the Republican Party. In 1952, this faction would fight for the nomination of Senator Robert Taft over Dwight Eisenhower and it would continue to fight trade liberalism, benefit little from the full implementation of the Bretton Woods system, and resurface in the Goldwater coalition of 1964.

That the Truman administration succeeded in militarizing fiscal policy, even as its pursuit of the Fair Deal seemed to cool, was due in part to the support of southern Democrats and some northeastern Republicans. These two groups tended to oppose the Fair Deal but had a more internationalist perspective on the trade/aid/military spending continuum. In the case of the internationalist or "liberal" Republicans such as Arthur Vandenberg (Michigan), John Foster Dulles (New York), and Henry Cabot Lodge (Massachusetts)—to name probably the three best known to history—they represented states with significant interests in rebuilding the European capital or consumer markets. Their constituencies also contained better organized New Deal coalition elements, and these politicians (particurly Vandenberg) were willing to give occasional mild support to the Fair Deal as well.

Southern Democrats of this period are a study in how the particularities of the U.S. federal state can mediate business conflict. The election of 1946 had wiped out liberal Democrats in the North but had not affected the secure incumbency of Democrats in the South. The 1948 elections had reinvigorated the size of the liberal Democratic faction in Congress, but these new members lacked the seniority of their southern counterparts. The seniority system worked to the advantage of the southern Democrats, who could use their embedded positions to channel military spending to their home states and districts, thus adapting regional economic development strategy to the new fiscal politics of the militarized Fair Deal. With relatively less industry facing incipient competition from Europe and an interest in maintaining export markets for agricultural and other industrial commodities (such as food processing; e.g., Coca-Cola), the southern

Democrats joined with moderate Republicans and nearly all of the liberal Democrats in a Cold War internationalist bloc that reflected the broad interests of U.S. business, including export-oriented manufacturing, defense-related industries, investment banking, and export-oriented agriculture.[45] Meanwhile, the southern Democrats strenuously opposed the Fair Deal agenda on civil rights and the Taft-Hartley repeal, as one would expect in a region of low unionization and labor-intensive industry low on the product life cycle curve.

The election of 1948 resulted not only in a return to a Democratic Congress but also in the surprising re-election of Harry Truman after a campaign in which the president ran on the Fair Deal platform and excoriated the "do-nothing" Republican Congress for failing to make popular social reforms. The Fair Deal was to include expanded public housing, national health care, civil rights legislation, and the repeal of the Taft-Hartley Act. None of the above occurred. The major accomplishment of the Fair Deal was the expansion of the Social Security program.[46] This expansion, however, was essentially an increase in benefit levels for the categories of workers already included; domestic and agricultural workers remained outside of this most basic of New Deal reforms. Despite strong popular support in a housing market that would remain tight into the 1950s, public housing was cut. Taft-Hartley remained unaltered, despite immediate postelection expectations to the contrary, even in the business press, that it would be repealed or at least significantly modified in a pro-labor direction.

Wartime restraint of business, designed to maintain uninterrupted production, had aided the growth of organized labor. Yet the regulation of labor in wartime also set the stage for a postwar counterattack on labor's newfound influence in the U.S. political economy. Although wartime planning and control did increase the rate of unionization, it was in a manner that severely restricted the rank and file insurgencies so widespread in the late 1930s. To strike or otherwise engage in militant action was portrayed as traitorous by both business and government. In order to stem a groundswell of labor unrest, particularly evident late in the war and in the immediate postwar period, labor's erstwhile friends in government increasingly sought legislative authority to intervene in and halt strikes. The war had brought full employment, but wages had not kept pace with prices, owing in no small part to business's greater ability to dodge controls or bully the Office of Price Administration (OPA) with threats of congressional intervention.[47] Indeed it was Truman himself who had asked for legislative power to intervene in strikes at the opening of the Republican majority Congress in 1947. Taft-Hartley, of course, went well beyond what was politically acceptable to the administration and was vetoed. But there was elite consensus on both extending executive power to intervene in strikes in the national interest and decertifying of unions that refused to purge Communists or suspected Communists from leadership positions.[48]

Labor policy in the 1940s resubordinated unions to a subaltern position within the liberal-internationalist bloc. The purge of labor leadership, the outright destruction of several of the more militant CIO unions through anticommunism, and the spread of open shop laws in the South and the West broke the spread of the union movement at a time when it appeared to be taking control of the Democratic Party in some parts of the country.

Labor had few options other than the Democratic Party. Many labor activists favored a third party effort, although the increasing dominance of anticommunist rhetoric in this period placed severe hurdles along this path as it increasingly came to give the non-Stalinist left a pariah status as well.[49] Those who had backed Henry Wallace's third-party effort in 1948 frequently hid this association in subsequent years.[50] Further, organized labor at its peak represented less than a third of the workforce; it could give significant organizational support to issues and candidates in many states, but it could not mobilize millions of voters in an independent political direction, as the example of John L. Lewis's support for Wendell Willkie suggests. (It is easier to move millions of dollars from one campaign to another than to change the partisan loyalties of millions of voters, a structural advantage of business over labor in mass democratic politics that has yet to be fully explored.) Finally, and perhaps most significant of all, labor's leadership retained strongly conservative business union tendencies, especially in the AFL, and probably lacked the militancy requisite for mass action at a national level such as that pursued by the British and French trade unions in the 1920s and 1930s.

The evisceration of the broad left by anticommunism is exemplified by the domestic politics of the Korean War. While the war stalemated and became increasingly unpopular, the left played virtually no role in organizing domestic protest or opposition. The Progressive Party managed to maintain its existence and put forth the antiwar candidacy of Vincent Hallinan in 1952, but its votes were few and its support in the liberal journals of opinion nonexistent. The Cold War reconfigured the ideological environment in a manner helpful to resurgent business nationalism, adaptable to the needs of business internationalism, and distinctly detrimental to the progressive elements of the New Deal coalition.

The role of ideology in politics may be understood not only as the expression of interests but also as an indication of group confidence. In the context of the severe crises of the 1930s and 1940s, otherwise moderate business interests became increasingly attracted to isolationist, even autarchic perspectives and, in some cases, more so in Europe than North America, even to fascism.[51] By the same token, however, the industries that we have identified as liberal internationalist became more willing to support liberal interventionism in the domestic economy as long as it led to trade and international monetary, and fiscal policies consistent with their interests. In the postwar period, these business groups, while still broadly supportive of liberal spending policies and even a degree of planning, found that they could also achieve their interests within the context of a militarized budget and an anticommunist version of U.S. globalism. Indeed, for some industries, such as aeronautics and electronics, the shift to Cold War liberalism presented a more direct subsidy than did social welfare liberalism.

By 1951, the agenda of Fair Deal liberalism had been displaced by the "consensus" internationalism of the Cold War. Labor had been resubordinated within the liberal bloc and the left that briefly seemed to flourish in the Popular Front period effectively eliminated. Organized labor would remain at or near its postwar strength of 25–30 percent of the workforce until the crises and structural changes of the 1970s would sharpen the rate of its decline, but it had already passed its brief flourish of growth and heightened influence. Other new social movements, in particular civil rights, were still marginal at best.

Rather than develop toward a social democratic–style welfare state, the United States had made the fateful shift toward a permanent war budget, a change that would have determinate influence on the global position of the U.S. political economy in the decades ahead. Business nationalism had rallied from its New Deal and World War II era defeats and had been to a degree successful in its attacks on labor and the left. Yet business nationalism in its more isolationist forms had not been able to defeat the internationalist bloc's fiscal, trade, or international monetary policy preferences. The development trajectory of the U.S. political economy toward the capital export end of the product life cycle was furthered, with military spending in Europe and Asia playing no small part in that process.

NOTES

1. For a good overview of how international relations literature has dealt with these terms, see Greg Nowell, "International Relations Theories: Approaches to Business and the State," in Ronald W. Cox, ed., *Business and the State in International Relations* (Boulder, CO: Westview Press, 1996), pp. 181–197.

2. The leading accounts of the origins and development of the Bretton Woods regime emphasize state autonomy from business interests. See, for example, John Odell, *U.S. International Monetary Policy: Markets, Power and Ideas as Sources of Change* (Princeton, NJ: Princeton University Press, 1982); Joanne Gowa, *Closing the Gold Window: Domestic Politics and the End of Bretton Woods* (Ithaca, NY: Cornell University Press, 1983); and Fred Block, *The Origins of International Economic Disorder* (Berkeley: University of California Press, 1977).

3. The term "interest bloc" is borrowed from James H. Nolt, "Business Conflict and the Origins of the Pacific War," unpublished dissertation, University of Chicago, 1994. Note that our use of the term differs from that used by Nolt.

4. The increased importance of international linkages and, correspondingly, interest blocs, is a major theme in a body of work influenced by Gramscian international political economy, including Robert Cox, *Production, Power and World Order: Social Forces in the Making of History* (New York: Columbia University Press, 1987); Stephen Gill, *American Hegemony and the Trilateral Commission* (New York: Cambridge University Press, 1990); Stephen Gill, ed., *Historical Materialism and International Relations* (New York: Cambridge University Press, 1993); William Robinson, *Promoting Polyarchy: Globalization, U.S. Intervention and Hegemony* (New York: Cambridge University Press, 1996); and William Stant, "Business Conflict and U.S. Trade Policy," in Ronald W. Cox, ed., *Business and the State in International Relations* (Boulder, CO: Westview Press, 1996), pp. 79–108.

5. The theoretical model for such applications of the product life cycle is James Kurth, "The Political Consequences of the Product Life Cycle: Industrial History and Political Outcomes," *International Organization* 33, 1 (Winter 1979): 1–34. Also see Peter Gourevitch, *Politics in Hard Times* (Ithaca, NY: Cornell University Press, 1991).

6. For a good analysis of the relationship between Bretton Woods, the Marshall Plan, and increased U.S. foreign direct investment in the less developed world, see Robert Wood, *From Marshall Plan to Debt Crisis* (Berkeley: University of California Press, 1986).

7. For a theoretical overview of the relationship between federalism and business interests in U.S. political economy, see Colin Gordon, "New Deal, Old Deck: Business and the Origins of Social Security, 1920–1935," *Politics and Society* 19, 2 (1991):165–207.

8. For an examination of the relationship between business interests and congressional representatives in U.S. foreign policy toward Latin America, see Ronald W. Cox, *Power and Profits: U.S. Policy in Central America* (Lexington. University Press of Kentucky, 1994).

9. For the best historical overview of business interests involved in planning and implementing the Marshall Plan, see Michael Hogan, *The Marshall Plan: America, Britain, and the Reconstruction of Western Europe, 1947–52* (Cambridge: Cambridge University Press, 1987).

10. For background on the nationalist support for rollback policy during the Korean War, see Bruce Cumings, "Rollback and Nationalism," in *The Origins of the Korean War,* Vol. 2: *The Roaring of the Cataract* (Princeton: Princeton University Press, 1992), pp. 79–121.

11. For example, see Mira Wilkins, *The Maturing of Multinational Enterprise* (Cambridge: Harvard University Press, 1974). Wilkins's work is cited extensively by economists and political scientists examining the global investment patterns of U.S.-based multinational corporations. A central thesis of the work is that business interests get very little help from the U.S. government in promoting investment and trade objectives and that geostrategic factors drive U.S. foreign policy.

12. For the standard realist account, see Robert Gilpin, *The Political Economy of International Relations* (Princeton, NJ: Princeton University Press, 1987).

13. This chapter relies on the business press, especially *Fortune* and *Business Week,* and U.S. government publications, especially Commerce Department data, to trace U.S. foreign direct investment in Western Europe. Although providing important basic data regarding firm investments, these publications understate the degree of investment planning that took place during the interwar and immediate postwar period. For good archival research tracing the relationship between policymakers and

U.S. petroleum interests during this period, see David Painter, *Oil and the American Century* (Baltimore: Johns Hopkins University Press, 1986).

14. Council on Foreign Relations, *Studies of American Interests in the War and the Peace, Economic and Financial Series*, E-B, 67: 1–2.

15. Ibid.

16. See Eric Helleiner, *States and the Reemergence of Global Finance* (Ithaca, NY: Cornell University Press, 1994), pp. 63–64.

17. For a summary of the position of leading exporters on the Bretton Woods agreement and capital controls, see the testimony of the Business and Industry Committee for Bretton Woods, *Appendix to the Congressional Record*, Vol. 91, part 11, 79th Congress, 1st Session, March 23–June 8, 1945, p. A2649.

18. Charles Maier, "The Politics of Productivity: Foundations of American International Economic Policy After World War Two," in Charles Maier, ed., *In Search of Stability: Explorations in Historical Political Economy* (Cambridge: Cambridge University Press, 1987), pp. 138–139.

19. For a succinct summary of the views of an influential bloc of U.S. bankers, see the congressional testimony of the American Bankers Association, *Appendix to the Congressional Record*, 79th Congress, 1st Session, Vol. 91, Part 10, January 3–March 22, 1945, p. A538.

20. On the split between industrialists and bankers, see Charles Maier, "The Politics of Productivity," pp. 138–139.

21. For the political concerns of U.S. investors, see Hogan, *The Marshall Plan*, pp. 249, 253, 420, 437.

22. Council on Foreign Relations, *Studies of American Interests*, pp. 1–2.

23. For a list of some of the most prominent internationalists supporting Bretton Woods, see Business and Industry Committee, *Appendix to the Congressional Record*, p. A2649.

24. Robert Oliver, *International Economic Cooperation and the World Bank* (London: The Macmillan Press, 1975), p. 184.

25. Ibid., p. 242.

26. Ibid., p. 243.

27. William Domhoff, *The Power Elite and the State: How Policy is Made in America* (New York: Aldine de Gruyter, 1990), p. 179.

28. Robert Solomon, *The International Monetary System, 1945–1976* (New York: Harper and Row, 1977), p. 12.

29. Alfred Eckes, *A Search for Solvency* (Austin: University of Texas Press, 1975), p. 192.

30. Solomon, *The International Monetary System*, pp. 15–16.

31. Immanuel Wexler, *The Marshall Plan Revisited* (Westport, CT: Greenwood Press, 1983), p. 97.

32. European Recovery Program, *Hearings before the Senate Committee on Foreign Relations*, 80th Cong., 2nd session, May–June 1947, pp. 692, 707–709.

33. Ibid.

34. Wood, *From Marshall Plan to Debt Crisis*, pp. 40–44.

35. Ibid., p. 42.

36. Fred Block, "Economic Instability and Military Strength," in John Ikenberry, ed., *American Foreign Policy* (New York: HarperCollins, 1996), pp. 230–248.

37. James Boylan, *The New Deal Coalition and the Election of 1946* (New York: Garland Press, 1981) and Alonzo Hamby, *Beyond the New Deal: Harry S. Truman and American Liberalism* (New York: Columbia University Press, 1973).

38. Jeffrey Frieden, "International Investment and Colonial Control: A New Interpretation," *International Organization* 48, 4 (1994):559–594, and Cumings, *The Origins of the Korean War.*

39. Benjamin Fordham, *Building the Cold War Consensus: The Political Economy of U.S. National Security Policy, 1949–1951* (Ann Arbor: University of Michigan Press, 1998), quote at p. 1.

40. Michael Hunt, *Ideology and U.S. Foreign Policy* (New Haven, CT: Yale University Press, 1987), p. 181.

41. Hamby, *Beyond the New Deal.*

42. Ibid., p. 406.

43. Lynn Eden, "Capitalist Conflict and the State: The Making of United States Military Policy in 1948," in Charles Bright and Susan Harding, eds., *Statemaking and Social Movements: Essays in Theory and History* (Ann Arbor: University of Michigan Press, 1984).

44. Hamby, *Beyond the New Deal*, p. 393.

45. For Senate voting and sectoral industrial patterns, see Fordham, *Building the Cold War Consensus.*

46. Alonzo Hamby, *Liberalism and Its Challengers: FDR to Reagan* (New York: Oxford University Press, 1985), p. 64.

47. See Boylan, *The New Deal Coalition,* chapter 4.

48. R. Alton Lee, *Truman and Taft-Hartley* (Lexington: University of Kentucky Press, 1966).

49. Athan Theoharis, "The Rhetoric of Politics: Foreign Policy, Internal Security, and Domestic Politics in the Truman Era, 1945–1950," in Barton Bernstein, ed., *The Politics and Policies of the Truman Administration* (Chicago: Quadrangle Press, 1970).

50. Richard Walton, *Henry Wallace, Harry Truman, and the Cold War* (New York: Viking Press, 1976).

51. Eric Hobsbawm, *The Age of Extremes* (New York: Pantheon, 1995).

3

Business Conflict
and Cold War Ideology

The internationalist policies of foreign military aid and global market development pursued by the Truman administration did not lack for sharp challenges from nationalist interests and ideologues. Conservative politicians and businesses oriented toward the domestic market were concerned with the growth of government and organized labor, "subversion" from the left, and the potential threat of foreign competition assisted by the liberality of the United States. The early 1950s were a period of both opportunity and frustration for this right-wing coalition of interests.

The U.S. intervention in Korea raised administrative and policy questions about the mobilization of the economy on a war footing. In the face of concerted business opposition and public antipathy, the Truman administration shied away from the kind of public control of prices and product distribution that had characterized World War II. Yet although the right resisted the socialistic aspects of wartime governance, it expressed frustration at the apparently limited objectives of the U.S. military force in Korea and sympathized with General MacArthur's insubordination and extension of the conflict. As discussed in the previous chapter, a significant fraction of U.S. capital had a stake in the Asian market, now radically shrunk by the Chinese revolution and communist advances into Korea, and had reason to fear the further gains of revolutionary socialist-nationalist movements in East Asia.

The position of the 1950s nationalist right in the United States, as expressed by Senator Robert Taft, for example, was ultimately untenable. On the one hand, it yearned for a return to the pre–New Deal minimal state and a world without communist regimes. Yet, as critics of liberal containment strategies, they desired the rollback of communism abroad as well as the rollback of the interventionist state (and trade unionism) at home. One historian reports that Taft was "furious" at the modest size of the new Eisenhower administration's cuts to the federal budget for fiscal year

1954, reductions that were almost entirely decreases in Truman administration proposals for military spending.[1] In the end, as subordinate partners
in the Eisenhower administration, the conservatives helped achieve a containment of the welfare state and trade unionization, the McCarthyite
purge of some liberal elements in the State Department, and a trend toward
fiscal and monetary conservatism in federal policy that was apparent
throughout the 1950s.

In terms of organized business interest groups, local trade associations
and the National Association of Manufacturers (NAM) generally represented the more *revanchist* tendencies of business nationalism.[2] Yet on
closer examination of the political economy of the 1950s, we will see that
the globalizing interests of business internationalism, represented by such
groups as the Committee for Economic Development (CED) and the Business Advisory Council, remained predominant.[3] Overall, the pattern of fiscal, monetary, and trade policy throughout the 1950s continued to promote
the expansion of foreign markets and the export of capital. The policies of
the Eisenhower administration emphasized lowered trade restrictions (a
historical departure for a Republican) and the protection of the dollar's international position against threats to the dollar. Over the course of the
decade, an increasing balance-of-payments crunch developed as a result of
the dollar's gold convertibility. In short, the Eisenhower administration,
like its predecessor, pursued the maintenance and fuller implementation of
the Bretton Woods regime.

The 1950s did indeed witness the shift of the U.S. political economy to
the rule of a center-right administration supported by business nationalists.
Yet by decade's end this coalition would be challenged by a neoliberalism
that sought higher growth rates through more expansionist fiscal policy and
stronger commitments to foreign aid and interventionism.[4] That neoliberal
bloc was to entail a concatenation of interests of the military-industrial
complex, curtailed by the fiscal conservatism of Eisenhower, and business
internationalists. The internationalists grew increasingly concerned with the
macroeconomic growth rates of Europe, Japan, and even the USSR, which
were higher than those of the United States in the go-slow approach of the
Eisenhower years. Few now appreciate that Eisenhower's famous farewell
address warning against the military-industrial complex was directed to his
left, that is, to those who supported a strong Keynesian move toward more
guns and more butter (for education especially, post-Sputnik) that would
satisfy their own interest in higher growth.

THE PERMANENT ARMS ECONOMY

The final three years of the Truman administration witnessed a near quadru-
pling of military spending, from $12.2 billion in FY 1951 to $46.3 billion

in FY 1954. In fact, by the latter fiscal year, defense expenditures encompassed 70 percent of the federal budget.[5] Sloan depicts the policy approach set forth in National Security Council document 68 as an efficient factor in the military buildup. He interprets this surge in military aid as central to the U.S. response to the Chinese revolution and the development of Soviet atomic weaponry.[6] As such, NSC 68 reflected global trends in which the regional conflict on the Korean peninsula was a hot side theater of the central Cold War drama. Yet by this account, U.S. military-fiscal policy of the early 1950s amounted to little more than a stimulus response to the vagaries of international communism. But as Eisenhower himself emphasized, capitalist economic development was part and parcel of the Cold War struggle, and as such, military spending intertwined with business interests.

Eisenhower rejected the view taken by the authors of NSC 68 that 1954 was the year of "maximum danger" in the U.S. endeavor to contain communist expansionism. The new president perceived the Cold War as a long-range battle of attrition that might last as long as fifty years. In other words, Eisenhower was no partisan of the right-wing rollback strategy if that meant some form of short-range military ambition. In NSC 162/2 Eisenhower, Secretary of State Dulles, Treasury Secretary George Humphrey, and Joint Chiefs of Staff head Admiral Arthur Radford articulated the "new look" policy of balancing security needs, deficit-free budgets, and tax cuts.[7] The NSC 68 policy, one might say, had been contained but not before a permanent arms economy had taken hold. In fiscal matters, both military and civilian, the legacy of the Eisenhower administration was that it retained the essentials of the "warfare-welfare" state that it inherited without substantially diminishing or expanding it. But what was significant about Eisenhower's policies was their halt of spending growth, which in turn represented an increased strength of conservative nationalism in the 1950s.

Critics of the permanent arms economy debate if, and to what degree, the United States became dependent on the permanent arms economy. The monopoly capital school argues that the "main problem of accumulation under monopoly capitalism was . . . to find ways in which this increasing surplus could be absorbed. . . . The system became increasingly dependent on the promotion of economic waste, both through the private channel[s] . . . and the public channel of military spending (which accounted for the greater bulk of the federal expenditures on goods and services)."[8] Yet other analysts portray the military budget as a drain on U.S. investment resources and a significant cause of the relative economic decline in the United States in contrast to low-military-spending industrial powers such as Germany and Japan.[9]

Although we are skeptical of the degree to which the U.S. economy during the early postwar period (or at any time since) could be fully identified as monopoly capitalism, the problem of surplus was a potential crisis and was recognized as such by U.S. business and political leaders of this period. This surplus was manifest in monetary terms by the inability of the weaker European currencies to go to full convertibility at fixed rates as envisaged by Bretton Woods. The dollar surplus in turn reflected the dominance of U.S. industrial production and productivity, a strength with the Achilles' heel of dependency on soft world export markets. In other words, the very conditions of U.S. hegemony threatened the sustainability of the prosperity that underwrote that hegemony. Increased military spending, then, could help cope with a multiplicity of problems:

1. Military spending would provide profit for capital investment in new production and technology at a time of nascent recession.
2. Military aid to NATO countries and elsewhere would help strengthen the currencies of U.S. trading partners.
3. Industrial exports, both military and civilian, would find export markets.
4. The development or redevelopment of allied markets would provide foreign investment opportunities for firms at more advanced stages of the product life cycle.

By the end of the 1950s in the United States, more than nine-tenths of final demand for aircraft and parts was a result of government military-related expenditures. Nearly three-fifths of the demand for nonferrous metals, over half of the demand for chemicals and electronics goods, and over one-third of the demand for communication equipment and scientific instruments was dependent on military spending. In the United States, the 100 largest companies consistently received close to three-fourths of army outlays.[10]

Nonetheless, increased military spending is not an unalloyed benefit for all business interests. Higher spending means higher taxes, or at least deferred tax cuts and more borrowing, which in turn harm undercapitalized businesses and worry credit markets. In the 1950s many core industries in the United States did not relish the onset of foreign competition as European industry in particular was stimulated by U.S. policy. The question of the ultimate macroeconomic impact of government spending may be academic, and it is Janus-faced in the context of a privatized economy, but above all it is ideological, because to emphasize the damaging effects of the permanent arms economy is to criticize a key method by which U.S. policy facilitated the globalization of the postwar economy. By contrast, certain sectors in finance and defense-related industries are dependent on the permanent arms economy, but to identify their interests with those of the capitalist system or class as a whole is to make an analytical error similar to that of statist theory by implicitly identifying particular interests as an agency that acts for the whole.

PROBLEMS OF THE TRUMAN ADMINISTRATION

The absence of wartime wage and price controls in 1950–1953 meant that the fiscal stimulus of increased military spending would create inflationary pressures in the domestic economy and, as candidate Eisenhower pointed out in 1952, decrease the purchasing power of the dollar. Inflation, increasing budget deficits, and the declining value of the dollar both nationally and internationally would provide issues for the narrowly successful Republican recapture of Congress in 1952 and increase the comfortable margin of victory of candidate Eisenhower. The stresses of the economic crunch on labor would encourage an increase in strikes and work stoppages in the early 1950s that some saw as a new resurgence of the militant 1930s.[11] But the Truman administration could and did use the Taft-Hartley Act against labor in the ensuing strikes. Additionally, liberal Democrats and labor leaders had fostered a Cold War fervor through the suppression of communist-organized CIO unions, the red-baiting of supporters of progressive critics of Truman's foreign policies such as Henry Wallace, Vito Marcantonio, and W. E. B. Du Bois, and the administration of loyalty tests in government, labor, and elsewhere. The politics of anti-communism ultimately tended to undercut the centrist support among both elites and the masses that the Truman administration relied upon for its combination of limited intervention abroad and modest Fair Deal objectives at home. Fair Deal liberalism was portrayed as communist dupery and creeping socialism in an ideological context that was apparently moving sharply to the right.[12]

Some might think that the downfall of the New Deal/Fair Deal coalition in 1952 was the product of the Truman administration's ineffectiveness at rallying public opinion for the necessary sacrifices of the conflict, including the reimposition of economic controls. Although elite opinion favored Truman's policy toward Korea, the broader public seemed quite disaffected, and many longtime Democrats supported the candidacy of the unimpeachably patriotic General Eisenhower, who promised a quickly negotiated end to the conflict.

However, the inflation and deficits of the early 1950s were not in any specific sense the product of Korean War spending. Approximately 10 percent of the military budget after the drastic increases of 1951 (see the previous chapter for further discussion) was related to the military usage of men and material on the Korean peninsula. The bulk of spending was to combat the Cold War on the European front, precisely where the balance-of-payments problems faced by NATO governments reinforced the problem of the "dollar overhang" and frustrated the search of business internationalists for commodity and capital markets. Western Europe was and remains the primary locus of U.S. foreign direct investment, hence the consistent importance of U.S. (and European) macroeconomic policy as it affects the underlying play of market forces that could stabilize or undermine the Bretton Woods framework.

Mass public opinion may have been disaffected by the possibility of renewed economic rationing in the Korean War years even as political elites maintained a broadly united supportive front, save only for the elite militants of the right who openly sought an expanded war in Asia. Yet it was economic elites' resistance to the political economy of wartime-style macroeconomic management that significantly forced up the deficit in 1951–1953. During World War II the Federal Reserve banks had purchased U.S. government securities from the Treasury Department at or above par value under a policy of pegged interest rates. In 1951, however, the Federal Reserve entered into a conflict with the Treasury, refusing to maintain the peg and insisting instead on the purchase of Treasury-issued bonds at market rates.[13] In effect, then, Federal Reserve member banks could now profit from increased military and domestic spending while the higher rates forced up the deficit. Alternatively, the Treasury could finance at lower short-term rates (which it did), creating the likelihood of a near-term fiscal crunch with a recessionary impact (there was a recession late in 1953 extending into 1954).

EISENHOWER AND THE "CORPORATE COMMONWEALTH"

Historiographical interpretations of the Eisenhower administration debate whether these years represent change or continuity in the basic patterns of U.S. politics and public policy.[14] Our approach appreciates the continuities in a political economy that were fundamentally beneficial to the business internationalists as well as shifts within the power bloc and, most crucially, the dynamics of global accumulation and their impact on domestic class structure.

In a November 1953 memo to Bureau of Budget Director Joseph M. Dodge, Eisenhower stated: "I believe it a necessity for this administration to announce broad and liberal objectives in certain fields . . . and [determine] which service to fix in the public mind the character of our political thinking." These were (1) public housing/slum clearance; (2) the development of water resources, and (3) the extension of Social Security. The president's memo in effect summarizes what were then the most basic

and popular elements of the New Deal/Fair Deal framework that he had inherited from his two immediate predecessors. By pursuing these moderately liberal policies, the first post–New Deal Republican president could
reach directly into the heart of the New Deal coalition with a set of programs that would have mass appeal for working-class voters[15] and local
and regional economic interests such as housing and agriculture that had
depended on federal support for recovery and development. In particular,
the appeal to the western region of the United States is unsurprising given
the Eisenhower Republicans' notable electoral gains in the region that had
saved Truman from what had famously appeared to be certain defeat in
1948. By adopting the New Deal as a given, and indeed something to be
embraced, the Eisenhower administration's actions manifest the importance of the broad "middle class" constituencies' electoral power and the
symbiosis of their interests with established public policy.

The Eisenhower administration's embrace of a moderate and business-
oriented welfare state strongly suggests the continued ideological hegemony of the internationalist liberal bloc throughout the 1950s. In other
words, a political economy of state-supported aggregate demand, foreign
market development, "high-volume production," and high wages with a
liberal mix of public and private welfare benefits was by then institutionalized and would remain so regardless of the party of presidents or congressional majorities.[16]

The politics of corporate liberalism is well illustrated by the reform of
the Social Security Administration (SSA) in 1950–1953. As McQuaid
points out, the Business Advisory Council supported, indeed authored, the
Truman-Eisenhower expansions of public pensions (Social Security) as an
alternative to a European-style developed welfare state. The SSA reform
sought to protect larger firms from competition from smaller companies
that had not previously been required to pay Social Security taxes and to
rein in more liberal state welfare spending, providing "fiscal integrity" otherwise "undermined by dole programs that state politicians were using to
their own political advantage." Additionally, modifications were made in
corporate tax regulations to give corporations incentives to rejuvenate the
pre–New Deal pattern of welfare capitalism by providing private health and
pension plans to employees.[17] The social welfare framework created by the
mid-1950s was the now familiar pattern of public pensions somewhat more
generous than public assistance, augmented for workers in the relatively
privileged core sectors by private pension and insurance schemes.

More conservative business interests such as the NAM advocated a
"voluntary" approach to Social Security. This position was adopted by the
more conservative elements in Congress such as Senator Barry Goldwater,
who would remain far enough to the right to espouse this unpopular position during his 1964 presidential bid. In effect, the conservatives were

supporting a dole for the low-income elderly rather than a public-private mixture of pension and pension-like policies advocated by the business liberals. At least this was the critical view taken by corporate leaders such as Marion Folsom of the Eastman Kodak Company, who chaired the Business Advisory Council's Social Security Committee at the time.[18]

This liberal bloc became hegemonic, despite the notable, continued, and widely articulated presence of voices on the right that did not accept, and indeed never have accepted, the legitimacy of the New Deal. Eisenhower's slogan of "corporate commonwealth" is an expression of this hegemony insofar as it refers to a distinct departure from the pre-New Deal Republican pattern of laissez-faire in relation to welfare, taxes, and the compensation of labor and protectionism with regard to foreign trade. Yet Eisenhower's Republican electoral and congressional support networks also included conservative and right-wing business nationalists. The influence of party as a mediating factor in U.S. public policy was such that the interests of businesses and voters who chafed under increased federal payroll taxes, favored high tariffs, and supported McCarthy had to be assuaged. Throughout its eight years, the Eisenhower administration would be internally conflicted by the interests of a corporate commonwealth type of liberality and the drive to cut spending, taxes, and foreign aid.

By referring to a liberal *bloc,* we mean to indicate a coalition of interests in which certain groups, that is, internationally oriented businesses, were dominant. A bloc is a coalition to the extent that all parts of it gain some advantage for their support. However, the interests contained are not in equal relationship and the overall direction expresses the long-term aspirations of the leading elements. For example, labor made definite short- to medium-term gains in status and organization as a result of the New Deal, yet the long-run trend toward global liberalism would hardly seem to sustain these gains. We can also validly speak of an alternative conservative bloc, with business nationalists in a leading role, or even the makings of a social democratic bloc, had organized labor achieved truly national strength. To delimit the term "bloc" we refer only to those coalitions that have national reach and coherent national policy agendas. A bloc obviously need not be hegemonic and, given the loose structure of political parties "in the American mold,"[19] should not be reduced to party; rather, a block seeks the cooperation of interest groups in policy advocacy and development. Further, it must be emphasized that blocs are not static, but rather historical; always in conflict and in dynamic flux. As Adamson puts it, "Hegemonies always grow out of historic blocs, but not all historical blocs are hegemonic." Further, a social group (in our approach an organized business sector) that forms "political alliances with other such groups may or may not develop [those alliances] into a hegemonic relationship" with other social groups or policymakers.[20]

Running through all political coalitions are the fissures of particular interests that may, in times of crisis, become virtually irreconcilable and lead to the dissolution of the bloc, a fate that occurred to pre–Great Depression conservatism. Historical and material context, then, is often of decisive importance insofar as it structures the policy options available. As Sloan puts it, "The end of the Korean War and economic prosperity allowed Eisenhower to avoid a hard choice between his conservative and liberal propensities. The president was confronted with far more difficult choices in his second term" and tilted right on issues of fiscal and monetary policy.[21] But this rightward tilt would leave the administration in a bind when it came to coping with the 1958 recession and encourage the resurgence of the Democratic Party of Lyndon Johnson, Sam Rayburn, and John F. Kennedy.

If there actually was a liberal internationalist hegemony in the 1950s, as we claim, this hegemony also required an effective intellectual expression. In Gramscian terms, the ideological interests of social groups are voiced by "organic intellectuals."[22] One instance of such an intellectual figure in the Eisenhower years is the Council of Economic Advisers (CEA) chair Arthur Burns (1953–1956), who had previously succeeded in translating his academic credentials as an economist into market value as a management consultant. Burns was Keynesian but conservative. In the 1960s, Burns would develop a conservative critique of Kennedy CEA chair Walter Heller's theories on macroeconomic fine-tuning. In Sloan's account, Burns was especially effective in his role of presidential adviser during the 1954 recession: "Burns introduced and helped legitimate some Keynesian thinking in Eisenhower economic policy making. A Republican administration could intervene . . . and sustain business confidence."[23]

The influence of intellectuals on public policy is often mistakenly taken as evidence for state autonomy, but this conclusion requires an unfounded empirical leap. Intellectuals in the U.S. sociopolitical structure do not derive their status from state sanction through membership in a corporatist body such as a national or royal academy; rather, U.S. political intellectuals are defined through a complex of private and public institutions such as consulting firms and think tanks. Their political economy is rooted in the corporate world rather than in a purportedly autonomous state. In the case of Arthur Burns, the "organic intellectual" of modernizing Republicanism helped legitimate, from his position in the CEA, relatively liberal fiscal policies during the first term of the Eisenhower administration. It is interesting to note that the CEA was created by the Employment Act of 1946, wherein Congress, with CED and Business Advisory Council support, adopted an official policy goal of full employment and mandated annual reporting by the CEA to Congress and the president on the progress of the national economy and employment.

In 1955, Treasury Secretary George Humphrey, a manager of the Ohio-based Mark Hanna holding company, challenged the Burns-authored CEA annual *Economic Report* as "socialistic."[24] Humphrey had direct ties to a historically significant Republican firm,[25] a financial conglomerate; although of more direct relevance was his reputation as a conservative voice on the Business Advisory Council. According to Morgan, his "public rhetoric reassured the Republican right and the corporate community about the administration's intentions and deflected liberal attacks away from Eisenhower."[26]

The measure of the influence of the Humphrey type of business conservatism can be taken by the trends of federal fiscal policy during the Eisenhower years. By 1960 federal civilian expenditures plus transfer payments were equivalent to 6.0 percent of GNP, down from 7.4 percent in 1939. The ratio of federal domestic outlays to total public sector domestic outlays (federal plus state and local) was .64 in 1960, a decline from .82 in 1939. As Morgan puts it, "[T]he momentum towards a federal welfare state slowed markedly in the Eisenhower era,"[27] despite the singular federalization of the SSA.

INTERNATIONALISM AND WESTERN EUROPE

The political economy of internationalism intersects with the interests, ideologies, and bureaucratic positions of key actors in U.S. foreign policy. Both the Truman and Eisenhower administrations were committed to the broad outlines of the internationalist program for Western Europe: a foreign military aid program (NATO's Mutual Security Assistance Act) whose allocations could be adjusted to influence the political and economic direction of Western European allies. The major goals involved removing the intra-European trade barriers and currency controls that inhibited foreign direct investment and slowed U.S. exports to the region. Under the Truman administration, this internationalist agenda involved the simultaneous administration of Marshall Plan aid funds and military assistance via the Mutual Security Assistance Act. Business internationalists helped oversee the implementation of Marshall Plan funds and were also involved in mobilizing political support for NATO funding in Western Europe.

In fact, U.S. internationalists, by influencing the allocation of NATO funding levels through the Mutual Security Assistance Act, could simultaneously achieve geostrategic and economic objectives in promoting the integration of Western Europe. Business internationalists exerted influence on U.S./NATO policy through the U.S. ambassador to NATO and the head of the Mutual Security Administration, both highly susceptible to business influence. Two of the NATO ambassadors, George Perkins (1955–1957) and Randolph Burgess (1957–1961), had close connections to business internationalists. Perkins had been a trustee of the internationalist Foreign Policy Association during the mid-1950s and the director of a subsidiary of the National City Bank of New York (1935–1949), a leading lender to Western Europe. Randolph Burgess had been a high official of the National City Bank of New York from 1938 to 1952.

By the end of the Korean War, Congress approved approximately $5 billion in U.S. military assistance to NATO nations in Western Europe. Internationalists in charge of administering the Mutual Security Assistance Act could insist that military aid be conditioned on significant progress in integrating West Germany in a military alliance with Western European allies. The United States was quick to support the first proposal from France to rearm Germany: the European Defense Community (EDC), which was to include a collective European military structure with twelve West German divisions. The British had to come to the rescue, however, when the French parliament showed strong opposition to the EDC in 1954, threatening to defeat attempts to include West Germany in the Atlantic Alliance. The British made a commitment to maintain their troops on the European continent in perpetuity, in exchange for West German sovereignty and membership in both the NATO alliance and the Western European Union (WEU). The WEU consisted of the Brussels Treaty Organization—Britain, France, Belgium, the Netherlands, and Luxembourg—with the addition of Italy and West Germany. The integration of West Germany into the Atlantic alliance had been accomplished with the aid of a threat from Secretary of State Dulles to lessen (or even abandon) the U.S. military commitment to Western Europe unless West German rearmament was accomplished.

Integration of West Germany into the Atlantic Alliance had been a long-term project of U.S. foreign policy makers and business internationalists. Military integration would solve several pressing problems for U.S. planners: (1) It would reinforce political ties between the United States and West Germany in the face of Soviet challenges; (2) It would provide for further U.S. assistance to conservative political forces in West Germany (the Christian Democrats, in particular) and weaken their political opponents; and (3) it would provide an important infusion of military aid whose spinoff effects would help promote the preconditions for increased U.S. foreign direct investment in West Germany.

In short, U.S. policy toward West Germany would mirror U.S. policy objectives toward all of Western Europe during the 1950s. Internationalists within the State Department, the White House, and the private sector pushed for the political and military integration of West Germany throughout the early Cold War period. As early as 1950, the State Department was pushing for the rearmament of West Germany and by 1954 the United States had secured approval of West German membership in NATO. Most accounts of U.S. policy toward West Germany emphasize the geostrategic aspects of U.S.-Soviet competition, ignoring the role of business internationalists in pursuing long-term foreign economic policies toward West Germany. However, there is strong evidence that business internationalists took the lead in advocating specific policy proposals for West Germany.

As early as 1945, a series of investment banks linked to the Rockefeller group and Dillon, Read began lobbying the State Department for "a productionist approach" to West Germany that entailed increased U.S. economic assistance and cooperation between U.S. and German business elites through such entities as the International Chamber of Commerce, active in Western Europe by 1947; the U.S. Chamber of Commerce, active in Germany in 1949; the German-American Capital Commission, established in 1951 to increase investment opportunities for U.S. firms, and the German-American Economic Association.[28] On the U.S. side, corporations active as part of an internationalist effort to promote West German recovery included Chase Manhattan Bank; Dillon, Read; General Electric; National City Bank; Standard Oil of New Jersey; Armco; and Phoenix Rubber, a subsidiary of Firestone with investments in West Germany and France.

The military integration of West Germany, then, complemented efforts by business internationalists to promote economic regionalization in Western Europe as a precondition for increased U.S. trade and foreign direct investment. The Truman White House and State Department took the lead in promoting regional integration through the European Payments Union (EPU), a clearinghouse that allowed European countries to use their trade surpluses with one country to purchase goods from another, and through support for the European Coal and Steel Community (ECSC), a supranational agency created in 1953 that would control the coal and steel resources of member nations. U.S. planners viewed the ECSC as the first step toward liberalization of the European market and a precursor to a regional common market.[29]

The United States granted a loan of $100 million to the ECSC on April 23, 1954, administered by the Export-Import Bank with funds provided by the Foreign Operations Administration, to be extended over twenty-five years, with repayment beginning after three years at an annual rate of 3.875 percent.[30] The loan was made to modernize mining operations and expand capacity for the production of coal, coke, and iron ore. Business internationalists lobbied for the loan as a step toward the rationalization and integration of an important segment of the European market. Direct investors would benefit from the cheaper inputs and better infrastructure assumed to be products of the regionalization process. Exporters felt that greater price competition would encourage demand for U.S. products and lessen the stranglehold of a few producers over the European market.[31]

Overall, business internationalists favored the ECSC as a mechanism that would enhance the political and economic climate for increased U.S. foreign direct investment. However, U.S. exporters wanted to limit the ECSC to a small number of European countries in order to check the negative influence of a common market tariff on U.S. exporters. In fact, leading U.S. exporters to Europe made it clear that, although they supported liberalization of trade within Europe, they would oppose any common market scheme likely to significantly increase the discrimination against U.S. goods. By limiting the scope of the Common Market, U.S. foreign direct investors would be able to link operations in the Brussels pact nations, along with Italy and West Germany, while limiting the impact of a common market tariff on U.S. exporters. The exclusion of Britain from the Common Market appeased U.S. exporters, who feared that British inclusion would result in higher tariff barriers on exports to Britain.[32]

Under the Truman administration, divisions among internationalists were expressed in bureaucratic debates that pitted the State Department and the U.S. head of the European Cooperation Administration (ECA), Paul Hoffman, against the Treasury Department, the Federal Reserve, and the International Monetary Fund (IMF). The State Department and the ECA advocated a strong productionist approach to European recovery that maximized the amount of bilateral aid to Western Europe and minimized the political requirements and eligibility for such aid. Productionists privileged strong growth and political stability over orthodox economic measures. Business internationalists, anticipating an expansion of manufacturing investments in Western Europe, endorsed this approach to U.S. lending, favoring high levels of U.S. aid and the maintenance of capital controls as the best route to political stability in Western Europe.[33]

The orthodox internationalists within the IMF, the Treasury Department, and the Federal Reserve advocated limited amounts of U.S. bilateral aid and multilateral assistance conditional on verifiable steps by Western European governments to eliminate currency and capital controls. These divisions were most apparent in the debates over the EPU. Productionists supported the EPU as an outlet to increased growth and investment throughout Western Europe, despite the fact that the EPU allowed for only a limited regional currency convertibility. The orthodox internationalists opposed the EPU as "an unnecessary barrier to the early restoration of full, multilateral convertibility."[34]

The Eisenhower administration's policies differed in subtle ways from those of the Truman administration. In a Republican Party divided by nationalists and internationalists, with a strong base of fiscal conservatism linked to support for a balanced federal budget, the Eisenhower administration slowed the rate of U.S. military spending while maintaining the internationalist commitment to Western Europe. This was accomplished by relying more aggressively on nuclear weapons to deter the Soviet threat and strengthen the NATO alliance while reducing the deployment of conventional weapons and troops in various parts of the world. At the same time, the administration attempted to make U.S. foreign aid packages to Western Europe conditional on the adoption of particular foreign economic policies designed to benefit U.S. foreign direct investors, such as greater progress toward currency convertibility, further reductions in trade barriers, and additional incentives for increased U.S. foreign direct investment.[35] The conditionality of Eisenhower's foreign aid was designed to prevent the growth of a regional trading bloc in Europe that would be closed to U.S. investors. The administration also worked to ensure the stability of the dollar, the pillar of the Bretton Woods regime, by promoting international trade and investment.

In the 1940s some scholars had already expressed doubt that the key currency scheme of Bretton Woods was in fact workable in the long run. In the late 1950s, as the growth of the European and Japanese economies accelerated and their industrial technologies had gained some parity with those of the United States, the dollar was confronted with the strongest indications of slippage in its exchange value since the war (there had been some decline in the dollar's value during the Korean War–related inflation which, as noted earlier, Eisenhower made an issue of in the 1952 campaign).

The problem with the dollar in the late 1950s was related to its convertibility to gold at the fixed rate of $35 an ounce per Bretton Woods. International traders, anticipating future decline in the purchasing power of the dollar, began increasingly to convert dollars to gold in anticipation of a plausible future devaluation of the dollar. The administration's and the Federal Reserve's policies were to support the dollar through anti-inflationary fiscal and monetary policy. Despite the signs of recession, the view of the administration was that long-range economic health required a strong and stable dollar combined with the opening of foreign markets. As one scholar writes of the balance-of-payments (BOP) situation, "There was a tendency to believe that the problem might simply disappear when foreign nations eliminated their discriminatory restrictions against U.S. exports and rising incomes in these countries increased demand for U.S. products."[36]

While practicing and supporting fiscal and monetary conservatism, the Eisenhower administration also continued to encourage economic internationalization. A new treasury secretary, Robert Anderson, advocated the following response to the BOP issue: U.S. allies must reduce trade barriers; U.S. companies should be encouraged to export (in some cases with government-supported financing), and the budget must be kept in balance.[37] Anderson, like Humphrey, was considered a strong fiscal conservative and anti-interventionist regarding the government's role in the affairs of business who had no proclivity toward protectionism. Anderson had been the manager of the Texas-based W. T. Waggoner Estates, which had interests in cattle, oil, and banking, and his background was in southwestern industries that had developed in symbiosis with the state and had been the right wing of the New Deal.[38] Anderson was Eisenhower's preferred successor but Anderson "had no mass appeal" nor a base in the Republican Party.[39] The elite from Anderson's region were just then becoming a major component of the Republican Party; their move toward playing a key role in a new conservative hegemony was still two decades away.

The Eisenhower Republicans succeeded to a notable extent in gaining the support of western and southern interests and middle-class voters who were drawn to many elements of its center-right internationalism. These traditionally Democratic groups were already export-oriented, and the Eisenhower administration supported suitable modes of infrastructure development such as dams and interstate highways. Further, the New Deal's positioning of the state as guarantor of the banking system was more than useful in controlling risk in these developing regions. The sun-belt elite also stood to benefit from a fiscal conservatism that could hold down the costs of capital and labor, which was considerably disenfranchised by racism and almost completely unorganized, and limit the federalization of domestic government. There were flaws, though, particularly the Eisenhower administration's holding the line on military spending, its willingness to back the tight money policies of the Federal Reserve, and its antipathy to agricultural subsidies. The most fundamental problem for the Eisenhower administration was an ongoing division between internationalists and nationalists within the Republican Party.

THE INTERNATIONALIST/NATIONALIST DIVIDE

The divisions between internationalists and nationalists continued to surface during the 1950s, as various members of each coalition attempted to maneuver for advantage. A survey of senatorial voting patterns on national security issues and foreign aid issues from 1949 to 1951 illustrates the political economy of these divisions. Internationalist senators are defined as those who consistently voted in favor of the Truman administration's national security and foreign aid programs to Western Europe during this time. If our argument is correct, we would find that there is a strong correlation between the voting pattern of these internationalists and the preferences of leading business elites in their home states. Internationalist senators should come from states characterized by a relatively high number of U.S. firms with foreign investments in Western Europe. Nationalist senators should come from states that have a relatively low or nonexistent number of U.S. firms with investments in Europe. In addition, there should be some correlation between nationalist voting patterns and states with a relatively high level of import-competing industries.

Table 3.1, drawn from Benjamin Fordham, looks at over 400 roll-call votes on national security issues to derive a score for individual senators based on their degree of support for the Truman administration national security agenda. Votes in favor of administration proposals were coded "1," while votes against the administration were coded "−1." Thus a higher positive ranking indicates a stronger tendency to support the administration's foreign policy agenda. NS Mean refers to the mean voting score on the national security program. The voting patterns of internationalist senators coincide with the presence of business internationalists in their respective states, providing a data fit for the insights of this study regarding the political economy of internationalism.

In addition, senators are grouped into categories according to their level of support for the Truman administration's Fair Deal domestic programs, as well as the administration's national security agenda. A higher negative rating indicates a greater propensity to support the Fair Deal domestic agenda of the Truman administration (see Tables 3.1 and 3.2).

Examination of the aggregate data reveals a strong correlation between the senators' voting patterns and the lending and investment patterns of corporations located in their respective states. In the private sector, commercial banks with extensive loans to Western Europe were concentrated in the Northeast, Southeast, Midwest, and San Francisco in the West. The overwhelming majority of all portfolio lending came from New York commercial banks whose political influence extended throughout the Northeast in the form of branch plants located in the New England area (see Table 3.3).

The strongest support for the Truman administration's national security and foreign aid programs toward Europe came from internationalist senators located in the Northeast, who included both Democrats and Republicans. Meanwhile perfect internationalist voting records were also obtained by both senators from Illinois, correlating with the importance of Chicago as an area of portfolio investment. The California Democrat Downey received considerable support from the San Francisco financial sector and voted consistently with internationalists in Congress. Additional aggregate data assembled by Fordham indicates that there is also a strong correlation between a senator's internationalist voting record and the presence of U.S. firms with foreign direct investments in Western Europe.[40] The presence of internationalist senators from the South is likely a reflection of the dominance of export agriculture from this region. A leading objective of southern Democrats throughout this period was the promotion of export agriculture.[41]

Clearly the differences in national security scores cannot be explained solely by the political economy of various states. Disaggregated data would tell us more about the influence of particular firms in financing senatorial campaigns and might well suggest that firms that appear underrepresented in aggregate data are in fact powerful in terms of their monetary access and influence. In addition, party affiliation also correlates with diverse scores on national security. Congressional internationalists are clearly more dominant in the Democratic Party, whereas the Republican Party is significantly divided between nationalists and internationalists.

By the mid-1950s, import-competing firms would be lobbying nationalists in the Republican Party in an attempt to secure protection from European and Japanese imports. This effort would form the basis of a drive by nationalists to take control of the party from internationalist influence. The culmination of this move would be the nomination of Barry Goldwater in 1964. This would effectively drive internationalists away from the Republican Party and toward the Democrats, helping to account for Lyndon Johnson's landslide victory in the 1964 presidential election.

Import-competing industries filed petitions in 1955 with the Office of Civil and Defense Mobilization to ask the federal government for protection from imports that posed threats to U.S. industries "vital to the national defense of the United States." Producers of twenty-one different commodities, seventeen of which were manufactured goods and four of which were minerals, urged restriction of imports on the grounds of national security.[42] In a special report filed with the National Security Council, the OCDM identified two special characteristics of the import-competing industries requesting government protection: (1) They were heavily dependent upon defense procurement for a substantial—in some cases major—part of their sales. Sharp cutbacks in government procurement for these industries have reduced demand, making them more vulnerable to foreign competition. Examples included the stencil silk industry, the tungsten, fluorspar, and cobalt industries, and wool textiles firms. (2) The bulk of the manufacturing firms requesting protection were precision-built products or commodities in which labor constituted a higher-than-average element of cost.[43]

The nationalist concerns articulated in this memo would become the basis for a larger right-wing movement of disaffected Republicans, which identified internationalists as their enemy, within both the Democratic and Republican Parties. Homer Ferguson, a Republican from Michigan and a member of the Senate Committee on Appropriations, articulated the views of conservative Republican nationalists in a 1952 letter to former president Herbert Hoover. In the letter, Ferguson warned that the Eisenhower candidacy represented "the effort of a small minority . . . who are not only outside the party but actually in opposition to the principles held by the overwhelming majority of the Party."[44]

Table 3.1 Voting Scores of Democrats in the 81st Congress

Liberal Democrats	FD Mean	NS Mean	Southern Democrats	FD Mean	NS Mean
Group Mean	*-0.88*	*0.92*	*Group Mean*	*-0.20*	*0.60*
Std. Deviation	*0.07*	*0.10*	*Std. Deviation*	*0.30*	*0.29*
Anderson (D–NM)	-0.75	1.00	Chapman (D–KY)	-0.23	0.81
Benton (D–CT)	-1.00	1.00	Connally (D–TX)	-0.16	1.00
Clements (D–KY)	-1.00	1.00	Eastland (D–MS)	0.24	0.41
Douglas (D–IL)	-0.79	0.79	Ellender (D–LA)	-0.14	0.47
Downey (D–CA)	-0.85	1.00	Fulbright (D–AR)	-0.26	0.82
Graham (D–NC)	-0.85	0.97	George (D–GA)	0.18	0.41
Green (D–RI)	-0.88	0.97	Hoey (D–NC)	0.04	0.75
Hill (D–AL)	-0.84	0.86	Holland (D–FL)	0.00	0.66
Humphrey (D–MN)	-0.92	0.97	Johnson, L. (D–TX)	-0.38	0.95
Hunt (D–WY)	-0.87	0.61	Johnston (D–SC)	-0.68	0.18
Kefauver (D–TN)	-0.90	0.93	Long (D–LA)	-0.72	0.40
Kerr (D–OK)	-0.75	0.90	Maybank (D–SC)	-0.64	0.55
Kilgore (D–WV)	-0.92	0.97	McClellan (D–AR)	0.15	-0.01
Leahy (D–RI)	-0.93	1.00	McKellar (D–TN)	-0.53	0.68
Lehman (D–NY)	-1.00	0.95	Robertson (D–VA)	0.18	0.76
Lucas (D–IL)	-0.86	0.97	Russell (D–GA)	0.04	0.05
Magnuson (D–WA)	-0.87	0.79	O'Conor (D–MD)	-0.10	0.76
McGrath (D–RI)	-0.90	0.91	Smith, W. (D–NC)	-0.33	1.00
McMahon (D–CT)	-0.79	0.94	Stennis (D–MS)	-0.16	0.57
Miller (D–ID)	-0.88	1.00	Tydings (D–MD)	-0.06	0.84
Murray (D–MT)	-0.92	1.00	Withers (D–KY)	-0.68	0.93
Myers (D–PA)	-0.92	0.95			

(continues)

Table 3.1 continued

Liberal Democrats	FD Mean	NS Mean
Neely (D–WV)	-0.92	0.95
Pepper (D–FL)	-0.94	0.89
Sparkman (D–AL)	-0.81	0.86
Thomas, E. (D–UT)	-0.80	0.92
Thomas, J. (D–OK)	-0.86	0.70
Wagner (D–NY)	-0.89	1.00
Outliers		
Byrd (D–VA)	0.48	-0.31
Frear (D–DE)	-0.53	0.39
Langer (R–ND)	-0.77	-0.57

Western Democrats	FD Mean	NS Mean
Group Mean	*-0.50*	*0.44*
Std Deviation	*0.19*	*0.37*
Chavez (D–NM)	-0.68	0.75
Gillette (D–IA)	-0.36	0.47
Hayden (D–AZ)	-0.69	1.00
Johnson, E. (D–CO)	-0.29	-0.09
McCarran (D–NV)	-0.47	0.05
McFarland (D–AZ)	-0.55	0.84
O'Mahoney (D–WY)	-0.73	0.83
Taylor (D–ID)	-0.91	0.42

Source: Benjamin Fordham, *Building the Cold War Consensus: The Political Economy of U.S. National Security Policy, 1949–1951* (Ann Arbor: University of Michigan Press, 1998), pp. 80–81.

Note: FD Mean refers to support for Fair Deal programs. NS Mean refers to mean voting score on the national security program.

Table 3.2 Voting Scores of Republicans in the 81st Congress

Internationalist Republicans	FD Mean	NS Mean
Group Mean	*-0.06*	*0.31*
Std. Deviation	*0.38*	*0.19*
Aiken (R–VT)	-0.71	0.43
Baldwin (R–CT)	0.11	0.26
Dulles (R–NY)	-0.20	0.50
Flanders (R–VT)	-0.21	0.29
Gurney (R–SD)	0.69	0.12
Ives (R–NY)	-0.42	0.19
Lodge (R–MA)	-0.25	0.45
Morse (R–OR)	-0.61	0.53
Reed (R–KS)	0.59	0.04
Saltonstall (R–MA)	0.07	0.20
Smith, H. (R–NJ)	0.07	0.44
Smith, M. (R–ME)	-0.23	0.43
Thye (R–MN)	-0.15	0.17
Tobey (R–NH)	-0.27	0.12
Wiley (R–WI)	0.35	0.04
Vandenberg (R–MI)	0.27	0.72

Nationalist Republicans	FD Mean	NS Mean
Group Mean	*0.56*	*-0.61*
Std. Deviation	*0.18*	*0.22*
Brewster (R–ME)	0.51	-0.67
Bricker (R–OH)	0.80	-0.75
Bridges (R–NH)	0.68	-0.63
Butler (R–NE)	0.81	-0.89
Cain (R–WA)	0.70	-0.58
Capehart (R–IN)	0.54	-0.82
Carlson (R–KS)	1.00	-0.60
Cordon (R–OR)	0.64	-0.37
Darby (R–KS)	0.36	-0.57
Donnell (R–MO)	0.30	-0.06
Dworshak (R–ID)	0.64	-0.68
Ecton (R–MT)	0.70	-0.81
Ferguson (R–MI)	0.57	-0.41
Hendrickson (R–NJ)	0.20	-0.18
Hickenlooper (R–IA)	0.64	-0.33
Jenner (R–IN)	0.61	-0.94
Kem (R–MO)	0.69	-0.92
Knowland (R–CA)	0.46	-0.27
Malone (R–NV)	0.39	-0.92
Martin (R–PA)	0.72	-0.72

(continues)

Table 3.2 continued

Nationalist Republicans	FD Mean	NS Mean
McCarthy (R–WI)	0.20	–0.48
Millikin (R–CO)	0.39	–0.38
Murdt (R–SD)	0.56	–0.49
Nixon (R–CA)	0.33	–0.60
Schoeppel (R–KS)	0.62	–0.63
Taft (R–OH)	0.53	–0.46
Watkins (R–UT)	0.49	–0.64
Wherry (R–NE)	0.70	–0.90
Williams (R–DE)	0.73	–0.76
Young (R–ND)	0.37	–0.70

Source: Benjamin Fordham, *Building the Cold War Consensus: The Political Economy of U.S. National Security Policy, 1949–1951* (Ann Arbor: University of Michigan Press, 1998), pp. 80–81.
Note: FD Mean refers to support for Fair Deal programs. NS Mean refers to mean voting score on the national security program.

**Table 3.3　International Lending by U.S. Banks in 1950
(millions of dollars)**

Federal Reserve City	Total Loans by Member Banks	Total Claims on Foreigners	Europe	Latin America	Asia
New York	13,900.6	1,002.7	410.6	343.2	81.4
San Francisco	6,559.1	133.2	59.9	33.4	25.4
Chicago	6,278.0	45.0	20.8	17.2	0.9
Philadelphia	4,451.7	10.8	5.2	2.4	0.1
Boston	4,056.0	49.0	12.2	29.2	0.1
Dallas	2,263.2	9.6	2.0	7.1	0.0
Atlanta	2,260.8	6.3	0.3	5.8	0.0
Richmond	2,405.3	0.2	0.0	0.1	0.0
Cleveland	2,042.0	24.0	11.5	11.2	0.3
St. Louis	2,033.4	2.9	0.2	2.4	0.1
Kansas City	1,667.6	0.0	0.0	0.0	0.0
Minneapolis	1,226.0	0.5	0.1	0.1	0.0
Total	49,143.7	1,284.2	522.8	452.1	108.3

Source: Benjamin Fordham, *Building the Cold War Consensus: The Political Economy of U.S. National Security Policy, 1949–1951* (Ann Arbor: University of Michigan Press, 1998), p. 96.

Ferguson goes on to characterize Eisenhower as a "Truman candidate," who in foreign affairs would promote "the continuation of the Truman disastrous foreign policy, permanent conscription and military service for all young men and women, permanent stationing of American troops in foreign countries, permanent economic and military support of Europe, permanent distribution (by loans and gifts) of American resources to more than half the world, and American substitution for the role played by the British Empire in world politics."[45] Indeed the tenor of the letter suggested signs of the Goldwater movement in its earliest phases, articulated by a Republican member of the Senate Committee on Appropriations whose views were supported by other conservatives within that influential committee. Seven of the committee's members came from western states; of these seven, several Republican senators—including Guy Cordon of Oregon, William Knowland of California, Zayles Ecton of Montana, and Milton Young of North Dakota—had a close connection to import-sensitive industries that would form the core of opposition to liberal internationalism. Joined by Joseph McCarthy, a Republican from Wisconsin and Ferguson himself, all had consistently voted against the national security programs of the Truman administration.

　　The scaling down of the military budget during the first Eisenhower term was part of an effort by the administration to appeal to diverse wings of its constituency. The administration's commitment to internationalism was evident in its support for European regionalism as a step toward reducing barriers to U.S. trade and investment. At the same time, the administration emphasized that it could accomplish internationalist goals at a lower cost than those pursued by the Truman administration, an obvious appeal to nationalists and budget balancers in the Republican Party who were advocating reductions in foreign aid and cuts in government expenditures.

INTERNATIONALISTS IN THE EISENHOWER ADMINISTRATION

Unlike their nationalist counterparts, internationalists had the advantage of being able to establish a policymaking agenda from the highest offices of the foreign policy establishment. The Eisenhower White House and State Departments were dominated by internationalists committed to the active promotion of trade and investment on behalf of U.S. firms that had reached the final stage of the product life cycle: foreign direct investors who had moved from exporting to Europe to establishing branch plants there. All the major Eisenhower foreign policy officials, with the notable exception of Treasury Secretary George Humphrey, had close connections with business internationalists with considerable investments in Western Europe. Secretary of State John Foster Dulles was the senior partner in one of the world's largest corporate law firms, Sullivan and Cromwell, which was closely linked to its most important client, the Standard Oil Company of New Jersey. Standard Oil of New Jersey was active in European investments and in promoting an integration of the European market through such internationalist bodies as the German-American Economic Association. The association's vice chairman was a leading board member of the German affiliate of Standard Oil.[46]

The administration's secretary of defense, Charles E. Wilson, had no prior governmental experience. He had been president of General Motors from 1941 to 1953, director of the National Bank of Detroit from 1942 to 1953, and a member of the Business Advisory Council from 1947 to 1951. All three entities were important conduits for internationalist causes, including increased economic and military aid to Western Europe, support for European integration, and a reduction of European barriers to U.S. trade and investment. In fact, as head of General Motors, Wilson had worked with the Truman administration in urging a strong U.S. effort to rebuild West Germany and integrate its economy into the Atlantic alliance.[47]

Secretary of the Army Robert Stevens (1953 to 1955) had no previous governmental experience but had been president or board chairman of the J. P. Stevens Corporaton from 1929 to 1952; a member of the Business Advisory Council from 1941 to 1955; and director of General Foods Corporation

(1946–1952), General Electric Co. (1947–1952), and New York Telephone Co., an AT&T subsidiary (1946–1952).[48] All of Stevens's affiliations reflected a strong internationalist orientation toward Western Europe, especially his association with General Electric, which had investments in West Germany after World War II and worked politically to expand the investment climate throughout the European region.

Numerous Eisenhower officials were affiliated with the Business Advisory Council, one of the most important internationalist groups in the post–World War II period. The BAC, created during the New Deal as a corporate advisory body for matters of domestic and foreign policy, had considerable access to the State and Commerce Departments during the Eisenhower period. In the area of foreign economic policy, the BAC and a counterpart entity, the Business and Defense Services Administration, advised foreign policy officials regarding whether to approve Export-Import Bank and World Bank loans. The BAC also worked with the State and Commerce Departments in promoting more profitable access to foreign markets through such measures as foreign direct investment tax breaks, the breakdown of intra-European barriers to trade and foreign investment, and U.S. government subsidies to foreign exporters and direct investors.[49]

Despite this degree of institutional power, internationalists still faced considerable challenges from U.S. firms threatened by reductions in trade barriers. The trade battles of the 1950s help illustrate the ongoing importance of the nationalist/internationalist divide in U.S. politics.

TRADE POLITICS IN THE "NEW REPUBLICAN" ADMINISTRATION

In January 1954, the Council on Foreign Economic Policy's Randall Commission (named for its head, a former CEO of Inland Steel) submitted a report to the president calling for the extension and furtherance of the policies embodied in FDR's Reciprocal Trade Agreements Act (RTAA). The Commission had been established in 1953 through joint appointments from Congress, which appointed ten of its members to serve in the commission, and the Eisenhower administration, which appointed seven commissioners. Six of the Eisenhower appointees were business internationalists. Three conservative Republican members of the commission dissented from its free trade views. The commission's recommendation was to extend the RTAA for three years, a goal that was secured only in 1955, after the election of a Democratic Congress. Congress approved the extension of the RTAA from 1955 to 1958 and then again through 1962, at which time the Kennedy Round of GATT would continue the internationalist agenda. Further, the Randall group endorsed a 5 percent across-the-board tariff cut per year, to be implemented at the president's discretion. The commission also supported abandoning farm price supports and advocated the free convertibility of European currencies.[50]

On the issue of the RTA we see again the pattern of internationalist interests in close cooperation with the executive branch in order to check efforts by the congressional nationalists to defeat their agenda. Reflecting the strength of the agricultural lobby with both the Republican and Democratic Parties, the administration did approach the farm subsidy issue very gingerly and gained only modest decreases in price supports. However, business internationalists helped lobby Congress to extend the RTA and to secure a 15 percent tariff reduction over a three-year period. Formed in the summer of 1953, the Committee for a National Trade Policy (CNTP) initiated a campaign to influence Congress and public opinion to support the Randall Commission approach to trade policy. The CNTP was formed as a kind of lobbying arm for the Committee for Economic Development, whose tax-exempt status would be jeopardized in broad lobbying campaigns of Congress. The first board members of the organization were drawn from some of the most prestigious internationalist firms of the country, including General Mills (Harry Bullis); the Gillette Safety Razor Company (Joseph Spang, Jr.); the Chase Manhattan Bank (John J. McCloy); Cleary, Gottlieb, Friendly and Ball (George Ball); and the Burroughs Manufacturing Company (chairman John Coleman).[51]

The CNTP based much of its lobbying efforts on documents drafted by the CED, including a 1953 report that addressed the subject of how to expand U.S. exports while overcoming the continuing worldwide shortage of dollars. The CNTP recognized that the congressional mood precluded any effort to expand U.S. aid programs beyond U.S. military assistance to NATO. The organization advocated a "trade, not aid" approach to U.S. foreign economic policy designed to promote U.S. trade and investment by reducing U.S. tariff barriers and promoting convertibility of foreign currencies. As Scofield notes in her assessment of the CNTP's lobbying efforts:

> The New York Times credited CNTP with helping secure passage of Eisenhower's 1958 renewal of the RTA: noting that the efforts of the President and House leadership were "fortified by pro-trade public opinion that resulted from an intensive publicity campaign throughout the country." The Times claimed that "much of the grass roots lobbying was guided by the CNTP with White House blessing." So close were the links between CNTP and the White House that Eisenhower was involved in the initial decision to select the Committee's Chairman. And a 1958 conference organized by the CNTP was addressed by the President, Vice President, four Cabinet members, and the Speaker of the House.[52]

The CNTP won important victories in gaining the extension of the RTA (twice) and in securing congressional authorization for 15 percent tariff cuts over the first three years of renewal. However, there were significant concessions made to protect agricultural, oil, and textile firms and to maintain trade restrictions between the United States and the Eastern bloc, which appeased logging and oil interests. In 1953 Congress passed Section 22 of the Agricultural Adjustment Act, which required the administration to impose "quantitative restrictions or special fees" on any agricultural imports to the United States that interfered with the U.S. price support program. Under Section 22, the United States imposed quotas to protect domestic producers of cotton, wheat, oats, peanuts, rye, barley, and manufactured dairy products. Since this measure conflicted with GATT regulations, the United States secured a waiver from GATT in 1955 to allow for the new provision.[53]

By 1954, the nationalist firms of the textile industry, in the midst of a move from the northern United States to the South, lobbied Congress and the Eisenhower administration to impose import restrictions against Japanese and European producers. The increasing concentration of the industry in the South allowed it to exert considerable influence with southern Democrats in Congress. Under pressure from lobbyists, and realizing that the votes of the southern Democrats were needed for the second extension of the RTA, the Eisenhower administration negotiated bilateral voluntary export restraint agreements on cotton textiles: a five-year agreement with Japan in 1957 and a similar agreement with Italy in 1958.[54]

Oil producers also sought protection from unfettered international trade. The oil industry was divided between large multinational producers, or "seven sisters," with their production facilities concentrated in the Middle East, and smaller independent producers based in the southwestern United States. The multinational producers had long bolstered their profits by setting up and managing a global cartel. However, by the mid to late 1950s, global oil prices had declined dramatically owing in part to the end of the Korean War, the opening of the Suez Canal, and increased global competition that resulted in a tripling of U.S. crude oil imports between 1948 and 1957.[55] In response, the domestic petroleum industry, eastern U.S. coal producers, and mining unions all called for increased protection.

The first approach of the Eisenhower administration was to try a voluntary import control plan. When that failed, the administration, in an effort to appease both the big producers and the independents with congressional influence, established a mandatory oil import control program, administered by the Oil Import Administration of the Department of the Interior, on March 10, 1959. The secretary of the interior was authorized to limit oil imports to approximately 9 percent of total projected demand. From the end of 1959 until 1962, imports of crude oil and unfinished imports declined by approximately 22 percent, or about 200,000 barrels a day.[56] The Eisenhower administration invoked a national security trade clause that allowed it to impose the quota.

At the same time, national security was invoked by the administration to maintain the Export Control Act of 1949, which allowed the Truman and Eisenhower administrations to restrict trade with Eastern bloc countries by establishing tariff rates at the high levels of the 1920s and 1930s. Influential business firms within the oil and timber industries lobbied aggressively to maintain the Export Control Act throughout the 1950s, insisting that the liberalization of trade with the East would greatly damage the profitability and market advantage of trade-sensitive U.S. products. John K. Evan, chairman of the National Planning Association, a business internationalist group committed to a broad liberalization of trade policy, explained that his group failed to release a report in 1959 on East-West commercial exchange because of the opposition of the oil subcommittee to the liberalization of trade with the Soviet Union.[57]

The ongoing battle between internationalists committed to the broad liberalization of trade and nationalists lobbying for protection of particular sectors continued through the 1950s. Business internationalists frustrated with the slow progress in the breakdown of trade barriers between the United States and Western Europe began to look more aggressively toward foreign direct investment as an outlet for increased global production, profitability, and market share. The ability to invest directly in the European market allowed firms at the high end of the product life cycle to tolerate ongoing trade restrictions between Western Europe and the United States. For U.S.-based investors in Europe, the reduction of intra-European trade barriers became a high priority.

INTERNATIONALISTS AND THE EEC

Throughout the 1950s, business internationalists expanded their investments into Western Europe, taking advantage of the reduced intra-European trade barriers facilitated by the European Coal and Steel Community. The Eisenhower administration supported the ECSC with loans as a first step toward the encouragement of a European Economic Community (EEC), which would represent the first effort to form a regional trading organization pledged to eliminate trade barriers gradually among member nation-states over a twelve- to seventeen-year period. U.S. direct investors, those at the high end of the product life cycle, lobbied the administration to support the EEC. Toward this end, business internationalists relied on political organizations established in West Germany and France to push for rapid integration of the European market.

The International Chamber of Commerce, the German-American Economic Association, the Federation of German Industries, and the French-American Committee brought together a broad coalition of European and U.S. industries promoting European regionalization. The French-American

Committee comprised a whole series of French subsidiaries of U.S. firms: IBM, Trailor, McCann-Erickson, and Gibbs-Hill France. The International Chambers of Commerce, consisting of all the major U.S. direct foreign investors, signed a 1954 Declaration of Atlantic Unity pledging industry-government cooperation in promoting a European Common Market. New investments by U.S. enterprises in the six-nation area reached $100 million a year in the early 1950s and jumped to $150 million in both 1955 and 1956.[58] By 1957 the total book value of U.S. private investment in plants and facilities in the area was $1.3 billion.[59]

Major U.S. firms with stakes in the emerging Common Market included Johnson & Johnson, Caltex (an oil-distributing firm); Ford (with its plant in Cologne, West Germany); Standard Oil of New Jersey (with Esso subsidiaries in France and Germany); Honeywell in Paris; Libby, McNeil and Libby; International General Electric; Wrigley; California Spray and Chemical (an arm of Standard Oil of California with a $1.5 million plant to make agricultural fungicide in France); U.S.-controlled British Carborundum, a company with affiliates in the U.K., Germany, and Norway; Minnesota Mining & Manufacturing (with affiliates in Britain, France, and Germany, which expanded production in Germany in anticipation of the Common Market).[60]

The growth of U.S. trade and investment in Western Europe did not simply materialize because of the invisible hand of the marketplace. Instead, business internationalists established political organizations committed to expanding their capital investments throughout Western Europe. Under the Eisenhower administration, the State Department worked to promote integration and investment opportunities for U.S. firms by channeling bilateral and multilateral assistance to European governments willing to undertake currency convertibility. The United States also took steps to prevent any resurgence of bilateral trade and payments agreements within Europe, tying U.S. support for the European Payments Union to progress in reducing bilateral European trade barriers.[61]

U.S. business internationalists, namely exporters of capital to Western Europe, aggressively stepped up their political efforts to promote a European Common Market by 1956, when economic trends indicated a slowdown in the total output of factories and mines in the United States. An address by the former head of the Council of Economic Advisors, Arthur F. Burns, to business executives at the Sixth Annual Management Conference of the University of Chicago, summarized the recent economic trends. Burns noted that the U.S. domestic economy had been increasingly sluggish during 1956 and 1957, as the Index of Industrial Production had stagnated from December 1955 through the third quarter of 1957. While total output of factories and mines had remained roughly constant during this period, business outlays on plant and equipment (capital spending) had risen steadily, by 27 percent between the third quarter of 1955 and the third quarter of 1957. Investment expenditures by manufaturing firms rose still more—by 37 percent, leaving a wide gap between capital investment and productive output.[62]

Although Burns did not refer to the discrepancy between factory output and capital investment as "underconsumption," his analysis suggested that U.S.-based firms had increased capital expenditures at a rate that was exceeding their capacity to increase production of finished goods. Internationalists hoped that the European Common Market would allow for increased foreign direct investments to compensate for sluggish demand at home, thereby maintaining profitability. At the same time, business internationalists pressed the Eisenhower administration for increasing the foreign aid budget in order to enhance opportunities for investments in the less developed world. Liberal internationalists were concerned that government foreign economic expenditures were too small to generate the demand necessary for profitable expansion of foreign capital investment.[63]

THE CONTAINMENT OF LABOR

While the Eisenhower Republicans juggled the interests of internationalists and nationalists in foreign and domestic policies, their efforts vis-a-vis labor were far more tepid. Eisenhower did appoint the president of the more conservative plumbers' union to his cabinet, but Labor Secretary Martin Durkin was generally considered to be well outside the business-dominated administrative inner circle. Eisenhower supported the Taft-Hartley framework and in 1959 signed off on the further restrictions of organized labor, such as secondary pickets and boycotts, embodied in the Landrum-Griffin Act. Meanwhile, conservative politicians working at the state level led the implementation of antiunion right-to-work laws throughout the South and the West.

Labor reached its organizational peak by the mid-1950s, representing slightly over 30 percent of the workforce by the time of the 1955 AFL-CIO merger. But it was a political force effectively contained within the industrial heartland of the Great Lakes region, with some strength in New England and on the West Coast as well. Organized labor has never been more than a regional power in U.S. politics, and it has never achieved any significant reform at the national level other than as a supporting player in a corporate liberal bloc. Its political influence has been confined to its occasional ability to block legislation that threatens the limited role it has.

Labor's own leadership has been quite complicit in its containment. McQuaid reports that as of 1955 George Meany, the president of the newly merged federation, showing an astounding lack of comprehension, "believed that the central core of America's economy had already been unionized and that organizing the unorganized in new industries and regions was not a priority."[64] We cannot help but ponder how the subsequent history of the civil rights and liberation movements of African Americans and women might have had a different trajectory had these groups, among others, been even somewhat better represented in the councils of labor, where A. Philip Randolph of the Pullman Porter's union remained an isolated critical voice in support of a more progressive labor agenda. Further, the AFL-CIO's supportive role in busting left-oriented unions in Latin America during this period could only exacerbate the problems of wage differentials that have increasingly threatened the standard of living of the U.S. working class.

George Humphrey depicted the relatively high wages of the United States as a comparative disadvantage for United States industry in international trade,[65] and both Humphrey and Eisenhower agreed with the CED and BAC position that increasing wages at a rate faster than productivity gains would encourage inflation. Eisenhower himself wanted Congress to amend the Full Employment Act of 1946 to include a policy goal of zero inflation as well as full employment. Congress did not adopt this proposal, a failure to support the president that one source attributes to labor's lobbying efforts to block it.[66]

In our view, the welfare state is a product of both business and class conflict. However, the designs of U.S. social policy have consistently followed the methods favored by business to support domestic and global markets without redistributing income or influence. "Citizenship rights," in T. H. Marshall's sense, of the effective ability to participate in the broad society without the bars of class, status, and wealth "have been achieved in some substantial degree through the active intervention of labour movements in the political arena" according to Giddens.[67] This frequently heard claim, which adumbrates the autonomy of the state from business, may be true to a certain extent elsewhere in the world, but we find no evidence to support this interpretation of U.S. public policy since World War II.

Concerning the theory of state autonomy, Giddens adopts Claus Offe's view that the capitalist state is "dependent upon processes of valorization and accumulation of capital which it itself does not directly control." Specifically, that the "state's revenue is dependent upon the accumulation process, upon the valorization process but it does not control these directly."[68] In other words, the claim is made that while the state is institutionally autonomous from business, it is fiscally dependent upon business. Giddens defines the issues in such a reified manner that the state appears to be a univocal agency. It might be more useful to note the consistency with which policymakers attend to the problems business faces in "the valorization process" and the full extent to which national interest is defined as continual profitability and accumulation.

THE BALANCE-OF-PAYMENTS AND POLICY RESTRAINT

> I felt that a rapid return to a balanced budget would help reassure other nations as to America's ability to pay her debts and lessen their desire to turn their dollars into gold. . . . We are the world's banker. If our money goes pflooey, the whole thing collapses. Our vaunted high wages will turn into bread lines.
>
> —Dwight D. Eisenhower[69]

Although this chapter has described the impact of industrial internationalists on U.S. public policy, it would be mistaken to conclude that the underlying tendency of the Bretton Woods regime was simply to make the world safe for U.S. exporters. Exporters of commodities did have some influence on the direction of foreign economic policy, and many exporters supported Marshall Plan aid. However, the most influential group of internationalists were those at the high end of the product life cycle who were able to engage in foreign direct investment in Western Europe. These internationalists pushed for a strong dollar and the formation of a European Common Market, policies that did not benefit most U.S. exporters. After all, the maintenance of a strong dollar does little in the short run to benefit exporters, whether they be exporters of autos, consumer durables, or agricultural commodities. To the contrary, a strong dollar can make foreign consumers unable to afford U.S. products. However, if we consider the global economy from the viewpoint of the investment banker and the exporter of capital, then the interest in a strong and stable dollar becomes much more pronounced, as does U.S. support for the EEC.

The dollar's convertibility to gold under the Bretton Woods agreement made U.S. policy highly vulnerable in international markets to inflation or even the possibility of inflation. As Sloan describes the circumstances faced by the Eisenhower administration: "Since 1953, foreign holdings of U.S. currency had exceeded U.S. gold stocks required for conversion. . . . If inflation continued it would lead to declining exports and an eventual loss of confidence in the dollar. Foreign governments would then cash in their dollars for gold, which would disrupt world trade."[70] For 1951–1957 the United States averaged a BOP surplus of $957 million per annum. By 1958–1960 a deficit of $3.7 billion had developed. By December 1956 the consumer price index was rising at an annual rate of 3.5 percent, "a figure that was considered frightening during the 1950s."[71] Raymond Saulnier, Council of Economic Advisors chair from 1956–1961, considered 1.5 percent an acceptable limit, and Saulnier was more conservative than his predecessor Burns; no longer did CEA balance the more conservative interests at the Treasury and the Federal Reserve.

In response to the BOP deficit, the Federal Reserve and Robert Anderson's Treasury Department supported increased interest rates to "attract foreign capital and help correct the balance-of-payments." In clarifying policy priorities to Eisenhower, Anderson claimed, "We face a choice . . . preventing a little more unemployment or preserving the value of the dollar."[72] In effect, the political economy of capital export was to be given first priority.

In understanding developments during the late 1950s, it is important to keep in mind that the United States still had a favorable balance of trade; it was not the case that imports were outstripping exports. The problem lay in the role the dollar played as key currency convertible to gold at a fixed rate, as "anchor" of a stable system of world trade, and as assurance of value for international investors. The difficulty with the BOP was caused by the impact of marginal trends, as "the volume of its [U.S.] imports increased faster than the growth of its exports. The cost of U.S. imports soared as the country attempted to finance both its growing consumption needs and the demands of the defense program. Sluggish export growth meant that it began to experience" BOP difficulty.[73]

In 1949, the U.S. government's gold inventory was at an all-time high of $24.4 billion (as measured in the nominal terms defined by Bretton Woods). In 1950–1957 the stock of gold remained at a plateau of $22–23 billion. However, "this fell sharply" to under $18 billion by December 1960, when "total volume of foreign-owned dollar claims against the U.S. gold supply reached 16.8 billion."[74] In other words, the export of dollars, through both foreign investment and the purchase of imports, had created an observable and potential crisis for Bretton Woods.

Furthermore, after the November 1960 election of John Kennedy, whose campaign had consistently emphasized growth against Republican fiscal and monetary restraint, a run on gold had begun:

> On 30 October, Kennedy gave an unequivocal pledge to maintain the current value of the dollar if elected. As a further reassurance . . . he also announced a modified position on interest rates. A Democratic administration would place more emphasis on lowering long-term interest rates, which would boost domestic investment and production, rather than short-term rates that were carried by most foreign held obligations. This statement soothed the money markets and stemmed the gold drain for the time being. On the other hand, it had also closed off the easy-money route to economic growth. . . . Kennedy had accepted that the defense of the dollar's international position should have precedence over the domestic aims of monetary policy. The Democratic administrations of the 1960s would always be in the position of having to consider the effects of expansionary monetary measures on the balance-of-payments deficit.[75]

THE "NEW LIBERALISM"

The Democratic resurgence in the congressional and presidential elections of 1958–1960 was helped by recession as well as Sputnik. Eisenhower's policies of tight money and tight budgets may have protected the dollar but did little for the Republican Party. In this context, a liberal politics of growth and military nationalism gained broad appeal. Within the administration, Vice President Nixon had understood the political ramifications but was unable to move the administration back to its earlier partial embrace of Keynesian demand stimulus. As to the leading Eisenhower Keynesian fighter of the 1954 recession, "after leaving the administration, Burns became concerned about the slow pace of economic expansion and helped to draft the Rockefeller Brothers Fund panel reports which advocated tax reduction and higher government expenditures on selected programs, notably education, urban renewal, energy resources and highways to boost economic growth."[76] Along with the public, then, key members of the internationalist business sector were growing concerned with the relative slowness of U.S. growth rates as compared with those of Germany, Japan, and even the U.S.S.R. With due consideration for the dollar's constituency, the agenda for the Kennedy-Johnson years would be to encourage growth with more guns, more butter, lower taxes, and the continued pursuit of free trade within the Bretton Woods framework. However, the stresses in the Bretton Woods system, already apparent by the end of the Eisenhower years, would continue to fester and grow as the international context grew more competitive.

NOTES

1. On coming into office, the Eisenhower administration revised the FY 1954 budget expenditures from $78.6 billion down to $68.7 billion. John W. Sloan, *Eisenhower and the Management of Prosperity* (Lawrence: University Press of Kansas, 1991), pp. 69–73.

2. Interestingly, the Chamber of Commerce moved to endorse free trade during this period, despite its diverse and often combative membership at the local level.

3. In a generally sympathetic "revisionist" account of the Eisenhower administration, Iwan Morgan refers to the Business Advisory Council as "the executive committee of the nation's corporate elite." Iwan W. Morgan, *Eisenhower Versus the Spenders* (New York: St. Martin's Press, 1990), p. 8.

4. But it is significant that the Kennedy-Johnson period would witness the maintenance of relatively conservative monetary policy by a central bank that had gained greater autonomy in its 1951 showdown with the Truman Treasury Department.

5. Sloan, *Eisenhower and the Management of Prosperity*, p. 69.

6. Ibid., p. 74.

7. Ibid., p. 78.

8. John Bellamy Foster, *The Theory of Monopoly Capitalism* (New York: Monthly Review Press, 1986), p. 12. For the *locus classicus* of this approach, see Paul Baran and Paul Sweezy, *Monopoly Capital* (New York: Monthly Review Press, 1966).

9. Seymour Melman, *The Permanent War Economy* (New York: Simon and Schuster, 1985).

10. Michael Kidron, *Western Capitalism Since the War* (Baltimore: Penguin Books, 1968), pp. 50–53.

11. Robert Zieger, *The CIO, 1935–1955* (Chapel Hill: University of North Carolina Press, 1995).

12. Among political elites, support for the Korean War policy of the Truman administration ran from the southern Democrats and moderate Republicans on the right to Hubert Humphrey, the Reuthers, and Americans for Democratic Action (ADA) and CIO on the left all the way to Henry Wallace, who perhaps in atonement for his earlier heresies had now became a supporter of the Truman administration's military intervention in Northeast Asia. The Progressive Party continued through the 1952 election on an antiwar platform with candidate Vincent Hallinan receiving 0.23 percent of the vote. In New York state, Progressive Party Senate candidate W.E.B. Du Bois gained over 4 percent of the vote, making what could be considered a surprisingly strong showing given the candidate's race and advanced age. American Labor Party Congressman Marcantonio lost a re-election effort, however, as Liberal, Democratic, and Republican fused to effect his defeat. All of these figures would be targets of political harassment in the years to come, especially Du Bois, who was subject to a congressional investigation as well as charges of his acting as the agent of a foreign government for his involvement in the peace movement.

13. Donald F. Kettl, *Leadership at the Fed* (Washington, DC: Brookings, 1986), and Anthony Campagna, *U.S. National Economic Policy, 1917–1985* (New York: Prager, 1987).

14. The "traditional" view on Eisenhower was that his administration was a period of stasis during which serious economic, social, and foreign policy issues were left unattended; Emmit J. Hughes, *The Ordeal of Power* (New York: Atheneum, 1963). Revisionist readings that emphasize the significant changes effected in U.S. politics by the Eisenhower leadership, of which our work could be considered a critical variant, include Stephen Ambrose, *Eisenhower: The President* (New York: Simon and Schuster, 1984); Gary Reichard, *The Reaffirmation of Republicanism* (Knoxville: University of Tennessee Press, 1975); Fred Greenstein, *The Hidden Hand Presidency* (New York: Basic Books, 1982); and Robert A. Divine, *Eisenhower and the Cold War* (New York: Oxford University Press, 1981). For a postrevisionist interpretation that re-emphasizes the limited and frustrated goals of the administration, see Piers Brenda, *Ike: The Life and Times of Dwight D. Eisenhower* (London: Martin Secker and Warburg, 1987).

15. Eisenhower's appeal to wage earners is, of course, to be distinguished from his antipathy to organized labor.

16. The phrase "high volume production" is from Robert Reich, *The Work of Nations* (New York: Vintage Press, 1992), and denotes industrial output with economies of scale and productivity sufficient to provide both high social wages and profitability. This approach also requires expanded and therefore "open" trade.

17. Kim McQuaid, *Uneasy Partners: Big Business in American Politics, 1945–1990* (Baltimore: Johns Hopkins University Press, 1994), pp. 84–86.

18. Ibid., pp. 86–87.

19. Leon Epstein, *Political Parties in the American Mold* (Madison: University of Wisconsin Press, 1987).

20. Walter L. Adamson, *Hegemony and Revolution* (Berkeley: University of California Press, 1980), pp. 177–178.

21. Sloan, *Eisenhower and the Management of Prosperity,* p. 71.

22. Antonio Gramsci, *Selections from the Prison Notebooks* (New York: International Publishers, 1971), p. 19.

23. John W. Sloan, "President Eisenhower, Professor Burns, and the 1953–1954 Recession," Melvin J. Dubnick and Alan R. Gitelson, eds., in *Public Policy and Economic Institutions* (Greenwich, CT: JAI Press, 1991), p. 58.

24. Ibid., p. 37.

25. Mark Hanna managed William McKinley's 1896 presidential campaign, mobilizing a $1 million corporate fund-raising effort on behalf of McKinley's tight money and protectionist platform against the populist insurgency of William Jennings Bryan. Historically speaking, then, Humphrey was the protegé of the very epitome of midwestern business nationalism.

26. Morgan, *Eisenhower versus the Spenders,* pp. 8–9.

27. Ibid., p. 19.

28. Kees Van Der Pijl, *The Making of an Atlantic Ruling Class* (London: Verso, 1984), pp. 144–145.

29. Foreign Operations Assistance, "The European Coal and Steel Community," White House Office, National Security Council Staff Papers, 1953–1956, Council on Foreign Economic Policy (CFEP), 520, Box 5, Eisenhower Library.

30. Ibid.

31. Subcommittee of the Council on Foreign Economic Policy, "Regional Economic Integration," White House Office, National Security Council Staff Papers, 1953–1961, CFEP File, 539, Box 7, Eisenhower Library.

32. Fred Block, *The Origins of International Economic Disorder* (Berkeley: University of California Press, 1977), pp. 99–100.

33. Eric Helleiner, *States and the Reemergence of Global Finance: From Bretton Woods to the 1990s* (Ithaca, NY: Cornell University Press, 1994), p. 64.

34. Ibid., p. 68.

35. Council on Foreign Economic Policy, "Overall U.S. Foreign Economic Policy," March 30, 1954, White House Office, National Security Council Staff Papers, 1953–1961, 510/1, Box 4, Eisenhower Library.

36. Sloan, *Eisenhower and the Management of Prosperity,* p. 129.

37. Ibid., p. 130.

38. Morgan, *Eisenhower versus the Spenders,* p. 10. See also, Harold Vatter, *The U.S. Economy in the 1950s* (Chicago: University of Chicago Press, 1984).

39. Morgan, *Eisenhower versus the Spenders,* p. 11.

40. Benjamin Fordham, *Building the Cold War Consensus: The Political Economy of U.S. National Security Policy: 1949–1951* (Ann Arbor: University of Michigan Press, 1998).

41. For details of the relationship of southern Democrats (and exporters) to the Democratic Party, see G. William Domhoff, *The Power Elite and the State: How Policy Is Made in America* (New York: Aldine de Gruyter, 1990), pp. 235–245.

42. Memo from Leo A. Hoegh, Office of Civil and Defense Mobilization (OCDM), to Clarence Randall, Chairman of Council on Foreign Economic Policy, regarding contents of a discussion paper drafted by the OCDM on "U.S. Import

Competition as Exemplified by Section 8 Cases," March 29, 1955, White House Office, National Security Council Staff Papers, 1953–1961, Trade Competition Between U.S. and Europe, Eisenhower Library.

43. Ibid.

44. Letter from Senator Homer Ferguson to Herbert Hoover, May 8, 1952, Hoover Post Presidential Individual File, Eisenhower, Dwight D. correspondence, 1952, Box 53, Herbert Hoover Presidential Library, West Branch, Iowa.

45. Ibid.

46. Philip Burch, *Elites in American History, Vol. III* (New York: Holmes and Meier, 1980), pp. 128–129.

47. Tom McCormick, *America's Half Century* (Baltimore: Johns Hopkins University Press, 1994).

48. Burch, *Elites in American History,* p. 133.

49. Gabriel Kolko, *Main Currents in Modern American History* (New York: Pantheon Books, 1984), p. 314.

50. Sloan, *Eisenhower and the Management of Prosperity,* p. 126.

51. Jerri-Lynn Scofield, *Foreign Policy as Domestic Politics: The Political Economy of U.S. Trade Policy, 1960–1975* (Ph.D. dissertation in progress, Oxford University, 1997), pp. 75–77.

52. Ibid., p. 77.

53. Ibid., pp. 105–106.

54. General Agreement on Tariffs and Trade, *Textiles and Clothing in the World Economy* (Geneva: GATT, July 1984), p. 64.

55. Robert Keohane, "State Power and Industry Influence: American Foreign Oil Policy in the 1940s," *International Organization* 36, 1 (Winter 1982): 174.

56. Scofield, *Foreign Policy as Domestic Politics,* pp. 109–110.

57. Ibid., p. 115.

58. For details of U.S. firms engaged in efforts to expand their European investment and production opportunities, see "Common Market Plan Will Spur U.S. Firms to Boost Plant Building in Europe," *Wall Street Journal,* July 12, 1957, pp. 1, 15.

59. Ibid.

60. Ibid.

61. Council on Foreign Economic Policy, "Overall U.S. Foreign Economic Policy," January 10, 1955, White House Office, National Security Council Staff Papers, 1953–1961, 510/1, Box 4, Eisenhower Library.

62. Arthur Burns, "The Current Business Recession," address presented at the 6th Annual Management Conference, Chicago, March 22, 1958, Dwight D. Eisenhower Papers, Ann Whitman File, Administration Series, Box 2, Robert Anderson, Eisenhower Library.

63. For details of this shift from "trade, not aid" to "trade and aid" in U.S. policies toward the less developed world, see Ronald W. Cox, *Power and Profits: U.S. Policy in Central America* (Lexington: University of Kentucky Press, 1994).

64. McQuaid, *Uneasy Partners,* p. 98.

65. Sloan, *Eisenhower and the Management of Prosperity,* p. 129.

66. Ibid., p. 124.

67. Anthony Giddens, *A Contemporary Critique of Historical Materialism,* 2nd ed. (Stanford, CA: Stanford University Press, 1995), p. 14.

68. Ibid., p. 212.

69. Quotes in Sloan, *Eisenhower and the Management of Prosperity,* pp. 128–129.

70. Ibid., p. 28. See also, Robert B. Anderson, "The Balance-of-Payments Problem," *Foreign Affairs* 38 (April 1960): 419–433.

71. Sloan, *Eisenhower and the Management of Prosperity,* p. 41.

72. Ibid., p. 123.

73. Ibid., p. 127.

74. Ibid., p. 128.

75. Morgan, *Eisenhower versus the Spenders,* p. 175.

76. Ibid., p. 7. See also, Rockefeller Brothers Fund, *Prospect for America,* 1961. For a critical review, see "Editorial: The Rockefeller Report," *Fortune* 57: 97–98.

4

Liberal Globalization in the 1960s

> The flaw in the pluralist heaven is that the heavenly chorus sings with a strong upper class accent.
> —E. E. Schattschneider, *The Semi-Sovereign People*

Beneath the intense partisan conflict of the 1960 election a business-elite consensus was emerging on the basic issues of the political economy of the day. Even during the preinauguration transition period, the new administration began to lay the practical political groundwork for the extension of Eisenhower's foreign economic policy. Progressive and liberal critics of the Kennedy administration at the time believed that the priority given to trade policy was detrimental to important aspects of the liberal social agenda such as the extension of the Social Security system to health care coverage. Arthur Schlesinger, usually a leading celebrant of "Camelot," critically termed trade expansion the "unifying intellectual principle of the New Frontier." This typification is accepted by one of Kennedy's foreign economic policy advisers, who has stated that liberal trade legislation "would test the Congress, test the temperature of public opinion, and serve as an educative device. So that there was in this sense a 'grand design,' there's no question about that."[1]

Despite the flutters of the financial markets subsequent to the election of a liberal Democrat in 1960, the Kennedy administration and, for that matter, the Johnson presidency up to 1965 would maintain a cautious, even conservative approach to domestic spending and monetary policy. Given Vice President Nixon's pragmatic move to the center in the late 1950s as the sluggish economy jeopardized his electoral ambitions, it is very difficult to identify how Nixon would have differed from Kennedy in the essentials of trade and fiscal policy.

President-elect Kennedy appointed Republican financier C. Douglas Dillon to Treasury, the relatively obscure but well-connected Dean Rusk[2] to State over more liberal and prominent candidates such as Adlai Stevenson, and the auto industry's wunderkind Robert McNamara to Defense. The executive branch of the 1960s, like that of the 1950s, would continue to share the outlook and personnel of the internationalist bloc. The two Democratic administrations of the 1960s would pursue a liberal globalism that emphasized expanded trade, economic growth, and technical innovation within the parameters of a restrained fiscal and monetary policy that was predicated on maintaining the dollar's key currency role in the Bretton Woods order. Ultimately, the dynamics of the world economy and the upheavals within U.S. society would undo their desired consensus and set the stage for the major crisis of the postwar system in the 1970s.

THE POLITICAL DESIGN FOR BUSINESS CONSENSUS

A primary legislative priority of the new Democratic administration was to move toward greater liberalization of trade. Already during the preinauguration transition period, Kennedy staffers initiated a thorough research effort to identify the sources of U.S. exports by state and congressional district in the nation.[3] This material was used during 1961–1962 as part of the administration's efforts to lobby every member of Congress, creating the capacity to identify specific industries, firms, and workers in every part of the country who had direct interests in expanded trade.

The Trade Expansion Act of 1962 (TEA) was the product of the administration's efforts on behalf of trade liberalization. This legislation essentially extended the framework of the earlier Reciprocal Trade Agreements Act by broadening the president's power to reduce tariffs in accordance with multilateral arrangements worked out under the GATT framework. In prioritizing the TEA, the Kennedy administration was pursuing a theme already articulated by the Committee for Economic Development. Indeed, CED vice chair Howard C. Peterson was appointed special assistant to the president on international foreign trade. In this White House staff position, Peterson acted as liaison to the business community and played a key role in facilitating business lobbying efforts on behalf of trade expansion.

The policy rationale for the TEA was that it offered a means of relieving the balance-of-payments crunch, promoting sustained growth, and preventing inflation. Additionally, the administration argued, it was necessary to achieve reciprocal tariff reduction vis-à-vis the developing European Economic Community, particularly in the anticipation that Britain would join the organization. In a memo to the cabinet and major executive office heads, Peterson wrote:

> If we fail to protect our access to Europe's markets, we risk a favorable mer-
> chandise trade balance which was $4.7 billion in 1960. Moreover, we would
> not diminish the incentive to a large flow of U.S. direct investment in West-
> ern Europe provided by the existence of a high tariff wall. Both considera-
> tions would aggravate our vexing balance of payments problem and propel
> us toward the last resort of import restrictions. . . . If we fail to achieve rec-
> iprocal tariff reductions with the EEC, we cast away a powerful tool for re-
> straining inflation and [promoting] innovation in the American economy.[4]

In formulating a policy strategy for liberalizing U.S. trade policy, the
Kennedy administration relied on numerous corporate think tanks, interest
groups, and individuals. In addition to the CED, the most influential corporate organizations included the National Foreign Trade Council, the International Chamber of Commerce, and the Committee for a National Trade
Policy (CNTP), which all drafted position papers advocating a reduction of
U.S. trade barriers. These organizations also provided members to work
with Kennedy officials in lobbying Congress to pass the Trade Expansion
Act. The CNTP, essentially a lobbying arm of the CED, took the lead in organizing the lobbying efforts of free trade groups and communicated
closely with the White House regarding congressional lobbying efforts.[5]

The membership of the CNTP was drawn from those capital-intensive
international business firms that had long supported U.S. government efforts to promote free trade and foreign investment opportunities. Led by
such corporations as Caterpillar, Gillette, IBM, Westinghouse, and General
Electric and commercial banks such as Chase Manhattan, these firms ad
vocated a free trade policy as one of the most essential steps toward a
long-term effort to reduce the balance-of-payments deficit. Capital-intensive internationalist firms were concerned about the potentially restrictive
policies of the European Economic Community. An examination of private
correspondence between these firms and the Kennedy administration reveal a mutual priority in working to ensure progress in negotiating lower
tariff barriers between the United States and the EEC.[6]

Internationalists supported the Trade Expansion Act for several reasons. First, U.S.-based foreign investors were concerned that a closed EEC
market would mean higher prices for inputs used in production. Tariff barriers would force U.S. investors to rely on European-based producers for
supplies needed in the production process and keep out potentially cheaper
imports from non-European sources. Second, U.S.-based foreign investors
had been busily expanding their investments in the less developed world.
The ability to export from the less developed world to the advanced markets of the United States and the EEC were considered important to the
long-term success of relocation strategies. In communication with the
White House over the importance of the EEC to U.S. operations in the less

developed world, David Rockefeller's Business Group for Latin America voiced the opinion that future corporate expansion into manufacturing production in Latin America and elsewhere was tied to the continued effort to open markets in the United States and the EEC.[7]

Internationalist business groups were prepared to expand their investments inside regional common markets and even to support common tariff walls around those markets as a mechanism to expand production and sales opportunities. Still, most internationalist firms and lobbying organizations viewed regional common markets as a step toward reducing trade barriers that limited corporate expansion, not as permanent features of the international economic landscape. Internationalist organizations worked with the Kennedy administration to secure congressional legislation that was aimed primarily at reducing the trade barriers of the European Economic Community, despite the fact that in 1957 many of the same internationalists supported the creation of the EEC as an important first step in reducing trade barriers throughout Europe.

However, the administration's free trade objectives were not limited to Europe, as Peterson's memo indicates: "Our broad objective is to ensure that the EEC market is available to the export interests not only of this country but also of other nations not in a position to bargain effectively, such as those of Latin America."[8] This global perspective is consistent with the growing interest of U.S. business internationalists in developing prospective markets in the Third World as described by Cox and Gibbs.[9] In a letter of September 9, 1961, to the U.S. commander in the Panama Canal Zone, Peterson describes the increasing importance that the CED was placing on Central America and assures the general that the region's significance will not be overlooked in the development of trade policy.[10]

Among business internationalists at the time there was some ambition to reduce many tariff rates to zero as well as eliminate the "no injury" to domestic industries standard that had limited trade liberalization efforts since 1934.[11] However, these aspirations were frustrated by the Kennedys' political coalition with textile interests in the South as well as in New England. Effectively, a side agreement was worked out with the textile industry as early as 1960 to the effect that trade expansion policy would retain protections for this industry.[12] A practical consequence of this agreement was that it split protectionist opposition by allying the administration with a major protectionist interest, thereby increasing the political isolation of other business nationalists.

In order to secure the TEA, the Kennedy administration and internationalist business organizations recognized the urgency of curtailing the influence of the textile industry and other nationalist business sectors on Congress. Kennedy administration officials understood that congressional approval for a significant extension of the Reciprocal Trade Agreements

Act hinged on the acquiescence of traditionally protectionist industries. The most politically powerful protectionist industries included textiles, oil, and timber. Firms within each industry were able to extract significant concessions from the Kennedy administration prior to congressional approval of the TEA. The extent and nature of the concessions illustrate the continuing political importance of the nationalist versus internationalist divisions in U.S. foreign policy and how those divisions were manifested in executive-congressional negotiations over the Kennedy trade bill.

The strength of the textile lobby requires some understanding of the geographic concentration of the industry in the southern United States and apparel production in New York. In 1960 and 1961 the textile industry relied on two influential House members, Carl Vinson and Harold Cooley, to broaden House support for textile protection. Both Vinson and Cooley controlled awarding of defense contracts and based the awarding of such contracts to a representative's district on whether or not that representative had voted for textile protection. This log-rolling mechanism best explains how the textile industry was able to gain political influence beyond the votes of House members from the South and New York. Support for textile protection came from members of Congress from all parts of the United States, making the textile lobby a political force that the Kennedy administration could not ignore in its efforts to pass the TEA.

As early as February 1961, the Kennedy administration developed a plan to guarantee monetary assistance and specific minimum levels of protection to textile firms affected by the Trade Expansion Act. The plan, formulated by President Kennedy in close coordination with the Commerce and Treasury Departments, was designed to limit any opposition to the TEA by offering concessions to nationalist firms. The administration appointed a Textile Advisory Committee to develop a seven-point program of assistance to the industry.[13] The Commerce Department launched a research program to assist textile firms in modernizing their plants and equipment to cope with new international competition. The Treasury Department reviewed the extension of depreciation allowances on textile machinery, and the Small Business Administration assisted in financing the modernization of the industry. Most important, the administration moved to reduce import competition significantly by continuing the established trend of cartelizing the world textiles market among existing producers and severely restricting the growth of exports from those countries new to textile production.[14]

Other nationalist sectors were able to win significant concessions from the Kennedy administration in exchange for cooperating in the legislative passage of the TEA. Two powerful champions of domestic oil interests, Representative Wilbur Mills, chairman of the House Ways and Means Committee, and Senator Robert S. Kerr of Oklahoma, threatened to oppose the TEA unless the administration guaranteed the extension of the oil import quota policies. Bureaucratic debates emerged over the import quota program, which Kennedy's Budget Bureau described as having "grown out of domestic industry pressures rather than defense considerations."[15] The bureau argued that "the oil import program had done little to achieve its stated goal: to encourage domestic companies to develop new capacity."[16]

The Interior Department, however, staunchly defended the oil import quotas, citing national security interests as the primary reason for continuing the quota system. The Interior Department lobbied to expand the quota system to reduce oil import levels further by 100,000 barrels per day while increasing the quota level to 12.2 percent of the domestic oil supply. Under significant pressure from congressional representatives and senators close to the oil industry, the Kennedy administration adopted many of the Interior Department's recommendations to expand the program, despite the bureaucratic opposition from the Budget Bureau and the Council of Economic Advisers, both represented, along with the Interior Department, in the Petroleum Study Committee established by the Kennedy administration to review the quota. The administration ultimately sided with the Interior Department in order to deflect a potentially powerful oil lobby from opposing the TEA.

The administration also moved to placate opposition to trade expansion from other nationalist sectors, including timber, carpets, and sheet glass. For the timber industry, the administration proposed a six-point support program for domestic producers that included "a preferential military procurement plan and a promise to negotiate a voluntary restraint arrangement with Canada."[17] At the same time, the administration guaranteed existing tariff levels for carpets and sheet glass in an effort to further neutralize protectionist opposition. As a side effect of these concessions, the administration was able to secure considerable legislative support for its trade expansion efforts, securing passage of the TEA by the sizable margins of 298–125 in the House and 78–8 in the Senate.[18]

The administration's lobbying efforts were aggressively supported by capital-intensive internationalist business groups and by leading Republicans such as Henry Cabot Lodge and Alfred Landon. On the other side, Senator Barry Goldwater led a protectionist coalition that aggressively opposed the administration's trade policy. The later Goldwater presidential nomination would reflect a highwater point for protectionists within the Republican Party, as firms that perceived themselves damaged by the TEA would gravitate toward the maverick Republican. For example, despite temporarily acquiescing to the terms of the TEA, nationalist firms in textiles, independent oil, sheet glass, steel, timber, and coal fled from the Democrats after securing further promises of protection from the Goldwater Republican camp in 1964.[19] Nonetheless the Kennedy period represented a time in which free trade and protectionist firms could peacefully, albeit temporarily and uneasily, coexist, buttressed by a Keynesian tax bill that united diverse wings of the business community and tempered opposition to the internationalist foreign policy pursued by the administration.

The Hegemony of Business Internationalism Under Kennedy

Even among the traditionally protectionist ranks of business, the opposition to the Kennedy initiatives was less than stalwart. For example, the Manufacturing Chemists Association, which "always had problems with . . . liberal trade policy," formally opposed the TEA. But the association's opposition was attenuated by its president, Robert Semple of Wyandotte Chemical, which, like others in this industry, "had changed a good deal . . . over the years. It was a very substantial exporter."[20]

More significant, perhaps, the National Association of Manufacturers voiced its opposition to the elimination of tariffs on imported manufactured goods. The NAM did not oppose reciprocal trade reduction per se but chafed at the idea of increasing the percentages by which tariffs could be reduced and strongly opposed a proposal that the Labor Department administer trade adjustment assistance programs for workers who might be adversely affected. Speaking to the NAM, Howard Peterson criticized its emphasis on the supposed disadvantage that U.S. manufacturers faced in world markets because of higher wages in the United States. His remarks contain a remarkable passage that seems more than prescient in light of later developments:

> You are much too sophisticated to pull that old line about wage rates. You know as well as I do that American productivity is higher than that of any other country. You know that the dollar's strength in the world rests on that fact more than all the gold in Fort Knox. Once we lose our advantages in productivity over other nations, you won't have to worry about wage differentials. . . . Foreigners will simply start selling the dollar cheap and that is the quickest way in the world to narrow the gap in money wages between our country and other free countries.[21]

It would be less than a decade before the scenario described here by Peterson took place, when the end of dollar-gold convertibility forced the effective devaluation of the dollar, hence cheapening it and making U.S.-manufactured exports more price competitive in world markets.[22] Our theory is that the global economic design of the Kennedy administration was to stimulate innovation and investment in the United States through increased international competition and public sector stimulus via tax cuts, tax expenditures for investment and depreciation, and direct expenditures for military purposes, education, foreign aid, and other government services. This agenda was largely endorsed by a broad range of business interests and wholly opposed by almost none.

Peterson encouraged JFK to lead on trade policy by making trade expansion his top legislative priority in the 87th Congress and by supporting the concept of zero tariff rates in the Atlantic trade zone. In a September 1961 memorandum to the president, the special assistant on international trade notes that the trade expansion initiative was already supported by the apparently unlikely coalition of the U.S. Chamber of Commerce, the U.S. Council of the International Chamber of Commerce, the AFL-CIO, the Farm Bureau, and the League of Women Voters.[23] Yet the administration did not rely solely on these interest groups to fight the legislative battle for TEA; Peterson was also directly involved in organizing the Committee for a National Trade Policy, co-chaired by CED member John Hight.[24] The CNTP was essentially an extension of CED business internationalism that included prominent multinational corporate leaders such as Roger Blough of U.S. Steel, who would later have a famous confrontation with Kennedy over pricing policy in his industry.

The constitution and tax exempt status of the CED did not allow it to lobby expressly, but in this case as in others, the organizational pattern was to create an *ad hoc* interest group that would promote business internationalist interests in the legislative process. This formation of a temporary interest group appeared to give business internationalism a more ephemeral quality than the better known business lobbies of the NAM and the U.S. Chamber of Commerce. It is ultimately misleading to look at business dominance of U.S. national politics as a question of interest group politics because the factions of capital that have most consistently maintained close ties to the executive branch and have had a direct hand in policy development throughout the postwar period are represented through what we term the "informal corporatism" of such bodies as the CED and the Business Advisory Council, which also officially took no position on the issues. Yet one should not get the impression that the close relationship between the executive branch and the internationalist sector of business gives state managers power over the political expression of these business interests. As Commerce Secretary Luther Hodges ruefully noted when he attempted to exert appointment powers over the BAC, "I don't think even the President of the United States could get a member in there except as the BAC agreed."[25] After a confrontation with Hodges over the appointment issue, the BAC broke official ties with the Commerce Department and reconstituted itself as the Business Council and continued its policy of self-co-opting membership as a nonpartisan and unofficial private advisory group to U.S. government.

Neopluralist analysts of business and politics focus almost entirely on conventional interest groups—those with a mass membership and a primary emphasis on legislative liaison—as their unit of analysis.[26] This systematically underemphasizes the symbiotic relationship between the executive branch and the internationalist bloc that is represented via the informal corporatist networks of the CED, the Business Council, and other similar organizations. As Miliband put it in his classic study of state-capital relations:

> As the state has increasingly come to assume greater powers in all fields of economic and social activity, so have the major "interests" in society also naturally come to direct their pressure activities towards government and administration. . . . the most significant part of pressure group activity must now bear on the executive power; it is now only the weakest groups which seek to wield influence primarily through legislatures, precisely because they have little or no hold over the executive. The major "interests" use both means, with the greater emphasis on the government and the administration.[27]

Concerning the political role of the CED, Vogel states that its educational efforts and public statements on policy "do not so much reflect corporate preference as shape them."[28] We agree with that assessment; the CED and other "informal corporatist" organizations have often been able to play a leadership role, anticipating future problems and strongly influencing the direction of public policy both through ideas and through the strength of professional networks.[29] In Vogel's view the opinion-shaping role of the CED does not extend to government policymakers; further, he believes that without a peak organization, U.S. business interests remain fragmented and therefore weaker than many analyses, such as our own, would argue.[30] Vogel's perspective appears to rely on a model of political action in which governmental policy is a response to pressure from organized interests and the best organized interests therefore have the most influence. This is not a bad starting point; however, it fails to attend to the structural role that organizations like the CED play in the intellectual development of policy and the legitimation of policy that is consistent with the present and future success of capitalists and capitalism. Vogel's argument also relies on a contrast between the fact that business lacks a peak organization and that labor gained such an organization after the AFL-CIO merger. Yet this contrast is fundamentally flawed even on pluralist methodological grounds insofar as virtually every business in the United States, large or small, has membership in one or more business-oriented interest groups.[31] By contrast, only a small fraction of workers and consumers have ever had direct interest group representation. The fundamental economic interests of the vast majority remain represented only as atomized "citizens" whose acquiescence and votes are the outer circle of the political process.

The CED was, in the political design of the 1960s' liberal internationalist consensus, a public educator, which is to say that it actually showed the capacity to articulate a systemic agenda, making it something more than an interest group. By expressing a more broad-minded conception of government policy than other sectoral business interests, the CED fit the Gramscian description of the intellectual leadership that is necessary for a social group to attain ideological primacy. By contrast, there are no labor, consumer, or even business nationalist equivalents to the unique organizational ties to the state that have been enjoyed by the CED and the Business Council.

The TEA is a perfect example of the hegemonic leadership of, or the "organic intellectual" role played by, the CED. The CED, in response to the economic slowdown of the late 1950s, advocated and developed concrete proposals for the policy mix of tax cuts, credits, and trade expansion that were later adopted by Kennedy. Kennedy's economic policies were in all fundamental respects consistent with CED positions. Kennedy himself had ties to the CED dating back to 1953, the year he entered the U.S. Senate and perhaps began to seriously lay plans for seeking national office.[32] While the liberal- and labor-oriented wing of his party wished to move ahead on the social welfare and civil rights agendas, Kennedy wanted to avoid both a civil rights agenda that would alienate his white southern supporters[33] and any social welfare programs that would undermine business confidence. White House staffer Myer Rashish, a liberal academic economist with previous staff experience in the State Department and on the House Ways and Means Committee, and who preferred Stevenson to Kennedy, "thought that President Kennedy exhibited in those early months, and . . . this was true later on as well, more of a concern and worry about the U.S. balance of payments position than the problem merited." Rashish claimed that treasury secretary Dillon "found it to his advantage to make the balance of payments problem a central problem of American public policy."[34]

With legislative success in 1962 on the TEA, the Kennedy administration would still face signals of a possible economic downturn later in the year. On December 14, 1962, in what John K. Galbraith termed "the most Republican speech since McKinley," JFK called for tax cuts, especially in the higher income brackets and on corporate income, designed to stimulate private spending and investment and raise profit rates.[35] Galbraith, by contrast, had advised Kennedy to pursue stimulus through social spending designed to alleviate "public squalor." Yet Kennedy again showed a preference for private capital to play the leading role in economic growth; he had already by this point effectively supported both liberalized depreciation rules and the investment tax credit.

On tax policy we again find Kennedy pursuing a policy line already articulated by the CED and other business groups. The CED-organized Commission on Money and Credit had been advocating the need for tax cuts and investment credits since the late 1950s and had been frustrated by the Eisenhower administration's fiscal caution. On the same day as Kennedy's tax cut speech, the CED published a call for a tax cut "not off-set by spending cuts." Earlier in 1962 the U.S. Chamber of Commerce (COC) called for a tax cut that "if enacted would result in a budget deficit." The COC's newfound "liberalism" angered its former director, Senator Harry Byrd, so much that he publicly rebuked the organization for its pro-administration posture from the Senate floor.[36] The NAM, which declined to support the Kennedy proposal, did support a tax cut "even in the face of a current deficit"; however, given the group's concern to avoid pressure for wage increases, it favored limiting the tax cut to business investors rather than the across-the-board income tax rate cuts favored by all the other major players.[37] The product of this consensus was the Revenue Act of 1964, which lowered the highest marginal income tax rate from 91 to 70 percent and the corporate income tax rate from 52 to 48 percent.[38]

The Committee for Economic Development took the lead in drafting tax cut proposals that were circulated to important members of the Kennedy cabinet, including Secretary of the Treasury Douglas Dillon and Kennedy himself.[39] The committee had begun endorsing Keynesian policies for the stimulation of the domestic U.S. economy since the late 1950s and were joined in the early 1960s by the U.S. Chamber of Commerce and the National Association of Manufacturers. In December 1962, as the Kennedy administration was preparing to submit an economic stimulus package to Congress, Kennedy drew upon the recommendations of the CED for his plan. At the request of the Kennedy administration, copies of a proposed tax reduction drawn up by the CED were circulated to each member of Congress.

The CED proposal called for a two-part tax rate cut amounting to a total of $11 billion over two years. The first part of the program called for a reduction of all individual income tax rates by 8 percent, with a proviso that no rate would exceed 70 percent, plus a reduction of the corporate tax rate from 52 to 47 percent.[40] The committee justified the proposal by declaring that such a cut was necessary to help stimulate the nation's economic activity and raise national income. Using a straightforward Keynesian logic, the committee emphasized the tax cut as a counteractive measure designed to reverse the slow growth of the U.S. economy since 1958. The CED thought that tax rate reductions would increase economic activity to such an extent as to compensate for any loss in revenue to the U.S. government.

Other business groups endorsed this line of thinking, even those organizations such as the National Association of Manufacturers, whose membership had tended to support the balanced budget policies of the Eisenhower administration. George Hagedorn, a leading NAM economist, testified to Congress in August 1962 that "the problem before us is one of chronic suboptimum economic performance, rather than of a short-term cyclical downturn which may or may not be in the offing."[41] Spokespersons for the Chamber of Commerce echoed such Keynesian sentiments, with President Ladd Plumley warning that "a delay in cutting taxes might bring on an American recession which could easily spread to other Western-bloc nations."[42] The CED spoke of the "inadequate vigor" of the economy and of the need to establish "an economic climate that will nourish dynamic growth."[43]

Keynesian doctrine was shared by influential members of the Kennedy administration. Secretary of the Treasury Dillon worked with business leaders from the CED to form the Business Committee for Tax Reduction in 1963. Dillon called on four members of the CED to mobilize support for the formation of the Business Committee, a lobbying organization with a membership of 2,800 and a budget that made it the third largest spender among registered lobbying groups in 1963. The committee, led by Henry Ford II and railroad executive Stuart Saunders, lobbied aggressively for the tax reduction program drawn up by the CED in December 1962 and adopted in modified form by the Kennedy administration in 1963. Like the CED, the Business Committee justified its support of the tax cut in Keynesian terms, as a necessary demand stimulus that would help promote economic growth during a time of economic slowdown. The government deficit was viewed as an "investment in the future of the country."[44]

Walter Heller, head of the Council of Economic Advisers for the Kennedy Administration, argued for a tax reduction program that would "free the economy from the doldrums of long-run stagnation."[45] The Keynesian logic of demand stimulus was at the center of the Kennedy administration's tax cut program for 1963. In the Kennedy proposal the personal income rate schedule, then ranging from 20 to 91 percent, was to be slashed to rates ranging from 14 to 65 percent, across a period of steps starting in 1963 and continuing into 1965. The corporate income tax was to be cut from 52 to 47 percent, and capital gains taxes were to be reduced. The plan called for a total tax reduction of $10.2 billion and would reduce federal revenues by $13.6 billion. Of this amount, $11 billion was to come from individual income rate reductions and $2.6 billion from corporate income rate reductions. Certain reforms in the package would bring in an extra $3.4 billion in revenue, thus giving the net reduction of $10.2 billion.[46]

There were nuanced differences among business organizations that supported the Kennedy tax cut of 1963. The CED endorsed the proposal by embracing the Keynesian logic of demand stimulus, supporting not just a reduction of corporate taxes but a reduction of individual tax rates during a time of economic slowdown. The U.S. Chamber of Commerce, reflecting the views of a much more diverse business constituency, criticized the administration's "overemphasis on the need to stimulate consumer spending and called for larger cuts in corporate taxes and in the income tax at the middle and upper levels."[47] Still, the chamber leadership did venture the opinion that "lower-bracket reductions could be helpful in creating additional purchasing power."[48] In its lobbying efforts on behalf of the tax rate reduction bill, the chamber actually supported a larger first-year deficit than would occur under the Kennedy program.

The National Association of Manufacturers did not advocate tax reduction in the face of a budget deficit and avoided explicit approval of the Kennedy administration's tax reduction plan. Ultimately, the NAM supported the idea of tax cuts to spur investment but was reluctant to endorse a proposal that would extend the tax cuts to middle- and lower-income brackets. The NAM favored a reduction in corporate tax rates and an even greater reduction in taxes owed by the upper income brackets. The NAM proposals drew upon the so-called Maytag Plan, named for Fred Maytag II, chairman of the association's Taxation Committee, and on the Herlong-Baker bills, introduced to Congress in January 1959. These bills called for a five-year, five-step program of tax reduction, with the rate spread of individual income taxes being gradually lowered from 20–91 percent to 15–47 percent and the corporate rate dropping from 52 to 47 percent.[49] Still, the NAM avoided the Keynesian strategy of recommending such tax rate cuts during a budget deficit. In this regard, the organization maintained its allegiance to the budget-balancing doctrines of the right wing of the Republican Party, and it criticized the overspending of the Kennedy administration for its impact on the federal budget deficit.

BUSINESS INTERNATIONALISTS AND THE GREAT SOCIETY

Lyndon Johnson reaped the political benefit of business consensus and prosperity in 1964. With the economy growing and LBJ maintaining fiscal restraint, significant numbers of businesspeople shifted their votes and contributions from the Republicans to the Democrats. Notable business supporters of Johnson "included two former Eisenhower cabinet members—Robert B. Anderson and Marion B. Folsom—and other former Republican sub-cabinet officials and White House assistants. . . . Polls showed strong business and professional support for the Democratic ticket, and influential members of the Business Council . . . endorsed President Johnson."[50]

The overwhelming defeat of Goldwater, among many other factors, represented a crushing loss for business nationalism, protectionism, and pre-Keynesian fiscal policy. Goldwater was one of only ten Republicans to vote against the Revenue Act of 1964. He had also opposed the elimination of the protectionist "peril point" procedure under the TEA and was an outspoken opponent of nonmilitary foreign aid.[51] On social policy, he had voted against the Medicare program and even had the audacity to challenge the Social Security system.

In the high growth phase of the mid-1960s the Democratic administration at last moved toward the implementation of long frustrated liberal goals of expanding the social welfare system. In 1964, subsequent to the income tax cuts, Congress voted in favor of a regressive increase in payroll taxes to fund the Medicare program. The next Congress elected in the 1964 landslide enacted a broad array of programs in health, education, housing, and welfare under the Johnsonian auspices of the Great Society and War on Poverty.

In our view, the increased emphasis on social welfare in this period must be attributed, at least in part, to the social upheavals of the time. The African American struggle in particular played a crucial role as national Democrats sought to capture the support of newly enfranchising and primarily low-income, working-class southern blacks. The Johnson administration pursued the type of expanded federal commitments to health care, education, job training, and housing that had been supported by labor-oriented liberals since the end of the New Deal era. However, the president eschewed universal coverage schemes in these areas, coverage that is common in most of the world's advanced capitalist welfare states, keeping the Great Society within fiscal bounds consistent with the interests of the liberal internationalist bloc.

In aggregate terms, the War on Poverty amounted to little more than a skirmish. By 1967 "federal, state and local programs in welfare, public health, education, social insurance, and veterans benefits was only 6.5 percent of the GNP" as compared to 6.0 percent in 1957.[52] In effect, the Johnson-Kennedy social initiatives amounted to an incremental shift in the allocation of surplus resources in a period of prosperity. In 1957 the share of GNP committed to social welfare in West Germany was 20.8 percent; in France, 18.9 percent; and in Great Britain, 12.1 percent. By comparison, the U.S. welfare state in 1967 was half or less the relative size of 1957 welfare states in these major Western European industrial nations.

Nonetheless, the Johnson administration's parallel escalation of military force deployment and subsequent increase of military expenditures provided the basis for a "fiscal crisis" in the latter part of the decade that undermined the dollar's position on international markets. Further, the fiscal crisis would continue through the 1970s, 1980s, and into the 1990s, in some part caused by the rise of entitlement spending. It should be noted, however, that spending cuts (public housing, legal aid) and entitlement abolition (AFDC) have been in precisely those programs whose primary beneficiaries are the poor. Conservatives since Goldwater have been far more circumspect to challenge those programs that benefit primarily middle-income groups. Welfare policy was and remains class politics despite the Kennedy-Johnson efforts to forge a consensual liberal bloc that downplayed class and racial differences.

For a brief period in the early 1960s under conditions of unprecedented prosperity, business conflict was diminished. In this period of consensus among the diverse interests represented by various business groups, liberal leadership fostered the implementation of a business-oriented and globalist Keynesianism. But the political economic conditions that gave rise to the liberal bloc's design for consensus did not endure beyond the middle years of the decade.

COMPETITION IN THE WORLD ECONOMY

The political efforts of the Kennedy administration to win congressional support for the Trade Expansion Act was led by corporate lobbyists whose firms enjoyed significant advantages over foreign competitors in the post–World War II period. The top 200 U.S.-based multinational corporations (MNCs) were able to rapidly expand their foreign trade and investments relative to their global rivals. This was due to several advantages enjoyed by the U.S.-based firms in the post–World War II period. First, physically untouched by the devastation of World War II and buoyed by the escalation of U.S. military spending during the war, U.S. firms were able to increase their economies of scale to allow for the rapid incorporation of new technologies. Meanwhile, potential foreign competitors were faced with the devastating consequences of the war and had to rebuild their industrial and technological bases. Second, the key role of the dollar in the global economy provided ready markets for products made in the United States. As we have seen, the extension of U.S. bilateral loans further increased the export and investment opportunities for U.S. firms. Finally, the domination of the U.S. economy by U.S. corporations unequaled in "size, scale, and scope" made penetration of the U.S. market difficult for foreign competitors. Through the period 1948 to 1966, imports averaged only 5.6 percent of GNP.[53]

There is abundant evidence of the ascendancy of U.S. firms in the global market. First of all, of the 100 largest businesses in the capitalist world by the mid-1960s, 65 were American, 18 belonged to the EEC, 11 were British, and 5 were Japanese.[54] The largest car manufacturer in the EEC made only a fifth of the number of cars produced by the largest U.S. auto manufacturer. The turnover of the twenty largest U.S. corporations almost equaled the gross national product of West Germany, and the turnover of the five largest U.S. corporations was almost the same as the gross national product of Italy.

By the mid-1960s, of the 500 largest businesses in the capitalist world, Philips, the largest firm in the EEC, was only 33rd. Volkswagen, the biggest German company, was 34th; the biggest French corporation, the Rhone-Poulenc, was 44th; and the biggest Belgian company, Petrofina, was 140th. By 1965 the turnover of General Motors was equal to the sum total of the turnover of the thirteen largest German companies.[55] At the same time, U.S. chemical firms had cornered 41 percent of world trade, compared with only 20.5 percent for the EEC.[56]

Such an international environment was conducive to broad cooperation among U.S. firms in supporting the Trade Expansion Act of 1962. However, almost as soon as the act had been forged into law by strong margins in the House and in the Senate, firms that had originally supported the agreement defected into an opposing protectionist camp that migrated to the Republican Party and the presidential candidacy of Barry Goldwater. The source of increased business conflict was a dramatic rise in import competition in the U.S. market. Aggregate data indicate a significant increase in import competition between 1966 and 1973, with imports rising from 5.6 to 8.6 percent of U.S. GNP. Disaggregated data reveal a more extreme jump in import penetration of particular sectors between 1960 and 1970: Imports rose from 4 percent to 17 percent of the U.S. market in autos, from 4 percent to 31 percent in consumer electronics, from 5 percent to 36 percent in calculating and adding machines, and from less than 1 percent to 5 percent in electrical components.[57]

At the same time, growing domestic competition emerged as a major challenge for U.S. firms. This was the result of several factors, including the economic boom of the 1960s, which opened the door for outsider firms to break into markets previously controlled by insiders. Accelerated government spending on military goods rebounded to benefit a wide array of new firms in the aerospace, steel, metal mining, textiles, rubber, and shoe industries. At the same time, non-military domestic spending benefited financial, real estate, and construction industries involved in urban economic renewal.[58] In addition, the Justice Department pursued increasingly effective antitrust regulation, further opening the door to increased domestic competition during the 1960s. According to economist William Shepherd:

> The U.S. economy experienced a large and widely spread rise in competition during the period from 1958 to 1980. . . . Tight oligopoly still covers nearly one-fifth of the economy, but that share is down by half from 1958 to 1980. Pure monopoly and dominant firms have shrunk to only about 5% of the economy, while the effectively competitive markets now account for over three-fourths of national income. Most of the shift

appears to reflect three main causes: rising import competition, antitrust actions, and deregulation.[59]

U.S. firms responded differently to such import pressure. Leading computer and electronics firms accelerated the relocation of parts production to the less developed world, especially East Asia. Other firms relied on external borrowing from financial institutions to cover the financing of new investment designed to maintain market share. Prior to 1965 the overwhelming majority of U.S. firms financed new investment from internal profits. After 1965 that trend changed dramatically, as corporations increasingly borrowed money from banks to finance new investment. Economist Herman Minsky provided an overview of corporate debt trends in testimony before Congress in 1980, concluding that "the data for nonfinancial corporations indicates that something changed in the middle of the 1960s." Minsky noted that "the ratio of debt to internal funds, or liabilities to demand deposits, and of the open market paper to total liabilities indicates that the corporate sector not only has greater debt payments to make relative to cash flows but also that the margin of safety for debt to cash on hand has decreased, and the reliance by business on volatile and relatively uncertain sources of financing has increased."[60]

In short, Minsky's findings indicated that corporations increased their reliance on outside sources of finance to pay for the costs of expanding their foreign investments, in many cases as a way to maintain market share in the face of increased domestic and global competition. In addition, corporations, in an effort to raise funds to cover debts, began relying on investment banks to speculate on short-term stock and bond markets in order to pay off the costs of mounting debt. Foreign markets became even more important for U.S.-based MNCs in raising the capital necessary to sustain corporate expansion. Of special interest was the potential for borrowing capital from the emerging deregulated Euromarkets established in Paris and London, where U.S.-based commercial banks established low-cost centers for expanding their overseas lending.

BANKING INTERNATIONALISM:
FINANCE CAPITAL AND THE EURODOLLAR MARKET

Most accounts of the Eurodollar market explain its creation as a result of private sector initiative to bypass the capital controls implemented by the Kennedy and Johnson administrations in the 1960s. In this scenario, multinational banks moved their operations to the deregulated London Euromarket to avoid the interest equalization tax (IET) imposed by the Kennedy administration in 1963. The tax, designed by Douglas Dillon and

Robert Roosa, was applied to all new issues of foreign securities and equities sold in the United States. In 1964, the IET was strengthened to cover bank loans with a duration of one year or more and nonbank credits of one to three years.

Bankers did attempt to evade the capital controls by locating abroad. However, the U.S. government promoted such evasion by encouraging bank relocation of operations to the London Eurodollar market. Multinational bankers worked with sympathetic officials in the Treasury Department and the Federal Reserve to establish new branch banks in the emerging Euromarket. First, the Treasury Department exempted foreign currency loans of foreign branches of U.S. banks from IET regulation. Second, following considerable bank pressure in 1967, offshore dollar loans were also exempted from regulation.[61]

The rationale of the U.S. government in encouraging the relocation of U.S. branch banks to the Euromarket was twofold. First, there was direct response to increased pressure from the multinational financial sector, which enjoyed close ties to treasury officials in both the Kennedy and Johnson administrations. Second, the U.S. government hoped to use the favorable investment conditions of the Eurodollar market to persuade foreigners to hold dollars. The absence of reserve requirements and taxes in the Euromarkets of London and Paris meant that interest rates were higher than in the United States or the rest of continental Europe. U.S. officials perceived that the Euromarket might stop the drain on the U.S. gold supply and help stabilize the dollar.[62]

The United States' support for the Eurodollar market occurred within the context of maintaining the Bretton Woods financial system. During the 1960s, there was unanimity among various U.S. executive branch bureaucracies regarding maintaining the stable and, in the case of the U.S., fixed par values allowed by Bretton Woods. The key to maintaining the Bretton Woods system was the allowance of capital controls for member states of the IMF and the World Bank. Capital controls shielded governments from unregulated currency speculation that could threaten domestic spending programs and upset efforts by central banks to stabilize exchange rates. In fact, central bankers in both the United States and Western Europe were among the most ardent proponents of capital controls during the 1960s, fearing the destabilizing consequences of eliminating these controls.[63]

U.S. corporations that benefited from the overvalued dollar also supported capital controls. This support was reflected in the policy statements of the CED, especially U.S. foreign direct investors in manufacturing in Western Europe and the less developed world. Through 1965 the CED supported capital controls because of their perceived benefits in allowing the United States to maintain its extensive military and foreign aid commitments throughout the world and in maintaining the strength of the dollar.[64]

The committee, whose members benefited disproportionately from U.S. foreign aid programs that provided the preconditions for foreign investment, saw capital controls as important in maintaining U.S. geostrategic commitments and in preserving the stability of the exchange rate, which was viewed as essential for long-term fixed investments. In addition, U.S. domestic industries dependent on imports supported capital controls because of their interest in a strong, albeit overvalued, dollar.

By 1966, however, leading members of the CED began to shift their opinion regarding the desirability of capital controls. What explains the shift? First, U.S. multinational corporations were becoming increasingly dependent on external financing from multinational banks to maintain their market share and profitability in global markets. An aggregate comparison between investment financing in the 1950s and early 1960s and in 1973 illustrates the increasing linkages between U.S.-based multinational corporations and finance capital. Among the top Fortune 500 U.S.-based corporations in 1965, only 20 to 25 percent of corporate spending on capital formation was financed from external sources. The pattern then shifted so dramatically that by 1973 "external finance exceeded internal for the first time since 1950."[65] Long-term debt as a percentage of shareholdings in U.S. corporations rose from 87 percent in 1955 to 130 percent in 1965 and 181 percent in 1970.[66]

This trend led some multinational corporations to push for an elimination of capital controls as early as 1966. In a policy statement issued by the CED, the group urged the U.S. government to take the lead in promoting the elimination of capital controls, which had hindered access to global financial markets. Increasingly dependent on those markets for external financing, multinationals, especially in those highly diversified and mobile industries such as electronics, computer software, and telecommunications, pushed for an end to the restrictive Bretton Woods system of capital controls.[67]

It was ultimately the alliance between multinational high-tech industries and finance capital, coupled with the increasingly competitive international environment of the late 1960s, that shifted corporate interest groups such as the CED toward opposition to Bretton Woods. Restrictive capital controls imposed by European governments were increasingly designed to protect nationally based firms, often at the expense of foreign investors. In the late 1960s and early 1970s, both Britain and France launched intensified state subsidy and capital control programs designed to consolidate domestic industries and enhance their competitiveness relative to U.S.-based multinationals.[68] Opening capital markets would force disciplinary pressure on these European governments and would enhance the competitive position of U.S.-based firms.

The largest U.S.-based multinational investment and commercial banks supported the elimination of capital controls earlier than their counterparts in global manufacturing. However, their structural power was limited in the 1950s and early 1960s because of lower levels of interaction with U.S.-based multinational manufacturers. In the competitive climate of the late 1960s and early 1970s, two events coincided that served to integrate the operations of the largest U.S.-based financial institutions with multinational manufacturers. First, the ascendancy of Japanese and West German competition and the generalized, and often state-led, recovery of Western Europe posed new competitive pressures for U.S.-based multinationals. Instead of scaling back operations, U.S.-based MNCs increasingly relied on debt financing to expand their investments in an effort to maintain market share. Second, U.S.-based multinational banks also found themselves facing serious competitive challenges from abroad. Relocation to the Eurodollar market meant enhanced competitiveness and the ability to lend, on highly profitable terms, to U.S. corporations increasingly dependent on external financing.[69]

For high-technology firms, especially those in the computer industry, the increased access to cheap external financing meant the ability to expand their operations to take advantage of low-cost parts production. Computer giants led by IBM increased their external borrowing to maintain extensive research and development. For firms less able to shift investments, the elimination of capital controls was considered a mixed blessing. European-based steel firms, shipyard companies, coal firms, and other manufacturers dependent on generous government subsidies and capital controls, opposed efforts to dismantle the Bretton Woods system. Similarly, domestic U.S. firms in retailing and military production perceived the elimination of capital controls as undermining their ability to benefit from the strong U.S. dollar.

BUSINESS POWER AND THE MARKET CRISIS OF 1971

The U.S. state had conflicting objectives throughout the 1960s regarding international monetary policy. First, the geostrategic objectives of escalating U.S. military commitments in Vietnam and maintaining these commitments throughout the world rested on a strong dollar. White House and State Department officials throughout the decade sought to pass on the costs of an overvalued dollar to their European allies. The Kennedy and Johnson administrations took the following measures to stabilize the dollar:

1. Pressured Europe to open its economies to more U.S. exports. Goal: to keep demand for dollars high and reduce the drain on the U.S. gold supply.
2. Pressured Europe to shoulder more of the burden for NATO. Goal: to increase the foreign market for the U.S. defense industry without putting added pressure on the dollar.

3. Increased the rates of interest on short-term transactions for the purpose of keeping dollars in the United States. At the same time, in order to increase the prospects for capital investment in the United States, the administration kept long-term interest rates low. Goal: to provide a check on dollar outflows to prevent a further oversupply in global money markets.

4. Imposed the interest equalization tax (discussed in previous section). Goal: to check dollar outflows.

5. Created the Gold Pool of October 1961. Industrial countries contributed some gold to a fund whose purpose was to create a buffer stock that could be used to stabilize the free market price of gold. Goal: to provide disincentives for a run on the dollar.

6. Entered into the Basel Agreement, by which the central banks of Europe and the United States agreed to cooperate more closely in stabilizing exchange rates. Goal: to cushion the overvalued dollar by encouraging European countries to revalue their currencies.

7. Increased IMF capital subscriptions so that other countries would make their currencies available to countries suffering balance-of-payments difficulties. Goal: to check the outflow of dollars from the United States.[70]

Despite these measures, the United States was unable to check the downward pressure on the dollar. Starting with about $18 billion of gold in 1960, U.S. gold stock decreased by between $0.5 billion and $1 billion each year from 1960 to 1965. Between 1964 and 1965, during the so-called gold wars, the United States lost nearly $1.5 billion, a loss triggered in part by the French war against the dollar. By 1968, U.S. gold stock had dipped to $10 billion, an important level psychologically because it was considered the absolute minimum stock of gold needed to keep the dollar-based Bretton Woods system afloat.[71]

The Johnson administration responded in two seemingly contradictory ways. First, the administration increased the restrictions on flows of U.S. dollars abroad. All new foreign investment in Western Europe was to end, and new investment in Great Britain, Australia, Canada, and Japan was to be cut to 65 percent of its 1965–1966 levels. Second, as a major concession to multinational financial interests and U.S. investors, the administration allowed and encouraged increased outflows to the Eurodollar market. The increased importance of the Eurodollar market and the increased dependence on foreign investments led U.S.-based multinationals to organize politically to oppose capital controls.

First National City Bank, Bank of America, and the International Chamber of Commerce gathered in Burgenstock, Switzerland, in mid-1969 to propose alternatives to capital restrictions. By late 1968 and 1969, the *Wall Street Journal* and the *New York Times* editorialized in favor of greater exchange rate flexibility.[72] During this period, corporate leaders did not formally support ending the Bretton Woods system. However, their primary recommendations that U.S. and European governments move to relax and ultimately abolish capital controls would have the effect of undercutting the foundation of the Bretton Woods system. If governments abolished capital controls, then exchange rates would began to fluctuate under the pressure of increasingly mobile capital. Central bankers would be unable to effectively manage exchange rates under such circumstances, and the move toward floating exchange rates would not be far behind.

By 1969, First National City Bank joined Milton Friedman in advocating a flexible exchange rate regime, whereas Bank of America supported widening the bands.[73] Typically, multinational high-tech industries and manufacturers followed the lead of commercial and investment banks on matters of international monetary policy. This was increasingly the tendency in 1969 owing to a greater dependence by multinational investors on external bank financing. The explosive growth of the Eurodollar market, often attributed to the oil crisis and the subsequent inflow of petrodollars after 1973, actually started with increased dollar flows from U.S.-based multinational banks to their U.S. corporate clients. Both sought ways to cut costs in the increasingly competitive environment of the late 1960s. Both were also encouraged by the Johnson administration to invest in the Euromarket. While the administration attempted (and largely failed) to curb capital flows elsewhere, it systematically encouraged the growth of an unregulated Eurodollar market that increased the structural power of multinational financial corporation and their corporate clientele.

These structural conditions contributed to the collapse of the Bretton Woods system by 1974. For a complete understanding of these trends, we need to examine the international market conditions in which governments operated in the late 1960s and early 1970s. The structural market power of multinational finance had been enhanced by the willingness of the United States to promote the Euromarket. The explosive growth of financial transactions was anticipated both by the Euromarket trends and by increased global competition among multinational financial institutions. These structural market factors served to undermine and ultimately collapse the Bretton Woods system. By 1974, the goals of U.S.-based banks had been realized in the form of an elimination of U.S. capital controls and a shift to a flexible exchange rate system.

INTERNATIONAL MARKET CONDITIONS

The structural power of multinational finance was enhanced by the rapid growth of the Eurodollar and foreign capital markets in the late 1960s and early 1970s. The resources controlled by multinational financial corporations exploded in relation to central bank reserves. The Eurodollar market is estimated to have grown by $71 billion during 1971, whereas official reserves totaled $122 billion. The U.S. Tariff Commission estimated total short-term assets held at the end of 1971 by private international institutions at $268 billion. These figures illustrate the growing structural power of multinational capital and the increased speculation and borrowing by U.S.-based and competing MNCs during the late 1960s and early 1970s.[74]

Rampant speculation against the dollar had placed added pressure on other currencies. The German Bundesbank in 1971 took some steps to check market forces and ease the pressures of revaluation. The greater reliance on the Eurodollar market, however, distinguished this international monetary crisis from earlier crises. As a leading publication noted:

> The ever-growing Euro-currency pool was the main feature which distinguished the current crisis from its predecessors. It distorted German monetary policy and it helped fuel speculation against the main candidate for revaluation, the D-mark. Both involve the German authorities, who stand accused of the twin counts of refusing to take necessary corrective action on the Euro-dollar borrowings by German companies and contributing to the ease in which such dollars could be borrowed by allowing them to be relent into the market.[75]

The German Bundesbank did attempt, albeit briefly, to respond to the pressures toward revaluation. On the morning of May 5, 1971, with the intention of holding the mark at its ceiling, the Bundesbank purchased $1 billion in the first forty minutes of trading. Then German authorities, fearful of the inflationary consequences of such an approach, reversed course by withdrawing from the market and allowing the mark to float, taking with it the Dutch guilder, the Swiss franc, and the Austrian schilling. All of these currencies were revalued in the wake of the 1971 crisis.[76]

Meanwhile, there was growing pressure from a number of sources for the United States to depreciate the dollar. Treasury officials in the United States expressed alarm at the growing balance-of-payments deficits. During the summer of 1971, Nixon administration officials projected that the United States would have a $4 billion deficit in the current account for fiscal year 1972. At the same time, the executive directors of the IMF met in early 1971 to calculate the exchange rate alterations that would be necessary to offset the disequilibria in foreign currency markets. They concluded that an average dollar depreciation of about 10 percent would be required. A sample of the views of leading newspapers close to the international financial community also warned that fundamental adjustments would have to be made by the United States to avoid a further worsening of the balance-of-payments problem. A working paper by the Organization for Economic Cooperation and Development implied that some form of parity change would be necessary.[77]

These international market circumstances pushed the Nixon administration to act. The administration was growing increasingly alarmed about
the twin deficits of 1971. The United States faced both a growing payments imbalance and, for the first time since 1893, a yearly trade deficit.
Such circumstances prompted a greater range of U.S. business groups to
involve themselves in the debate over U.S. foreign economic policy. Leading U.S. exporters supported aggressive action to improve trade competitiveness. The multinational financial community continued its call for the
abolition of capital controls, insisting on unfettered access to foreign currency markets. Multinational investors, increasingly dependent on foreign
loans, also called for an end to capital controls.[78]

International market conditions help explain the timing of the Nixon
administration's decision to close the gold window. The administration
wanted to preserve U.S. domestic monetary autonomy in the face of a "run
on the dollar," which had reached its peak in the summer of 1971. The decision to close the gold window was an admission by the administration
that the United States was unable to check the dollar's precipitous decline
with the tools of the Bretton Woods system. The United States chose to act
unilaterally by implementing a variety of measures that startled its European and Japanese allies. In addition to taking the U.S. dollar off the gold
supply and effectively destroying the foundation of the Bretton Woods system, the Nixon administration imposed a 10 percent surcharge on imports
and unilaterally devalued the dollar by 10 percent.

The subsequent move toward the elimination of capital controls in 1974
lagged considerably behind the 1971 decisions and can be explained by a
combination of international market pressures, increased political mobilization by multinational financial interests, and the ascendancy of a neoliberal
ideology within U.S. policymaking circles. Most important, however, was
the oil embargo of 1973, which triggered the most aggressive expansion of
speculation on the Euromarkets.[79] The vast expansion of oil revenues of the
Organization of Petroleum Exporting Countries dramatically increased U.S.
private banks' Eurodollar holdings and provided tremendous structural constraints against the maintenance of capital controls.

In addition, the oil embargo price hikes had ripple effects throughout
the global economy that increased the costs of multinational investors dependent on the purchase of oil for the production of goods. Forced further
into debt to commercial banks, U.S.-based MNCs joined with their counterparts in Europe to campaign for access to cheaper sources of capital.
This, coupled with the structural pressures of market speculation, led to an
end to capital controls in the United States. The trend combined with and
was aided by the ascendancy of neoliberal officials to key positions within
the Nixon administration, most notably the appointment of George Shultz
as treasury secretary in 1972. This combination of factors helps explain the

timing of the 1974 elimination of capital controls and the shift toward floating exchange rates.

CONTRADICTIONS OF LIBERAL GLOBALISM

There was a decisive tension between the interests of business internationalists and the structural role of the U.S. in maintaining the world payments system. Specifically, this is the problem created by capital export through foreign direct investment and its strain on the dollar's position. This friction was noted at the time by the Business International Washington Roundtable, which at its January 22, 1962, meeting expressed itself "100 percent behind the President's program" but were also "critical of the President's suggestion that investment in the Common Market exports jobs, or is to jump over tariff walls."[80]

Despite the fact that the United States retained a trade surplus throughout this period, the balance of payments remained in deficit and this in turn continued the drain on U.S. gold reserves. The effective cause of the balance-of-payments problem was that U.S. export of capital was greater than the trade surplus, a situation that created a supply of dollars on the world's financial markets (mostly Eurodollars) in excess of global demand for dollars. The export of capital is carried out by either private or public investment. In the postwar era it is the U.S. government itself that has been the primary exporter of the dollar through foreign aid and international military deployment. Additionally, the spending of U.S. business investors and tourists abroad adds to the balance-of-payments deficit. However, as Mandel notes, the import and export of dollars as private capital remained in balance as late as 1968; it was the expenditure of government monies, mostly for military purposes, that would increasingly exacerbate the dollar crisis in the 1960s and early 1970s.[81]

The Kennedy and Johnson administrations would never be able to overcome the contradiction between a globally oriented political economy of growth and the tendency of U.S. capital to export itself. The expectation of U.S. policymakers at this time was that increased domestic growth and tax reform would increase profit rates and business investment at home. At the same time, they hoped that increasingly open market systems in Europe, Latin America, Asia, and even eventually Africa would continue to provide export markets for U.S. production. This liberal approach was unlike its nineteenth-century predecessor, however, in that it quite explicitly included a large degree of the global visible hand of military power to counter the threat posed by radical regimes that in various ideological manifestations (Nasser, Nehru, Perón, Mao, Nkrumah) all shared an opposition to the projected liberal trade regime of the leading capitalist power.

The liberal internationalist emphasis on economic stimulus was motivated by the recession of the late 1950s as well as by signs of trouble on corporate financial statements. During 1963 congressional hearings on tax reforms, Arthur Burns testified to the Joint Economic Committee that aggregate profit margins for U.S. firms had declined from a pretax profit rate of 22.6 percent of net output in 1948 to a rate of 17.4 percent in 1962. He also noted that business expenditure on new plants and equipment had stagnated since 1957. Burns favored tax reduction and reforms that would reinvigorate profit margins and investment, but not with deficit spending, which he warned would lead to inflation, increased deficits in the balance of payments, and the ultimate devaluation of the dollar.[82]

Initially, the Kennedy-Johnson strategy appeared to be successful as the U.S. balance-of-payments deficit, as measured on a liquidity accounting basis, declined from $3.9 billion in 1960 to $1.3 billion in 1965 and to $1.4 billion in 1966. In 1967, however, the deficit spiked back up to $3.6 billion, leading the administration to impose capital controls and suspend gold convertibility of the dollar in an effort to maintain its position.[83] The capital controls prohibited new net investment on continental Europe, restricted new investment in other developed countries (including Great Britain, Canada, Japan, and Australia) and the oil-producing nations to 65 percent of the 1965–1966 average, and limited new net investment in the developing nations to 110 percent of the 1965–1966 average. Additionally, U.S. foreign direct investors were required to repatriate increased shares of foreign earnings.[84] However, as we have seen, internationalist business firms and groups mobilized a strong counterresponse to lobby against capital controls. In addition, the explosive growth of the Eurodollar market limited the effectiveness of the capital controls policy.

The contradictions of state policies committed to promoting the preconditions for global investment through military spending, foreign aid programs, and a lengthy, costly war in Vietnam were reflected in rising business conflict by the mid-1960s. In short, U.S.-based firms with direct ties to military contracts and a stake in basic manufacturing industries, such as steel, rubber, and textiles, favored a continued escalation of military spending and a prolongation of the Vietnam War. Labeled by social scientist Eric Devereux as "conservative Republicans," these firms were already close to the Republican Party and conservative southern Democrats.[85] They saw the war as a way to maintain increased production and sales in the midst of macroeconomic problems. Critical of Johnson for his "moderate escalation" of the war effort, many of these same firms were also critical of Johnson for his liberal trade policies and had already flocked to Goldwater in 1964.

For their part, capital-intensive investors, especially commercial and investment banks, real estate, and home construction industries, opposed

the war because of its impact on the value of the dollar but were supportive of the administration's efforts to lower trade barriers. Mobilized in the
Committee for a National Trade Policy, these business internationalists, in
addition to their efforts to secure lowered trade barriers in Western Europe
during the Kennedy Round of GATT, advocated expanding trade and investment opportunities for U.S. firms in Eastern Europe and the Soviet
Union. Under the Nixon administration, these firms would be the leading
interest group support base for détente, especially the economic component that promised joint ventures between U.S. firms and state-owned industries in the East and financial opportunities for U.S.-based commercial
banks.[86] In addition, representatives of capital-intensive business internationalist firms lobbied the Johnson administration to remove capital controls and, failing in this effort, continued to seek the elimination of these
controls from the Republican administration of Richard Nixon.

In Congress Johnson and capital-intensive business internationalists
had confronted resurgent protectionist sentiment, especially from the textile industry, independent oil firms, timber interests, and the steel industry.
In 1967 the Kennedy Round of GATT was completed, automatically triggering further tariff reductions. During 1967 and 1968 Johnson had to
threaten the use of his veto power to contain several moves for increased
import quotas designed "to counter the effects of the Kennedy Round of
tariff cutting."[87] Additionally, Johnson was stymied in his efforts to expand
East-West trade as well as pass a new Trade Expansion Act, despite strong
internationalist business support for liberalizing trade with the Soviet bloc.
Caught between the protectionist pressures of renewed business nationalism from U.S. manufacturing interests under intensifying international
competition and the internationalism of the executive, Congress would not
legislate further tariff reduction negotiation powers for the president until
the Trade Act of 1974.[88]

The tumultuous events of 1968 revealed the disintegration of the popular components of the liberal bloc, business "desertions from Goldwater
generally returned to Nixon" in the 1968 vote.[89] During the campaign
Nixon promised to remove the capital controls immediately after his election, although once in office he pursued a policy of gradual decontrol. Regarding the Vietnam War, Nixon implemented a policy of an accelerated
bombing campaign coupled with increased reliance on the South Viet-
namese military as a long-term replacement for the continued deployment
of U.S. troops.

In office, the new Republican administration was confronted with the
worsening balance-of-payments crisis, the fiscal legacy of the previous
years, and increasing inflation. For over two decades Nixon had been trying to hold the support of both nationalist and internationalist wings of his
party. In the early 1950s he had been closely identified with McCarthyism,

but by the late 1950s he had shown a more moderate cast in his fiscal policy preferences. He had once declared "we are all Keynesians now," but he was the president who effectively ended the Bretton Woods fixed currency system. Nixon acquiesced to the elimination of capital controls but also imposed an import surcharge on foreign goods entering the United States as well as wage and price controls on the domestic economy.

The Nixon administration was conflicted by foreign direct investors who wanted free movement of capital, business nationalists who feared foreign competition, and U.S. commodity exporters whose access to foreign markets was frustrated by the overvalued dollar. The balance-of-payments deficit reached $9.8 billion in 1970 and would mushroom to $29.7 billion in 1971.[90] On August 15, 1971, Nixon announced the New Economic Policy (NEP), which ended dollar-gold convertibility at the $35 an ounce rate established under the Bretton Woods framework and imposed the import surcharge at the temporary rate of 10 percent. The import surcharge was lifted in December and a devaluation of the dollar was accomplished for the first time after World War II as a new rate of $38 per ounce was negotiated.[91]

By the early 1970s the U.S. was no longer in trade surplus, however. In fact, the trade deficit increased from $2.7 billion in 1971 to $6.9 billion in 1972. By the beginning of 1973 the dollar was again under devaluatory pressure and the balance-of-payments deficit remained comparatively high at $10.1 billion. On February 12, 1973, Nixon called for a further 10 percent devaluation of the dollar. Any further efforts to retain the fixed currency framework were doomed to failure. In the next decade the globalization of a free market in money would take hold as crises of stagflation, stagnant productivity, oil shocks, further devaluations, and falling profits would reverberate through the U.S. political system. The Carter administration would attempt to reconstitute a liberal coalition, but ultimately a neoconservative internationalist bloc would emerge by decade's end.

NOTES

1. Myer Rashish, oral history, 1965, JFK Presidential Library, p. 16; the quote from Schlesinger is at p. 15. Unlike Schlesinger, Rashish perceived no friction in the administration over the balance of emphasis between a domestic or global liberal agenda. Rashish was in the executive office and then on the White House staff, first as assistant to George Ball and then as assistant to Howard Peterson.

2. Rusk's tie to the liberal internationalist bloc was as president of the Rockefeller Foundation from 1952 to 1961; Phillip Burch, *Elites in American History*, Vol. III (New York: Holmes and Meier, 1980), p. 451.

3. The planning and purpose of this research project is discussed in a letter dated September 18, 1961, from White House staffer Myer Rashish to Jack Behrman, deputy assistant secretary of commerce for international affairs. Apparently, overseeing the project was Behrman's primary responsibility. Box 1, Howard C. Peterson—White House Staff Files, JFK Presidential Library.

4. Peterson memo to heads of CEA, OMB (Office of Management and Budget), NSC, and secretaries of state, labor, commerce, agriculture, and interior, "Proposals for 1962 U.S. Foreign Trade and Tariff Legislation," page 3, Box 2, Howard C. Peterson—White House Staff Files, JFK Presidential Library.

5. Jerri-Lynn Scofield, "Foreign Policy as Domestic Politics: The Political Economy of U.S. Trade Policy, 1960–1975" (Ph.D. dissertation in progress, Oxford University, 1996).

6. For an extensive account of administration and private sector efforts to lower the trade barriers of the EEC, see Steve Dryden, *Trade Warriors: USTR and the American Crusade for Free Trade* (Oxford: Oxford University Press, 1995), pp. 44–50.

7. On these and other matters pursued by the CED, see the Committee for Economic Development, *The European Common Market and Its Meaning to the United States* (New York: CED, 1959), and *National Objectives and the Balance-of-Payments Problem* (New York: CED, 1960).

8. CED, *The European Common Market,* p. 4.

9. Ronald W. Cox, *Power and Profits: U.S. Policy in Central America* (Lexington: University Press of Kentucky, 1994), and David Gibbs, *The Political Economy of Third World Intervention* (Chicago: University of Chicago Press, 1991).

10. Prior to service in the Kennedy administration, Peterson had been director of the Panama Canal Corporation; Box 1, Peterson—White House Staff Files, JFK Presidential Library.

11. In his oral history, Rashish indicates that the Commerce Department's resistance to zero tariff rates was effective. Former North Carolina governor Luther Hodges was commerce secretary at the time and served as a crucial administration tie to southern textile interests. The internationalist view that the "no injury" policy was an "embarrassment" and frustration for U.S. negotiators in the Geneva Round of GATT is expressed in a confidential memo from Rashish to Peterson of September 8, 1961, Box 1, Peterson—White House Staff Files, JFK Presidential Library.

12. Luther Hodges, oral history, 1965, JFK Presidential Library p. 10, discusses Kennedy's rapprochement with "textile leaders before the election."

13. Scofield, "Foreign Policy as Domestic Politics," pp. 152–153.

14. Ibid., p. 154.

15. Ibid., p. 156.

16. Ibid.

17. Ibid., p. 158.

18. Ibid., p. 162.

19. For a discussion of these and other nationalist firms, see Philip Burch, "The NAM as Interest Group," *Politics and Society* 4, 1 (Fall 1973): 120.

20. Rashish, oral history, pp. 24 and 25, for a discussion of Kennedy's alliance with textile industries, and especially with Carolina Democrats, including the key role played by South Carolina Governor Ernest Hollings.

21. Peterson speech to NAM, May 2, 1962, Box 1, Peterson—White House Staff Files.

22. Or conversely one could understand Nixon's NEP as allowing the world market to register the increasing value and productivity of labor in the economies competing with the United States, in particular Germany and Japan.

23. Peterson memo to JFK, September 12, 1961, Box 1, Peterson—White House Staff Files, JFK Presidential Library.

24. Letter to Peterson from John Hight and Robert Taft, August 22, 1961, concerning meeting with Peterson of August 21, Box 1, Peterson—White House Staff Files, JFK Presidential Library.

25. Hodges, oral history, p. 17.

26. For the best exemplar of this perspective, see David Vogel, *Kindred Strangers: The Uneasy Relationship Between Business and Politics in America* (Princeton, NJ: Princeton University Press), 1996.

27. Ralph Miliband, *The State in Capitalist Society* (New York: Basic Books, 1969), p. 161.

28. Vogel, *Kindred Strangers,* p. 60.

29. Vogel would seem to be implying that because the CED shapes business opinion rather than reflecting the state of business, it is not an effective organized business interest. To the contrary, if the CED does indeed have the power to shape business opinion, how much more legitimate its opinions in the eyes of elected officials!

30. Vogel, *Kindred Strangers,* p. 132.

31. COC membership is the broadest, although in more recent years the National Federation of Independent Business (NFIB) has gained a significant "market share" in the lobbying business. By the time of the Carter administration the NFIB had become a factor in national policy debates, which is described in the next chapter.

32. Karl Schriftgeisser, *Business and Public Policy* (Englewood Cliffs, NJ: Prentice Hall, 1967), p. 86.

33. Bruce Miroff, *Pragmatic Illusions* (New York: David McKay Company, 1976).

34. Rashish, oral history, p. 8.

35. Robert M. Collins, *The Business Response to Keynes* (New York: Columbia University Press, 1981), p. 182.

36. Ibid.

37. Ibid., p. 185.

38. At the low end, the income tax rate was dropped from 20 to 14 percent. Overall, the rate cuts were 19.7 percent, hence highest in percentage terms at the high and low ends of the income scale and more modest in the middle income brackets. The corporate income tax rate reduction was also modest but was coupled with other changes in investment credit and depreciation write-offs in this and other legislation of the period to effect the subsequent and continuing decline in the share of federal revenues provided by the corporate income tax.

39. Schriftgeisser, *Business and Public Policy,* p. 107.

40. Ibid.

41. Collins, *The Business Response to Keynes,* p. 108.

42. Ibid., p. 188.

43. Ibid.

44. Ibid., p. 192.

45. Ibid.

46. Schriftgeisser, *Business and Public Policy,* p. 109.

47. Collins, *The Business Response to Keynes,* pp. 192–193.

48. Ibid.

49. See Fred Maytag II, *Taxes and America's Future* (New York: National Association of Manufacturers, 1954), pp. 5, 7; and National Association of Manufacturers, *Tax Rate Reform Means Faster Economic Growth* (New York: NAM, 1960).

50. Herbert Alexander, *Financing the 1964 Election* (Princeton, NJ: Citizens' Research Foundation, 1965), p. 98.

51. The "peril point" procedure required the U.S. Tariff Commission to advise the president if a tariff reduction would harm a specific industry. If the president

still wished to lower that tariff, he would be required to explain his reasons for so doing to Congress. In effect, the procedure sought to deter tariff reductions by placing the president in a potentially awkward public posture. For Goldwater's votes, see *Congress and the Nation, 1945–1964*, Vol. 1 (Washington, DC: *Congressional Quarterly*, 1965), pp. 87a, 93a.

52. Edward S. Greenberg and Richard P. Young, *American Politics Reconsidered* (North Scituate, MA: Duxbury Press, 1973), p. 297.

53. David Gordon, "Chickens Home to Roost: From Prosperity to Stagnation in the Postwar U.S. Economy," in Michael Bernstein and David Adler, eds. *Understanding American Economic Decline* (New York: Cambridge University Press, 1994), p. 67.

54. Ernest Mandel, *Europe vs. America* (New York: New Left Books, 1970), p. 30; and Joe S. Bain, *International Differences in Industrial Structure* (New Haven, CT: Yale University Press, 1966).

55. Mandel, *Europe vs. America,* pp. 30–31.

56. Ibid., p. 32.

57. Gordon, "Chickens Home to Roost," p. 67.

58. Eric Devereux, "Industrial Structure, Internationalism and the Collapse of the Cold War Consensus: Business, the Media, and Vietnam," in Ronald W. Cox, ed., *Business and the State in International Relations* (Boulder, CO: Westview Press, 1996), p. 17.

59. William G. Shepherd, "Causes of Increased Competition in the U.S. Economy, 1939–1980," *Review of Economics and Statistics* (November 1982): 624.

60. Quoted in Joyce Kolko, *Restructuring the World Economy* (New York: Pantheon Press, 1988), p. 74.

61. Eric Helleiner, *States and the Reemergence of Global Finance: From Bretton Woods to the 1990s* (Ithaca, NY: Cornell University Press, 1994), pp. 88–89.

62. Ibid., pp. 90–91.

63. Jonathan Aronson, *Money and Power: Banks and the World Monetary System* (Beverly Hills, CA: Sage Publications, 1977), pp. 72–78.

64. James Hawley, *Dollars and Borders: U.S. Government Attempts to Restrict Capital Flows* (Armonk, NY: M.E. Sharpe, 1987), pp. 39, 74–75.

65. Kolko, *Restructuring the World Economy,* p. 73.

66. Ibid., pp. 73–77.

67. Committee for Economic Development, *The Dollar and the World Monetary System* (New York: CED, 1966).

68. Nigel Harris, *Of Bread and Guns* (New York: Pantheon, 1977), pp. 100–133.

69. For a careful examination of increasing global competition among multinational banks during the late 1960s and early 1970s, see Barbara Stallings, *Banker to the Third World* (Berkeley: University of California Press, 1987).

70. For a detailed account of the period of U.S. capital controls, see John Conybeare, *U.S. Foreign Economic Policy and the International Capital Markets: The Case of Capital Export Controls, 1963–1974* (New York: Garland, 1988).

71. Robert Walters and David Blake, *The Politics of Global Economic Relations* (Englewood Cliffs, NJ: Prentice Hall, 1972), pp. 74–78.

72. *New York Times*, December 2, 1968, p. 46; February 28, 1969, p. 53; and May 27, 1969, p. 62. Also see the *Economist's* "World Finance Survey," December 14, 1974.

73. John Odell, *U.S. International Monetary Policy: Markets, Power and Ideas as Sources of Change* (Princeton, NJ: Princeton University Press, 1982), p. 182.

74. Aronson, *Money and Power,* pp. 50–52.

75. Ibid., p. 100.

76. Odell, *U.S. International Monetary Policy,* p. 206.

77. Organization for Economic Cooperation and Development, "OECD's Code for Liberalization of Capital Movements," OECD Observer 55: 38–43.

78. "Report on the Cabinet Committee on Economic Policy," January 28, 1969, p. 6, document in the files of William Safire, Chevy Chase, Maryland, cited in Joanne Gowa, *Closing the Gold Window: Domestic Politics and the End of Bretton Woods* (Ithaca, NY: Cornell University Press, 1983), pp. 83–84.

79. For a good discussion, see Michael Hudson, *Global Fracture* (New York: Harper and Row, 1977), pp. 78–93.

80. Peter Davies memo to Howard Peterson, Box 1, Peterson—White House Staff Files, JFK Presidential Library.

81. Ernest Mandel, *Decline of the Dollar* (New York: Monad Press, 1972), p. 37.

82. Burns correspondence with JFK, February 7, 1963, Papers of President Kennedy, Presidential Office Files, General Correspondence, Box 16, JFK Presidential Library.

83. U.S. Congress, *Congress and the Nation,* Vol. 2, p. 175.

84. Ibid., p. 176. "Net investment" refers to adjustments that may be made for depreciation of foreign investment in plant and equipment.

85. Eric Devereux, "The Collapse of the Cold War Consensus," p. 29.

86. For a full account of U.S. business firms lobbying for increased East-West trade and investment during the Johnson and Nixon years, see Jerri-Lynn Scofield, "The Business of Strategy: The Political Economy of U.S. Trade Policy Toward the U.S.S.R., 1945–1975," in Ronald W. Cox, ed., *Business and the State in International Relations* (Boulder, CO: Westview Press, 1996), pp. 129–163.

87. U.S. Congress, *Congress and the Nation,* Vol. 2, p. 112.

88. The Trade Act of 1974 would authorize the executive to pursue trade liberalization in the subsequent Tokyo Round. After the conclusion of that round, Congress approved the Trade Act of 1979 as the pre-crisis of incremental negotiation and legislation toward free trade was re-established in the post–crisis period. For case studies of specific U.S. industries in the 1970s, see Helen V. Milner, *Resisting Protectionism* (Princeton, NJ: Princeton University Press, 1988).

89. Herbert E. Alexander, *Financing the 1968 Election* (Lexington, MA: D. C. Heath, 1971), p. 200.

90. U.S. Congress, *Congress and the Nation,* Vol. 3, p. 128.

91. Ibid., p. 119.

5

The End of Bretton Woods

THE POLITICS OF CAPITAL CONTROLS

In March 1969 the *Wall Street Journal* reported that the new Republican administration was eager to reduce the Johnson-imposed controls on foreign direct investment (FDI).[1] The Nixon approach was initially intended to be liberalization of capital controls combined with fiscal conservatism that would enhance the international position of the dollar. The Commerce Department issued new regulations increasing the amounts of investment exempt from control, particularly in mining and air transport, lowered the interest equalization tax (IET), and increased the amounts of foreign lending that could be made by U.S. banks.

However, Nixon's policy on capital controls was a far cry from the dismantling of controls he pledged to U.S. foreign investors during his campaign. Staff economists at the Chase Manhattan Bank believed that the effect of lowering the IET would be "minimal" because restrictive monetary policy made the cost of capital from U.S. investment banks uncompetitive. The Chase analysts also concluded that "it is probably premature to expect a complete dismantling of the controls, considering domestic inflation and the expected payments deficit."[2]

The balance-of-payments deficits for the next few years, as illustrated in the previous chapter, would exceed even the most pessimistic expectations. Further, inflation would worsen and the Nixon administration would, at least until after the 1972 election, be at pains to avoid the onset of recession. The perplexing combination of rising unemployment and increasing inflation that developed during the Nixon years confounded the search for coherent and ideologically acceptable policy within the established Keynesian framework. The continued worsening of inflation led to the famous imposition of domestic wage and price controls in 1971–1974. An administration that began with the intent of decontrolling international capital markets became in practice a government that both maintained capital controls and imposed the most thoroughgoing regulation of the domestic economy since World War II.

To better understand the developments of this period, it is useful to disaggregate the concept of "administration." Used as a singular noun in political science analysis and historical narrative, the term "administration" conveys the idea that a particular presidential government acts as a coherent agency. However, in actuality, administrations contain conflicting tendencies and interests. Further, it is useful to bear in mind that political choices among existing policy options at any given point in time are motivated by strategic as well as substantive reasons.

In response to the crisis of Bretton Woods, the economic policies of the Nixon administration were occasionally at odds with its own political predispositions and even somewhat erratic. In addition to crosscutting pressures from various business and economic interests, the administration faced international pressure on the United States to maintain the dollar's position as the key global currency. Also, the need for domestic popularity and legitimation made the president, whose own defeat in 1960 he attributed to recession, reluctant to engage in a thoroughly conservative fiscal policy upon taking office.

Economic policy during the 1970s crisis period manifests the conflicting interests that inhabit all governing coalitions but had been latent during the prosperity and consensus period of the 1960s. The Nixon administration had pledged liberalization of capital export but retained controls throughout its tenure. It briefly imposed tariff surcharges in 1970 as part of its proclaimed New Economic Policy, but then changed direction and rescinded these surcharges. It becomes clear when reviewing the primary sources that the administration itself was deeply divided over how to lead the U.S. economy out from the collapsing postwar framework.

The strongest pressures to liberalize capital controls came from export-oriented manufacturing interests. For example, on December 1, 1970, newly Nixon-appointed Federal Reserve chair Arthur Burns met with 3M chairman Harry Heltzer and six other executives from major U.S. manufacturing firms Caterpillar, B. F. Goodrich, ITT, Eastman Kodak, Honeywell, and Burroughs. They lobbied Burns's support for the abandonment of FDI restrictions and took the view that their firms helped rather than hindered the U.S. balance-of-payments position.

The capital controls were predicated on an effort to limit the glut of dollars on world financial markets. In the view of the export-oriented manufacturers group it "is the companies with overseas growth . . . that offer our country a significant expansion of exports and a rising share in overseas earnings through increased business activity abroad, and it is this growth that is being stifled by the program."[3] In a letter to Charles Colson,

Nixon's liaison to supportive constituent groups, Heltzer argued that "in order to maintain our strength and continued growth overseas, our growth companies must not be hampered to the extent that the managers of our foreign operations become . . . less aggressive in seeking out growth opportunities."[4] These firms had, in effect, reached a point in the product life cycle at which they were seeking to produce as well as sell abroad and were hindered in their attempts to do so by limitations on foreign direct investment.

In meeting with the export manufacturers, Burns had expressed the view that with one quarter of a favorable balance-of-payments, the controls could be relaxed and possibly eliminated. But, of course, such a favorable trend did not occur in 1970. Several months earlier the U.S. Chamber of Commerce had expressed to the president a view similar to that of Heltzer's group that "the emergency conditions which prompted the imposition of the controls have largely passed. . . . we believe the controls can safely be terminated at this time. Such action would serve to preserve the longer-range benefits of foreign direct investment for our balance-of-payments position."[5] Despite these arguments and with the balance-of-payments situation moving from a critical phase to a crisis, Burns remained unpersuaded and the policy essentially unchanged.

At the end of 1970, Charles Colson noted to George Shultz that "proponents of liberalization have, thus far, made no progress with Arthur Burns who I gather is unequivocally opposed to any modifications" of the FDI control program.[6] Colson was actively cooperating with business groups that were pressuring the administration for the elimination of capital controls. In the aforementioned memo to Shultz, Colson wrote that he and John Ehrlichman had met with top-level officers from ITT and that Colson had "assumed the responsibility of preparing a brief for liberalizing controls."[7] Additionally, Colson acted as an intermediary between the businesses that opposed capital controls and the White House, Commerce Department, Treasury, and the Federal Reserve.[8] Allied with Colson and the export manufacturing group was Commerce Secretary Maurice Stans, who had been a key fundraiser for Nixon during the 1968 campaign and also favored elimination of capital controls.[9]

At the beginning of July 1970, Colson complained to Peter Flanigan, Nixon's White House staff aide for economic affairs, that "a number of our major businesses have severe difficulties (IBM, ITT, in particular) with the Foreign Direct Investment program. . . . We have really not changed the program at all substantively from the way in which it was created during the Johnson Administration."[10] Flanigan replied by expressing concern about the "seriousness of this disagreement" between, on the one hand, Colson and Stans and, on the other, Burns, Treasury Secretary David Kennedy, and budget director Robert Mayo, who favored the retention of capital controls. Flanigan asked Richard Urfer, head of the Office of Foreign Direct Investment (OFDI), to provide the White House with memoranda detailing both sides of the capital controls dispute.[11]

In contrast to what would be considered the rational choice expectation of bureaucratic politics, the very agency that administered the capital control program favored its elimination. Urfer's OFDI was in the Commerce Department under the administrative authority of Maurice Stans. Neither Stans nor Urfer wished to maintain a program that restricted the ability of U.S. firms to engage in foreign investment. In an "eyes only" memo to Stans and Colson, Urfer expressed his view that "1970 is a crucial year for the Administration to decide whether these controls will be phased out . . . if the Administration is to maintain the cooperation of the business community by clear demonstration of steady progress toward the promised goal of complete abolition of controls."[12]

The business pressure for the elimination of the FDI program included investment bankers as well as export manufacturers. The bankers' interest, according to Urfer, was in the impact of the IET on their ability to *import* capital. "The main pressure for relaxation of the IET comes from part of the investment banking community which would like to see the U.S. capital markets opened to foreign issuers. Many of the foreign issuers have been heavily using the Eurodollar market, but they would presumably still find the U.S. market attractive."[13]

Responding to the interests of sectors of U.S. investment banking and manufacturing, both Colson and the Commerce Department sought to liberalize if not abolish capital controls. Their immediate proposal was that the percentage of foreign earnings that could be retained abroad should be raised from 30 percent to 50 percent.[14] Realizing that this would likely increase credit demand by U.S. foreign direct investors, Colson noted that the "Fed can take care of this as far as the domestic liquidity balance is concerned."[15] The Federal Reserve, however, distinctly lacked interest in so doing.

Explaining the support for retaining capital controls on the part of Treasury Secretary Kennedy and Arthur Burns appears difficult from a business conflict perspective. For Treasury and the Federal Reserve have, throughout our account, been consistently responsive to the interests of the internationalist sectors of U.S business. Their support of foreign investment controls would appear to be best explained from a statist or structuralist perspective as an interest in the maintenance of the dollar's position and the Bretton Woods system. Indeed, we believe that in crisis circumstances of this period, the need and the ability of state managers to act autonomously from dominant business interests were somewhat enhanced. The position of Burns and Kennedy could be seen as an attempt to save a postwar system that had, after all, facilitated an unprecedented degree of investment and trade liberalization. They were, then, willing to be illiberal toward the short-term interests of U.S. foreign direct investors in order to serve a broader internationalist purpose.

Block takes the view that "ruling class members who devote substantial energy to policy formation become atypical of their class, since they are forced to look at the world from the perspective of state managers."[16] Such an atypical perspective may have been held by Burns, whom we have previously described as an "organic intellectual" of business internationalism. However, in the case of David Kennedy, the treasury secretary was new to government work, having left the position of chairman of the Continental Illinois Bank of Chicago to take his position in the Nixon administration. We argue that Block's perspective has merit and may be somewhat applicable to the capital controls controversy. However, his argument would be more salient if the United States selected a more autonomous civil service elite rather than engaging in a pattern of drawing top administrative decisionmakers from the upper echelons of business and then recirculating this personnel in short, intermittent intervals back into the private sector (Kennedy, for example, left Treasury in favor of John Connally at the end of 1970).

Our explanation of the Nixon administration's retention of capital controls is twofold. First, there was indeed a growing sense of crisis among both business and government elites that made it difficult to judge precisely how best to protect what they considered vital U.S. interests. In addition to the balance-of-payments crisis, 1970 also witnessed the onset of a mild recession and an upsurge in inflation. Burns, as we shall discuss below, would soon do a complete about-face on incomes policy and reverse his long held laissez faire opposition to wage and price controls. Second, international pressures, especially from the Europeans, to maintain the dollar's position may also have contributed to U.S. efforts to maintain the dollar through capital controls in 1968–1971.

The International Economic Policy Association (IEPA), a Washington-based think tank with strong ties to export-oriented industries, communicated to Colson its view that "the European concern with the dollar glut and the U.S. payments deficit makes it difficult to abolish foreign direct investment controls now." The IEPA was antipathetic to capital controls and argued that despite Europe's concern, significant liberalization was nonetheless possible. Its agenda was to seek "coordinated" fiscal and monetary policy through the Organization for Economic Cooperation and Development (OECD) as a means of maintaining stable foreign exchange rates. In its view, the existing policy only frustrated the efforts of those firms that represented "America's few foreign exchange earners."[17]

However, groups such as the IEPA, the U.S. Chamber of Commerce, investment bankers, and capital-exporting manufacturers may well have been underestimating the fragility of the dollar's position at the time. Given the well-established liberal internationalist commitment to the Atlantic alliance, it would not be surprising that policymakers such as Burns and Kennedy would be reluctant to allow the Bretton Woods system to unravel. Yet before we conclude that state managers in the Nixon administration maintained capital controls in hopes of saving the Bretton Woods system, we must also note that other administration officials were anticipating the collapse of that framework and planning for the aftermath. A group of predominantly corporate economists, acting as consultants to the treasury secretary, argued in late 1969 that "the free market price should be allowed to drop below $35 [the dollar's fixed rate per ounce]" yet believed "that this would be prevented by support operations of some other governments."[18]

The corporate economists providing consultation to the treasury secretary represented primarily international banking interests: Chase Manhattan, Kidder Peabody, Manufacturers Hanover Trust, Morgan Guaranty, and the First National City Bank of New York (the present-day Citibank). One industrial firm, IBM, was represented, as well as a number of academicians, including Arthur Laffer and Alan Greenspan, who had previously headed up the Wall Street consulting firm of Townsend-Greenspan.[19] This group notably overlaps with those firms and interests that sought the liberalization of capital controls. In their discussions, the concern was not with the survival of the fixed exchange rates framework but with the potential fallout from the unregulated Eurodollar market.

The Eurodollar market was a substantial supply of dollars beyond the regulatory control of the U.S. government. The growth of this market was facilitated by the U.S. balance-of-payments deficit and reflected the increasing productive strength of the European economies, that of Germany in particular, relative to the United States since the end of World War II. The Europeans had, in effect, invested a portion of their increasing surplus in artificially overvalued dollars. If the Eurodollars were sold en masse as a result of the dollar's devaluation, it could severely damage the equity of U.S.-based foreign investors. The Treasury Department consultants group, however, took the view that the "Eurodollar market would not change if the dollar lost its position as a reserve currency *ceteris paribus*. The U.S. would always have the strongest currency because dollars were such a large proportion of the world's money supply. Europeans appeared to prefer to hold dollars rather than local currencies." Indeed, the consultants believed that capital controls were contributing to the growth of the Eurodollar market.[20]

U.S. business internationalists understood that the fixed exchange rate system was unsustainable, at least as it was constituted under the Bretton Woods agreement. The Nixon administration would maintain, at least by

outward appearance, its committment to Bretton Woods until an appropriate, efficient cause for crisis occurred. As Paul Volcker put it, "The United
States was committed to play the game straight until it was absolutely
clear the jig was up." By August 1971, after the Bank of England requested a guarantee of the convertibility of British dollar holdings into
gold (convertibility had been "temporarily" suspended by the Johnson administration), "Volcker concluded: 'the jig was definitely up.'"[21]

THE NEW ECONOMIC POLICY

On August 15, 1971, the Bretton Woods framework of fixed rates of international exchange, underwritten by the guaranteed convertibility of U.S.
dollars into gold at the rate of $35 per ounce, came to an end. As part of
the New Economic Policy, the dollar was devalued in relationship to gold.
A second official devaluation came in 1973. Yet there was still some discussion of how a method of fixed or pegged exchange rates in the style of
Bretton Woods might be reconstituted within certain bands or ranges. Regional groupings such as the European community could still maintain
currencies within a specific range and individual nations could continue to
peg their currencies to a fixed exchange of one or more of the world's
major currencies. As Treasury Undersecretary for Monetary Affairs Paul
Volcker claimed, when devaluation was imminent, "wider bands appear to
offer the best, though still a limited solution."[22] Yet without a fixed star by
which to set the international currency exchange system's compass,
schemes of maintaining constant relative currency values have been no
more than limited solutions. Ambrose makes the point succinctly, observ-
ing that after the 1971 devaluation "the dollar floated . . . requiring the creation of a whole new world monetary order."[23] The dollar was no longer
the fixed star around which international finance revolved. Unless some
new multilateral fixed currency structure could take the place of Bretton
Woods, an irrevocable step had been taken toward an unprecedented form
of a liberalized global market in currencies. By July 1974 the OECD governments abandoned comprehensive monetary negotiations.[24]

   One question that haunted some analysts was to what extent could the
international capitalist system function with liberalized rules of currency
exchange sans a fixed monetization of gold for the dominant currency.
Plausibly, without the protections offered by the Bretton Woods framework, individual nations would now more quickly and sharply feel the effects of international investors' displeasure with tax, spending, regulatory,
or labor policies that were designed to promote the interests of domestic
groups. The impetus toward economic nationalism, in other words, might
increase. Indeed, the liberal internationalist consensus of the 1960s has

never since been recovered and economic nationalists have been intermittently successful in their efforts to limit or hinder the postwar trend toward globalization.

Arthur Burns, alone among the top executive branch officials involved, opposed the 1971 decision to devalue the dollar. He worried that "*Pravda* would write that this was a sign of the collapse of capitalism."[25] Such was quite evidently not the case. Indeed, the "closing of the gold window" was not, after all, even the end of all the institutions created by the Bretton Woods agreements. The IMF/World Bank remained in place. Indeed, Volcker suggested to the Council of Economic Advisors that the IMF might now find a "restoration" of its role as "arbiter" in multilateral trade relations.[26] More to the point, the underlying purpose of Bretton Woods, to promote international trade liberalism, could, hypothetically, be pursued even more stringently in a world of floating currencies. Milton Friedman had advised the Nixon administration to end gold convertibility in 1969. Friedman claimed that "he foresaw that the dollar would have to be cut loose from gold . . . and that if it were not done immediately, the president would feel obliged to accompany this change with some kind of popular action—like imposing wage and price controls."[27]

The decision to impose wage and price controls was preceded by increased emphasis on the need to control rising inflation among the business elite. "In October 1970 the Business Council . . . harshly criticized the administration for failing to check excessive wage increases and price inflation."[28] In November, the CED called for the creation of an executive board that could set "broad norms of appropriate noninflationary wage and price behavior."[29] The administration's political economic strategy for 1971–1972 was control of inflation by administrative fiat coupled with tax cuts and spending increases, and monetary policy cooperation from Burns, designed to stimulate the economy at least until November 8, 1972. Decontrol, fiscal conservatism to fight inflation, and free trade were to be the agenda of the second term. But these priorities, along with the political consequences of the severe recession of 1974–1975, became the concerns of Gerald Ford's administration in the aftermath of the Watergate scandal.

BUSINESS CONFLICT AND THE NIXON ADMINISTRATION

Nixon's fall is the stuff of psychohistory and Hollywood drama of the first order. The social and economic conflicts of the period fostered a turbulent Zeitgeist that was the backdrop to the Watergate drama. Nixon's most prominent antagonists were "liberal" media like Bob Woodward and Carl Bernstein, congressional Democrats like Sam Ervin, and, perhaps above all, the pattern of paranoia and arrogance of power that ran through the administration. In the Nixon administration's own estimation, however, its worst enemies included a significant number of business liberals. The (in)famous Nixon enemies list provides an illuminating angle on the politics of business conflict in this period.

A number of prominent members of the Business Council appeared on the enemies list, such as Thomas Watson of IBM and Edgar Kaiser of Kaiser Aluminum. Their typical sin was that they had provided financial support to Democratic presidential candidates, Senator Edmund Muskie in particular, who was considered the likely Democratic nominee until after the New Hampshire primary. In terms of political economy, the business liberals opposed Nixon's continuation of the U.S. war in Vietnam and favored the expansion of East-West trade. The war, after all, was a drag on fiscal policy and a diplomatic barrier to détente.

The export manufacturers who had met with Burns to lobby for liberalization of foreign direct investment had argued that "real improvement in our balance-of-payments must come from reduction or reversal of the negative impact of the public sector."[30] In the context of the post-Johnson years, this could be understood as a conservative call for less butter or a liberal critique of the guns in Indochina. It was Colson, keeper of the enemies list, who noted to Flanigan that "the real cause of our balance-of-payments deficit is our trade deficit and our defense expenditures abroad."[31] The costs of the military state in Cold War as well as in combat exacerbated the problems of the dollar and inflation, the very conditions that led to the imposition of capital controls. Even firms such as IBM that benefited from the military-industrial complex had interests adversely affected by a hawkish foreign policy. IBM and five of the seven companies that had lobbied Burns for liberalized foreign direct investment regulations were, in Scofield's words, engaged in "significant commercial dealings with socialist countries" by 1973.[32]

Block argues that President Johnson's escalation of the war in Vietnam "ran afoul of declining business confidence."[33] Eric Devereaux concludes his empirical study of media opposition to the war by noting that "NBC and CBS broke with the Johnson administration on Vietnam at the same time as did multinational financial interests";[34] Nixon, however, had significant support from this group in 1968 as a candidate of de-escalation and fiscal conservatism and as president would eventually provide openings for significantly increased investment opportunities in both the Soviet Union and China.

Some staffers in the Nixon White House reacted to business internationalists' support of liberal politicians with a consternation that appears politically naive. For example, in Colson's papers a handwritten notation from one of his assistants appears next to the name of Henry Ford II, whose firm both Devereaux and Scofield associate with liberal interests in

East-West politics and who "seems to give to both sides." By "both sides" the memo writer meant that Henry Ford II gave to Democrats as well as Republicans, a fairly standard practice in big business circles, though it made Ford a nominee for the enemies list (his name does not appear there, however, perhaps because of Colson's greater savvy in these matters).[35]

The Nixon administration responded to dovish business internationalism in ways that were sometimes pathetic, sometimes sinister. For example, in October 1971 Colson intervened in the work of White House social secretary Lucy Winchester when he discovered that Edgar Kaiser had been invited to a state dinner held in honor of Indira Gandhi. Kaiser was at the time perhaps the largest single U.S. direct investor in India, but he was also a financial supporter of Hubert Humphrey. Colson took steps to ensure that such a mistake would not happen again.[36]

In a more substantive abuse of power, Colson requested that the Internal Revenue Service investigate a nonprofit organization associated with Robert Roosa, a former undersecretary of treasury during the Kennedy-Johnson years and a senior partner with the Wall Street investment banking firm of Brown Brothers, Harriman. Roosa was a political leftist in Colson's estimation, "a real bomb thrower."[37] Roosa's political activity after Nixon's inauguration had included advocacy of U.S. recognition of the People's Republic of China. It was this heresy that brought him to Colson's attention, quite ironically in light of Nixon's subsequent diplomatic initiatives.

Roosa was also concerned with how to reconstitute the foreign exchange system and with growing protectionist sentiment in the United States. In April 1975, he expressed to Assistant Treasury Secretary John Cooper his concern over "the strengthening isolationist attitudes so apparent in this country . . . with respect to international capital flows."[38] By then the Tokyo Round of GATT had commenced and capital controls had been lifted at the end of 1973. Nonetheless, Roosa felt that the role of exchange rates should be "reconciling the conflicting domestic objectives of nations, rather than mainly serve as a shield between them."[39] Roosa's view, according to one of Burns's correspondents, was that the best method for a nonprotectionist, stable world monetary system was a trilateral "linking [of] the dollar with the yen and the mark, thereby establishing three key currencies and three harmonized policies around which the international world would revolve."[40]

Ansell argues that the abandonment of the Bretton Woods monetary system, inflation, the oil price shock, and the recession all contributed to a conservative realignment of U.S. business, "including its multinational wing."[41] This shift was against the kind of liberal fiscal policies toward which business internationalists had been more favorably disposed in the 1960s. By the mid-1970s, the dominant explanation in elite business circles of the stagflation riddle was that a combination of low productivity and insufficient incentives to new investment were the fundamental causes of the complex problems of inflation and recession. In this view, public spending and wages would have to be held down and government regulation diminished for investment and productivity to increase. Roosa's own thinking was tending in this direction, for as he indicated to the more conservative Burns, floating exchange rates could result in greater "coordination" of fiscal and monetary policy between nations to hold down inflation.

EMERGING CONSERVATISM

The downfall of the Kennedy-Johnson consensus is often attributed to a liberal wish to have one's cake and eat it too. By attempting to provide guns, butter, and low taxes, the arguments goes, the policies of the 1960s created disenchantment with "big government," undermined the domestic economy, and contributed to the inflation, recession, political apathy, and an "unraveling" of the nation's social and cultural fabric.[42] However, we must bear in mind that Kennedy-Johnson liberalism was a politics of guns and butter and also a politics of free trade, low taxes, and the public subsidization of private investment. This bloc of interests was, in a changing global environment, increasingly untenable. For the state to continue to serve dominant business sectors, popular interests in higher wages, economic security, and job satisfaction would have to be diminished or at least contained.

Interpretations of 1960s liberalism as a case of too much welfarism are deeply flawed. If the U.S. war on poverty overburdened the fiscal capacity of the state, it surely defies all reason and logic that virtually every other advanced capitalist democracy sustained welfare states that in terms of comparative GNP were double, even triple, the size of the United States. Similarly, it is the relatively mean-spirited U.S. welfare system that coexists with high rates of crime, single parent households, and other signs of community decline. Conservative and neoliberal accounts of the "failure" of 1960s liberalism are coherent only if one looks at U.S. politics with heavy blinders on and ignores the role played by the dynamics of the global economy. The crisis of 1960s liberalism was to a large extent rooted in the relative decline, even stagnation, of U.S. capitalism. As Robert Roosa in his embrace of multilateralism effectively realized, the world economic hegemony the United States had experienced since the end of World War II was at an end. As Van Der Pijl puts it, in terms of U.S.-Europe relations, "American hegemony itself, and the entire structure of Atlantic integration developed in its context, lost its effectiveness as an expression of a presupposed general interest."[43]

The U.S. state was indeed faced with a crisis of capacity, but this crisis was the result of global change and the inability of the domestic economy to sustain itself without the visible hand of government. In Kolko's findings, for the three decades after 1950, half of new U.S. employment was created by state expenditure.[44] The devaluation of the dollar in 1971 signified the beginning of a process of reconfiguration of the U.S. political economy.

By the mid-1970s, elite opinion was shifting to the right, in the sense of growing acceptance of conservative accounts of the underlying causes of the economic decline. Crucial to the eventual conservative realignment of U.S. politics was the ideological function of explaining the crisis. The explanation that increasingly resonated in finance, industry, and government was the capital shortfall theory. In this view, the underlying problem of the U.S. economy in the early to mid-1970s was underinvestment by the private sector. This underinvestment was in turn traced to liberal taxation and spending policies that depressed the U.S. savings rate. The consequence of capital shortfall was sluggishness in productivity growth, which in turn caused both inflation and recession. In other words, stagflation had a single cause: the low rate of investment, which resulted in low growth rates as well as inflation because production could not keep up with the demand created by wages that raced ahead of productivity. Thus, it was argued, a vicious cycle of decline into both inflation and recession was created.

Ford's treasury secretary, William Simon, was one of the most forceful advocates of the capital shortfall perspective. In testimony before the Senate Finance Committee on May 7, 1975, Simon stated that during "the 1960s, the United States had the worst record of capital investment among the major industrialized nations." The secretary went on to note that, correspondingly, "our records of productivity growth during this period were also among the lowest." In global terms, the low investment rate in the United States "eroded our competitive edge in world markets." This investment deficit he blamed on Keynesian public policy: "the heavy emphasis we are placing on personal consumption and government spending as opposed to savings and capital formation." The practical implication of this line of reasoning was that "reasonable price stability" could be attained only through "a fundamental shift in our domestic policies away from continued growth in personal consumption and government spending."[45]

In the Ford administration, policy planners focused on capital shortfall as the cause of inflation. Capital shortfall was the presumption of the Domestic Council as it worked with business internationalists such as the Business Roundtable to promote a policymaking emphasis on fiscal conservatism. Paul Leach, Ford's head of the Domestic Council, coordinated a Capital Markets Working Group that supported deregulation of investment banks and utility holding companies in order to facilitate increased capital formation.[46]

The business internationalists continued to press for trade liberalization but now merged that concern with the capital shortfall concept to renew their emphasis on reducing the costs of capital through tax reductions. The Business Roundtable, an "informal corporatist" body similar in membership to the CED, argued that foreign investment was the key to overcoming the problem of capital shortfall. In its view, as the chairman of Rockwell International communicated to Paul Leach, "the income derived from these foreign investments . . . enters the U.S. capital stream, helping to create jobs in the U.S. . . . protectionist efforts to kill our overseas subsidiaries by excessive taxation and repeal of export incentives is extremely shortsighted."[47]

Not all elites concurred with the capital shortfall conservatives. Walter Heller, Kennedy's CEA chair, labeled Secretary Simon a "true believer" and, somewhat sardonically, pointed out in a *Wall Street Journal* editorial flaws in the capital shortfall argument: "In the good old days of low taxes and little progressivity, circa 1929, the nation's savings and investments came to 16% of GNP. In the bad new days of high and progressive taxes, circa 1973, the ratio happened to be the same 16%."[48] Liberal internationalists continued to favor increased federal support for education, community development at home, and foreign aid.[49]

The Business Council for International Understanding (BCIU), chaired by Richard D. Hill, also chairman of First National Bank of Boston, collaborated with the CED, the National Planning Association, and other business internationalists to support liberal trade and investment as well as "new forms of assistance to [less developed countries] LDCs," including the use of the IMF to finance loans to developing nations. Among the BCIU's core issues were technology transfer to spur growth in the LDCs (requiring unrestricted capital export), lowered tariff barriers, and support for foreign aid.[50] The BCIU's agenda was supported by the Kissinger-headed State Department and White House staffer John Vickerman, Ford's liaison to business and trade associations. However, a late 1975 White House conference organized by the BCIU on "what changes in U.S. foreign policy will and are taking place in view of today's new international economic order" was canceled for unexplained reasons. The upcoming primary season and Ronald Reagan's intensifying challenge to Ford's liberal tendencies in foreign policy may perhaps have been related to the cancellation. (The conference had been held the two years previous; 1975 was to have been the third and the agenda was preponderantly liberal internationalist.)

Joseph notes that in the immediate aftermath of the Vietnam debacle, there was a short-term trend toward a more liberal "policy current" in foreign economic issues.

The United States had failed—after more than thirty years of trying. The costs of that effort were enormous. For a brief time, both policy elites and the public at large, attempted to learn from the experience. . . . Unless social change was encouraged other Vietnams, and their attendant problems for the U.S., would mushroom. The proper response, the best way to blunt these revolutionary threats, was not armed threats but modification of the economic and political inequalities that existed between the developed and undeveloped nations. These policy elites . . . called for lower defense budgets and more foreign aid.[51]

The views of the erstwhile organizer of the aborted 1975 BCIU White House conference, Ogden White (chairman of the Bank of Boston), were consistent with the mid-1970s liberal policy current that Joseph identifies. In a memo to BCIU president Hill, White states, in approval of Secretary Kissinger's views, that "all nations must improve the system of international economic cooperation so that LDC's can share in . . . a growing world economy." White also suggests that the conference focus on the "special needs of the poorest countries," such as agricultural and health system development assistance. However, the BCIU also shared Kissinger's realpolitik and believed that the United States should "try to get the LDC's to talk in [terms of] national interest rather than in blocks [*sic*]; i.e. we should try to drive home our own wedge" against OPEC, United Nations Council on Trade and Development (UNCTAD), and other LDC transnational coalitions that potentially threatened the dominant interests of U.S.-based capital.[52] Both the Ford and Carter administrations did pursue moderately liberal approaches to global political economy by supporting foreign aid initiatives, trimming the military budget, and re-emphasizing trade and investment liberalization. The Carter administration in particular emphasized the need for political and social reform of repressive regimes in the LDCs as key steps toward effective economic development. Ford signed the generally liberalizing Trade Act of 1974 and Carter successfully fended off the auto industry's and labor's protectionist attacks on the Multilateral Trade Act of 1979.[53]

Cutting the rate of increase of the Pentagon's budget fit the liberal internationalist agenda, as well as a more generalized business interest in limiting any public expenditure that was perceived as a cause of stagflation. Yet by the late 1970s, U.S. defense expenditures were again on the rise and would grow rapidly in the next decade. As Joseph indicates, a more conservative policy current "argued that Soviet military strength was steadily growing, [while] in real dollars the U.S. defense budget was declining."[54] In Ansell's view, "Military force and preparedness increasingly were understood by certain sectors of the U.S. business community as being necessary to protect U.S. economic power against the challenges posed by the growing internationalization of the economy, the OPEC price hikes, the wave of Third World revolutions, and the declining competitiveness of U.S. firms vis-à-vis the economies of West Germany and Japan."[55]

The economic problems of the 1970s were a kind of Rorschach test of ideology. Their causes both efficient and latent were deeply complex and more than perplexing to established economic theory, which provided liberal prescriptions for recession and conservative medicine against inflation. But after 1973, both at once became a neologism: stagflation. As we have seen, business elites were drawn increasingly to the capital shortfall explanation. Alternative explanations, however, blamed the problems of the day on changes in the global economy.

Carter's CEA chair Charles Schultze thought that exogenous factors such as the oil price and supply shocks of 1973 and 1979 caused inflation,[56] although, as Castells points out, the global impact of the oil shocks was mitigated in the United States because the United States produces close to half of its domestic petroleum needs, far more than the other advanced industrial nations. In other words, the inflationary impact was much sharper in Europe and Japan and had the effect of actually favoring the overall U.S. balance-of-payments position.[57]

Castells offers the view that the political economy of détente provided an efficient cause for the inflationary surge of the early 1970s. Noting that the inflationary pressures began with rising food prices, Castells argues that the large grain sales made by the United States to the U.S.S.R. under the Nixon administration created a domestic shortage that led to inflation. By contrast, Bell dismisses this view without substantive argument: "A myth was fostered that the rapid rise in American food prices during 1973 was attributable primarily to this cause."[58]

The explanations of inflation had ideological significance, regardless of the ultimate truth of the matter. With the liberal coalition of the 1960s in disarray, the accounts of social distress offered by more conservative commentators gained predominance. Increasingly the idea that inflation was caused by too much social spending gained acceptance in mass and elite politics. In 1976 Democrat Jimmy Carter was elected by promising a balanced budget by the end of his first term, and indeed he did administer a declining deficit until the economic reversals of 1979.

In the 1970s the polity did not realign to a Republican majority and a new hegemonic conservative bloc did not gain power. That would come later, after a second wave of stagflation and international crises undid the Carter presidency and led to the election of Ronald Reagan. Nixon did make deep inroads into traditionally and culturally conservative Democratic constituencies of lower- to middle-income and southern whites and even some portions of organized labor. Yet a persistent problem for conservative coalition builders has been their inability to go beyond cultural appeals, based often on symbolic racism, to these mass constituencies.[59]

In the Nixon coalition and administration the outlines and tensions of an ideological bloc of the right emerged. The politics of capital controls and trade exemplified tensions among different business sectors. Yet these diverse business interests were increasingly unified in an ideological support of fiscal conservatism. Since his entrance on the national political scene in the late 1940s, Richard Nixon had successfully cultivated support from both the moderate internationalist and the conservative nationalist wings of his party. As a junior member of Congress, he had been publicly identified with the red scare on account of his high profile role in the Alger Hiss case and the anticommunist theatrics of his campaigns for the House and Senate elections. However, on the political economic issues of the day, he had voted with the moderate wing of his party in support of the Marshall Plan, foreign aid, and free trade. Similarly, the Nixon presidency's policies showed little favor to the old conservative nationalist Taft-Goldwater-Reagan wing of the party.

The emerging conservative coalition did include business nationalist elements as well as a distinctly conservative group of multinationalists.[60] In the 1968 Republican presidential nomination process, Nixon had been able to gain the support of powerful protectionists, such as Roger Milliken of the textile industry (who in the 1990s would become a key financial backer of Pat Buchanan's presidential campaigns). These interests may have preferred Reagan but supported Nixon for the practical reason of electability. Harry Dent, a former aide to Senator Strom Thurmond, whose key support for Nixon at the 1968 convention was conditional upon Nixon's assurances that textiles would retain their tariff protections, played a key role in conservative coalition building. Dent's role in the Nixon White House was as an advocate for the "Southern strategy" of gaining white social conservative support through opposition to the creation of racially integrated schools through court-ordered busing.[61] Dent later served as one of the U.S. negotiators at the Tokyo Round of GATT.

Despite the inclusion of business nationalist interests in the Republican governing coalition, the Nixon and Ford administrations continued the postwar pattern of seeking trade liberalization through GATT and legislative authority for tariff reduction. From "1945–75, U.S. tariffs on dutiable products declined from 32 percent to 8 percent while tariffs imposed by the industrial countries as a whole dropped to an average of 11 percent. Spurred in part by GATT trade liberalization agreements, merchandise trade among the industrial countries grew nearly twice as fast as their domestic economies from 1950 to 1975."[62]

All three presidential administrations of the 1970s sought to open up East-West trade and investment opportunities through the political economy of détente. However, protectionist forces in Congress were able to modify the Trade Act of 1974 in an expression of domestic opposition to detente. The Jackson-Vanik amendment to the Trade Act of 1974 linked the development of East-West trade ties to Soviet liberalization of Jewish emigration policy. The debate over the amendment was cast in the rhetoric of Cold War and human rights. But it was also a means by which protectionists, concerned with a potential influx of cheap imports from Eastern Europe, could express their opposition to administration policy. As Scofield comments, "Declining industries and labor unions . . . developed pressing interests in Soviet emigration issues almost overnight."[63] The amendment was added to the bill despite strenuous opposition from Presidents Nixon and Ford.

Although economic nationalists did show occasional strength in Congress, protectionism was not the foreign economic orientation of the emerging conservatism of the 1970s. Conservative internationalists (or multinationalists in Ansell's usage) included the full range of industrial and financial interests that wished to rectify fiscal and tax policy to promote capital formation, the military-industrial complex of interests that opposed budget cuts in defense, and export-oriented and foreign direct investment industries that opposed capital controls but increasingly sought governmental support for their efforts to gain increased access to foreign consumer and capital markets. These interests were commonly and increasingly opposed to liberal domestic and foreign policy, but they were not without conflicts either, especially over defense spending. The Reagan coalition would, however, include all these elements in 1980 after the Carter administration's efforts at resuscitating a liberal internationalist coalition.

INTERNATIONALISM WITHOUT LIBERALISM

For the liberal coalition, the 1970s were the beginning of a period of quickening decline. Significant components of U.S. civil society, particularly the organized working class, decayed in large part because of the stress and strain of the global political economy on domestic employment in the auto and steel industries and in related manufacturing and mineral industries, such as rubber and coal. To a large extent, self-limited to the industrial core by the leadership of George Meany, organized labor found its membership decreasing not only relatively but absolutely.

Throughout the 1960s, organized labor as a percentage of the workforce had experienced a relative decline as productivity and job growth in the manufacturing core slowed and other industrial nations gained greater shares of the world industrial market. Yet up to the 1974 recession, organized labor still represented a quarter of the workforce and continued to increase, albeit slowly, in membership (though its membership gains were increasingly limited to the public sector). Through the latter half of the

1970s an absolute decline in union membership began; a decline that became a freefall during the recession of 1982. From 1975 to 1983, total union membership fell from 23 million to 17 million.[64]

The collapse of the house of labor was manifest in the policy outcomes of the Carter years. Major defeats included congressional inaction on a labor-backed national health plan and Senate rejection of progressive labor law reform. This period also witnessed the effective end of full employment as a U.S. public policy goal.

The Bretton Woods framework had opened up the possibility of a Keynesian social compromise in which governments would pursue full unemployment policies without bringing immediate pressure on their currencies' international value. Under this framework the Europeans implemented advanced welfare states. In the more conservative United States, the Employment Act of 1946 officially, if not practically, committed the U.S. government to the pursuit of full employment. The Humphrey-Hawkins Act of 1978 was intended by its sponsors to strengthen the full employment commitment of the federal government by establishing a Job Guarantee Office that would provide public works employment to any adult who could not otherwise find employment. The Humphrey-Hawkins bill represented a coalition of liberal labor and African American civil rights groups. Candidate Carter had endorsed Humphrey-Hawkins during the 1976 Pennsylvania primary campaign, but once in office his support proved tepid as conservative critics emphasized the potentially inflationary effects of the legislation. Congressional conservatives successfully amended the bill, eliminating the Job Guarantee Office and incorporating a low inflation goal into the new law to counterbalance the supposed negative effects of low unemployment (the official target rates were set at 4 percent unemployment and 3 percent inflation). It is worth noting that in the late 1950s President Eisenhower had supported the CED's call to amend the 1946 Employment Act to include zero inflation as well as full employment but had been rebuffed by Congress.

The Humphrey-Hawkins Act had little or no impact on the subsequent course of U.S. economic policy. Dumbrell points out that the "President was given virtually unrestricted discretion to modify the goals and time schedules . . . the following spring [1979], when the White House, in submitting its 'austerity' budget, omitted any reference to full employment targets."[65] The failure of labor-liberals' domestic agenda during the Carter years was paralleled in foreign economic policy, where the administration pursued a business internationalist agenda of tariff reduction and executive reorganization.

The Tokyo Round of GATT concluded with a multilateral treaty signing in Geneva on April 12, 1979. Congressional approval of the subsequent 1979 Multilateral Trade Act, which gave legislative ratification to changes in domestic U.S. law necessary to implement the terms of the trade agreement, was swift; the Senate passed the bill on July 23, 1979. The Tokyo Round focused on decreasing nontariff barriers, such as domestic subsidy of exporting industries, and gave the International Trade Commission enhanced authority to regulate "dumping" of exports below cost as an international strategy to conquer competitors' national markets. The new agreement reduced U.S. tariffs from an average of 8.2 to 5.7 percent, including cuts in duties affecting the major declining industries of steel and textiles. Textile tariff rates dropped from 19.5 to 13.7 percent, and steel rates, from 6.1–6.2 to 4.3–4.6 percent. Tariffs on imported autos and aircraft were completely eliminated.[66]

Despite sharp tariff reductions affecting vulnerable industries, the 1979 Trade Act passed Congress with minimal opposition. This was due in part to the inclusion of language in the bill that streamlined and made more accessible the procedures for bringing countervailing duty and antidumping complaints. Additionally, a number of U.S. domestic industries that traditionally sought tariff protection had by 1979 made the transition to multinationalist or regionalist traders and investors. The U.S. auto industry had made substantial foreign investment, opening up plants as well as exporting to the European market, for example. Even significant portions of the once militantly protectionist textile industry had developed into trade regionalists with increased operations in the Americas.[67]

Trade reorganization under the Carter administration signaled a shift to trade and capital export promotion. An administration plan for reorganization of trade programs was announced prior to the passage of the 1979 Trade Act. As it was an internal matter of the executive branch, the Carter plan was implemented without the need for congressional approval. Efforts in Congress to pass a resolution of disapproval gained only limited support and failed.[68]

The Carter trade reorganization plan created a permanent Office of the U.S. Trade Representative. Additionally, the Carter plan shifted key administrative decisions from the traditionally internationalist Treasury Department to the Commerce Department, considered more sympathetic to the interests of export-oriented domestic manufacturers. Commerce would henceforth have jurisdiction over countervailing duties and antidumping claims. The rationale for this move was noted by Stephen Selig, a Carter liaison to business groups: "Those who believe Treasury to be dominated by 'free traders' are among those who seek the transfer of Treasury's import relief functions to Commerce or a new department expected to be more sympathetic to the protection of domestic industry."[69] Throughout the reorganization process, the White House staff focused on the plans and priorities of the affected business groups and noted the antipathy of exporters and domestic industries to the Treasury and State Departments.

The Carter administration is well known for its penchant for reform of bureaucracy and its desire to enhance administrative efficiency. In popular understanding, President Carter was by character and disposition a "micromanager." Hence, it might seem a function of Carter's own technocratic temperament that his administration made significant changes in the organizational chart of trade policy in response to the trade deficit challenge. However, on closer examination we find that in fact the trade reorganization plans were developed, promoted, and debated by business interests in government. The trade reorganization adopted by Carter was a compromise among the designs of competing business internationalists.

The Carter plan was a disappointment to the National Association of Manufacturers, which had developed and proposed a plan for the creation of a separate Department of Trade at the cabinet level. The NAM was no longer the protectionist interest group it had been at earlier phases of U.S. economic history. The NAM plan was a reflection of its membership's interest in a more aggressive export promotion policy; it foresaw the trade secretary as an advocate for opening foreign markets to U.S. producers. As noted in an internal administration memorandum: "NAM. Wants the strongest possible Trade and Commerce Department, including Treasury's enforcement functions, an Export-Import Bank tie-in, commercial attaches, enhanced export promotion, and sectoral analysis capability and, if they can get away with it, the lead responsibility for policy and negotiation."[70]

The NAM-supported plan for a separate Trade Department was developed by the Industrial Policy Advisory Committee (IPAC), an "informal corporatist" body created by the 1974 Trade Act that in 1979 was chaired by Robert Galvin of Motorola. This group represented such multinational interests as Del Monte, Eastman Kodak, Alcoa, St. Regis Paper, International Harvester, Hewlett-Packard, General Electric, Goodyear, International Paper, Union Carbide, and Armco. Its concern was to create "the government organization which will protect our interests under changed circumstances resulting from the multilateral trade negotiation package." This group also conferred with Senators William Roth, Abe Ribicoff, John Heinz, Lloyd Bentsen, and Bob Dole, who supported legislation to create a separate cabinet-level Trade Department or line agency.[71]

Aggressive export promotion through the creation of a separate Trade Department was opposed by the internationalist interests on the Business Roundtable and the Emergency Committee for American Trade (ECAT), which was linked to the Business Council and the U.S. Chamber of Commerce. These groups, which were more strongly representative of foreign direct investors, international finance capitalists, and multinationals with substantial production facilities developed abroad, opposed a plan that was suggestive of assertive economic nationalism and the possibility of increased tensions with foreign host governments. These more liberal internationalists favored retaining trade policy implementation within the executive office of the president.

ECAT was described by a key White House staffer as a "well-organized, highly effective group [that] represents some 200 of the largest U.S. multinational corporations. With high stakes in exports and imports, ECAT probably did more to assure Congressional passage of the Trade Act [of 1979] than any other private organization."[72] ECAT in particular opposed the creation of a line agency for trade that would lose its status as a "neutral" policy broker. Further, ECAT believed that "trying to give Commerce the trade policy lead would be like pushing back the clock twenty years."[73] Its idea of reform was to enhance the executive's discretionary power to lower tariffs and to negotiate trade concessions without congressional amendment, an advantage first given to the president in the 1974 Trade Act.

Internationalist interests that had been frustrated by capital controls a decade earlier now were able to effect changes in state structure and function designed to promote a more aggressive export orientation in U.S. foreign economic policy. The Carter plan was a shift toward export promotion, though without some of the nationalist overtones favored by the NAM and the IPAC. As governmental restructuring, it could be said to reflect the new world trade order that was developing in place of the Bretton Woods system. Trade reorganization was consistent with the goals of multilateral trade and investment[74] liberalization; indeed, it now projected the U.S. government on the world economic stage as an advocate of the export of goods *and capital.*

A new coalescence of business interests on trade issues and reformed institutions signaled a shift toward a more overt capture of the state by multinationalist business interests. This coalescence would in the 1980s and 1990s form the core of an increasingly hegemonic conservative multinationalist bloc. The rising conservative coalition would emphasize decreased costs of capital through lower taxes, less government regulation, reinvigorated subsidy of the military-industrial complex, government support of U.S. exporters, and the rollback of some of the more politically vulnerable portions of the welfare state.

NOTES

1. Richard E. Jansen, "Major Easing of Foreign-Investment Curbs Readied, but Key Domestic Decisions Remain," *Wall Street Journal*, March 17, 1969, p. 32.

2. Economic Research Division, "Easing of Capital Controls," internal corporate bulletin, The Chase Manhattan Bank, April 14, 1969, Arthur Burns Papers, Box 3, White House Central Files (WHCF), Staff Member and Office Files (SMOF), National Archives.

3. Harry Heltzer et al. to Arthur Burns, December 1, 1970, Burns Papers, WHCF, SMOF National Archives; Charles W. Colson, Box 38, Balance of Payments File, Charles W. Colson papers, WHCF, SMOF, National Archives.

4. Heltzer to Chuck Colson, December 3, 1970, Box 38, Balance of Payments File.

5. Arch N. Booth, executive vice president, Chamber of Commerce of the U.S.A., to the president, April 8, 1970, ibid. Booth's letter was directed to Kissinger and Colson for reply.

6. Memorandum, Colson to George Shultz, subject: OFDI, December 29, 1970, ibid.

7. Ibid.

8. Thomas Casey, Director, Corporate Planning, ITT, to Colson, April 27, 1970, ibid.

9. Memorandum for Peter Flanigan, July 2, 1970, signed by Colson, ibid. Stephen Ambrose, *Nixon,* Vol. 2 (New York: Simon and Schuster, 1989), after p. 123.

10. Memorandum for Peter Flanigan, July 2, 1970, signed by Colson, op. cit.

11. Memorandum for Colson from Flanigan, July 10, 1970, ibid.

12. Memorandum, Richard Urfer to Maurice Stans, subject: status of the FDIP, May 4, 1970, ibid.

13. Ibid.

14. Memorandum, Urfer to Colson, May 28, 1970, ibid.

15. Colson's handwritten note filed with Urfer memoranda, ibid.

16. Fred Block, "The Ruling Class Does Not Rule," in Margaret Levi, ed., *Marxism,* Vol. 2 (Aldershot, UK: Edward Elgar Publishing, 1991), p. 107.

17. IEPA did, however, take the view that FDI controls "can be substantially liberalized; and in our view they should be. Liberalization of OFDI controls would limit the distortions they cause for U.S. business." International Economic Policy Association, *Confidential Reporter* 41 (December 17, 1970), in Levi, *Marxism.*

18. Memorandum from Henry Wallich, senior consultant to the treasury secretary to CEA member Herb Stein, subject: "Summary of Treasury Consultants Meeting" of November 22, 1969, memo dated December 5, 1969, White House Central Files, Nixon Presidential Papers, National Archives; Herbert Stein Papers, Box 43, Treasury Consultants File, WHCF, SMOF, National Archives.

19. Letter from Herb Stein to Assistant Treasury Secretary Paul Volcker, December 30, 1971, provides the full list of treasury consultants, ibid.

20. Memorandum, Wallich to Stein, December 5, 1969.

21. James Reichley, *Conservatives in an Age of Change: The Nixon and Ford Administrations* (Washington, DC: Brookings Institution, 1982), pp. 223–224.

22. Memorandum, Volcker to the CEA, subject: "Where Should the IMF Be Going in the Flexibility Exercise?" June 10, 1971, Stein Papers.

23. Ambrose, *Nixon,* p. 459.

24. Joyce Kolko, *Restructuring the World Economy* (New York: Pantheon, 1988), p. 23.

25. Richard Nixon, *RN: The Memoirs of Richard Nixon* (New York: Grosset and Dunlap, 1978), p. 519.

26. Volcker to CEA, June 10, 1971.

27. Reichley, *Conservatives,* p. 223.

28. Ibid., p. 216.

29. Quoted in ibid.

30. Heltzer et al. to Burns, December 1, 1970.

31. Colson to Flanigan, July 2, 1970.

32. Jerri-Lynn Scofield, "The Business of Strategy: The Political Economy of U.S. Trade Policy Toward the U.S.S.R., 1945–1975," in Ronald W. Cox, ed., *Business and the State in International Relations* (Boulder, CO: Westview Press, 1996), p. 147.

33. Block, "The Ruling Class Does Not Rule," p. 119.

34. Eric Devereux, "Industrial Structure, Internationalism and the Collapse of the Cold War Consensus: Business, the Media, and Vietnam" in Ronald W. Cox, ed., *Business and the State in International Relations* (Boulder, CO: Westview Press, 1996), p. 38.

35. Memorandum, Gordon Strachan to Dick Howard, July 9, 1971, Charles Colson Papers, Box 41, WHCF, SMOF, "Black List" folder, National Archives.

36. Memorandum, Colson to Lucy Winchester, White House social secretary, October 14, 1971, Box 41, "Black List" folder.

37. Memorandum, Colson to George Bell, March 9, 1971, ibid.

38. Robert Roosa to John Cooper, April 18, 1975, Arthur Burns Papers, Box K29, Robert Roosa Correspondence File, Gerald R. Ford Presidential Library.

39. Robert Roosa, "The Parametric Function of Exchange Rates in a Market Economy," *Challenge*, accompanies January 12, 1978, letter to Burns, as in ibid.

40. Letter from Robert Axelrod to Burns, October 9, 1977, ibid.

41. Amy Ansell, "Business Mobilization and the New Right," in Ronald W. Cox, ed., *Business and the State in International Relations* (Boulder, CO: Westview Press, 1996), p. 60.

42. Allen Matusow, *The Unraveling of America: A History of Liberalism in the 1960s* (New York: Harper and Row, 1984).

43. Kees Van Der Pijl, *The Making of an Atlantic Ruling Class* (London: Verso, 1984), p. 245.

44. Kolko, *Restructuring the World Economy*, p. 19.

45. Statement by William Simon, secretary of the treasury, before the Senate Finance Committee, May 7, 1975, Paul Leach Papers, Box 11, Capital Formation file, December 1974–July 1975, White House Staff Files (WHSF) Gerald R. Ford Library.

46. Ibid., Capital Markets Working Group File.

47. Statement of Business Roundtable as attached to letter from W. F. Rockwell, Jr., to Paul Leach, September 19, 1975, ibid., Capital Formation File, August 1975–October 1975.

48. Walter Heller, "Taxes and the 'Capital Shortfall,'" *Wall Street Journal*, August 19, 1975, p. 12.

49. Thomas Ferguson, *Golden Rule: The Investment Theory of Party Competition and the Logic of Money-Driven Political Systems* (Chicago: University of Chicago Press, 1995).

50. John Habberton, BCIU president, to John Vickerman, January 14, 1976, John Vickerman Papers, Box 5, BCIU folder, WHSF, Gerald R. Ford Library.

51. Paul Joseph, *Cracks in the Empire* (New York: Columbia University Press, 1987), p. 287.

52. Memorandum, Ogden White to Richard Hill, October 15, 1975, Vickerman Papers.

53. Herbert Rosenbaum and Alexej Ugrinsky, *The Presidency and Domestic Policies of Jimmy Carter* (Westport, CT: Greenwood Press, 1994), p. 9.

54. Joseph, *Cracks in the Empire,* p. 288.

55. Ansell, "Business Mobilization and the New Right," p. 61.

56. Schultze in Rosenbaum and Ugrinsky, *Jimmy Carter,* p. 671.

57. Manuel Castells, *The Economic Crisis and American Society* (Berkeley: University of California Press, 1979).

58. Coral Bell, *The Diplomacy of Détente* (New York: St. Martin's Press, 1977), p. 206.

59. Dan Carter, *From George Wallace to Newt Gingrich* (Baton Rouge: Louisiana State University Press, 1996).

60. See discussion in Ansell, "Business Mobilization and the New Right," p. 67.

61. Carter, *From George Wallace to Newt Gingrich,* pp. 29, 34; Theodore White, *The Making of the President, 1968* (New York: Atheneum, 1969).

62. U.S. Congress, *Congress and the Nation*, Vol. 5 (Washington, DC: *Congressional Quarterly,* 1981), p. 271.

63. Scofield, "The Business of Strategy," p. 142.

64. Benjamin Ginsberg and Martin Shefter, *Politics by Other Means* (New York: Basic Books, 1990), p. 117.

65. John Dumbrell, *The Carter Presidency* (Manchester, UK: Manchester University Press, 1993), pp. 101–102.

66. U.S. Congress, *Congress and the Nation*, p. 271.

67. Ronald Cox and Daniel Skidmore-Hess, "The Politics of the 1993 NAFTA Vote," *Current Politics and Economics of the United States* 1, 2/3 (1995).

68. U.S. Congress, *Congress and the Nation*, p. 273.

69. Draft Memorandum by Selig, memo to Jimmy Carter from James McIntyre, OMB director, May 10, 1979, Papers of Stephen Selig, deputy assistant to the president, White House Office of Public Liaison, Box 186, Trade Reorganization File, WHSF, Jimmy Carter Presidential Library.

70. Memorandum to Tom Belford, Presidential Reorganization Project, for the file, June 7, 1979, ibid.

71. Memorandum, J. R. West, partner, Blythe, Eastman and Dillon, to Joel McCleary, deputy assistant to the president, Multilateral Trade Agreement File, August 14, 1978–July 10, 1979, ibid.

72. Memorandum, Selig to the special trade representative and White House staff liaison, August 15, 1978, Multilateral Trade Agreement File, ibid.

73. Memorandum for the file, June 7, 1979, Box 186, Trade Reorganization File, ibid.

74. Memorandum, Eric Hirschhorn to Selig, April 24, 1979, ibid. Notes that the Chamber of Commerce was "wondering why we weren't talking about" foreign investment as well as trade in the reorganization discussions.

6

The Reagan Revolution

Explaining the massive shift of business support to the presidential campaign of Ronald Reagan requires understanding the long-term and short-term trends within the global political economy during the last two years of the Carter administration. By the late 1970s, no effective political coalition could be built without taking into account the interrelationship between domestic and global politics. The most noteworthy political events of the second half of Carter's presidency involved a massive defection of liberal internationalists away from the Democratic Party and toward support for a Republican candidate who a short while earlier had been on the right-wing fringes of the party, unable to muster a broad base of business support beyond the "Goldwater coalition" of textile firms, independent oil producers, and military contractors.[1]

The movement of multinational corporate elites to the Reagan candidacy reflected a complex array of motivations that included considerable business support for rolling back the welfare state, especially aid targeted to the poor and the federal regulation of business, along with a commitment to increase military spending well beyond the limits of the Carter presidency. In addition, international financial interests, especially Chase Manhattan, Citibank, and the entire northeastern U.S. corridor of international commercial and investment banks, favored aggressive efforts to reverse the monetary plight of the dollar, in free fall during the last years of the Carter administration.[2]

The major events triggering support for a rightward shift of Carter's foreign and domestic policies in the last two years of his administration also led to increased and diverse business support for Ronald Reagan in the 1980 election. First of all, structural and long-term factors within the global political economy provided serious challenges to the array of U.S.-based multinational corporations that had previously supported the embedded liberalism of the Bretton Woods financial regime.[3] As detailed in previous chapters, the falling rate of profit had been a fact of life for most Fortune 500 firms since 1965, and in an effort to maintain competitiveness in global markets, most firms increased their rate of borrowing from commercial banks. Furthermore, U.S. corporations sought to cut their costs of production in other ways, either by sourcing out production of component parts to the less developed world (automobiles and electronics production in Latin America and Asia, respectively) or by relocating production of finished products to countries or regions with an adequate demand base (Western Europe or larger market countries in the less developed world).[4] Another corporate strategy involved reducing the competitive playing field by merging with or buying out competitors, but this approach was hindered by the antitrust provisions of the Justice Department and by the realities of increased global competition, which made oligopolies much more difficult to sustain than they had been in the 1950s and early 1960s. Corporations also began the process of restructuring in the U.S. domestic market, with manufacturing firms closing plants in the Northeast and moving to the South or Southwest, where right-to-work laws provided a conducive environment for reducing wages and benefits.[5]

However, a number of domestic and international obstacles stood in the way of U.S.-based multinationals reducing their costs of production and regaining market share lost to international competitors in Japan and West Germany. First, relocation strategies were often made more difficult by the complex array of government efforts to protect domestic firms from international competition. West Germany and Japan maintained significant subsidies and research and development expenditures for the most competitive of their export industries and discriminated in awarding lucrative state contracts to leading global competitors. By 1980 a high percentage of exports from the major industrial countries were dependent on state financing, with the Japanese state financing 39 percent of all Japanese exports; the British state financing 35 percent of all British exports; the French state financing 34 percent of all French exports and the United States financing 18 percent of its exports.[6]

Furthermore, virtually all Western European states relied on restrictive capital controls and foreign investment laws to limit U.S. penetration into the region. Although the United States and Britain had taken the lead in dismantling capital controls, the effort was far from uniform; vestiges of the old Bretton Woods system of capital controls and managed exchange rates were still intact in most Western European countries through the end of the 1970s.[7] Both U.S.-based multinational manufacturers and commercial and investment bankers sought to eliminate or weaken the controls on capital movement that ostensibly allowed governments to protect their domestic currencies and subsidy programs at the expense of foreign competitors.

Second, commercial bankers and foreign investors were increasingly concerned about the steady decline of the dollar, which increased the costs of foreign investment and made uncertain long-term investment strategies linked to the dollar. U.S.-based financial institutions feared that a lack of monetary stability and a steady weakening of the dollar might gravely weaken the position of U.S. banks vis-à-vis borrowers in the less developed world, especially after the major U.S. commercial banks lent 40 percent of the $400 billion that had been lent to governments in the less developed world by 1980.[8] By the late 1970s, the U.S.-based financial community overwhelmingly favored a restrictive monetary policy, which would have the advantage of placing the less developed governments in a financial squeeze by raising the costs of borrowing and, most important, the costs and terms of paying off the debt accrued during the 1970s. For U.S.-based foreign investors, a restrictive monetary policy would have the advantage of increasing the purchasing power of the dollar and thereby cheapen access to foreign inputs increasingly used in production. But most important, such a policy would provide an influx of needed capital from Western Europe, thus further internationalizing the U.S. economy and weakening the capital controls programs in Western Europe.[9]

A restrictive monetary policy would also serve to disorganize and weaken the position of organized labor in the United States, largely by generating a recession and creating a reserve army of labor that would be forced to compete for skilled and unskilled jobs. By the mid to late 1970s, multinational business increasingly financed right-wing foundations and interest groups that had warned of the prohibitive social costs of doing business in the United States. As the number of U.S. workers on strike for higher pay and better benefits increased steadily from 1967 to 1974, business foundations warned that a U.S. economy that operated at excessively high capacity was bound to result in periodic bouts with inflation that would increase the costs of doing business.[10] Despite the fact that the U.S. consistently lagged behind its Western European counterparts in the provision of unemployment and health benefits to organized workers, the business press increasingly predicted impending social and economic crises if wage rates continued to increase. Furthermore, business organizations formed with the explicit purpose of reducing the rate of unionization in the U.S. economy and facilitating the hiring of nonunion workers that was accompanied by the relocation of industries from the unionized states of the Northeast to the "right-to-work" states of the South and Southwest.[11]

Antilabor organizations with considerable multinational corporate financing mushroomed in the 1970s to promote an activist antiunion agenda in the courts and Congress. Examples include the Business Roundtable, which formed in the late 1960s in response to the increasing demands and wage successes of the construction building trades and fought successfully to increase the percentage of open shop or nonunion building contractors. The Roundtable worked with other business organizations to promote a broad antiunion agenda, including the National Association of Manufacturers'

Council for a Union Free Environment, the long-standing National Right-to-Work Committee, the small-business-dominated National Federation of Independent Business, the revamped U.S. Chamber of Commerce (which increased the proportion of its budget devoted to union-busting campaigns), and numerous trade associations.[12]

The efforts of increased business lobbying, an increasingly conservative trade union bureaucracy that valued cooperation over confrontation, and the effects of international competition on U.S. jobs combined to seriously reduce union membership over time. From 1969 to 1979, for example, the International Association of Machinists and Aerospace Workers lost more than 150,000 workers (nearly a quarter of its membership), the Amalgamated Clothing and Textile Workers lost 149,000 workers (a third of its membership), and the Railway, Airline and Steamship Clerks lost some 80,000 workers (40 percent of its membership).[13] Aggressive anti-union organizing by business groups contributed to the loss of union membership, which was reflected in the dramatic increases in business-sponsored decertification campaigns challenging union security clauses and the union's status as bargaining representative. In 1950 there were approximately 100 decertification elections involving close to 9,500 workers. In 1978 there were more than 800 decertification elections involving close to 40,000 workers.[14] Corporate hiring of union-busting consulting firms increased during the 1970s, with the explicit purpose of stopping union organizing drives.

Despite an activist effort to reduce union membership and cut labor costs, U.S.-based multinationals faced further problems during the slow growth, high inflation period of 1978 and 1979. During the first two years of the Carter administration, the U.S. economy continued to experience relatively high growth rates of between 4 and 5 percent annually. By the last two years of the Carter presidency, however, economic indicators were suggesting more problems for U.S.-based multinational firms. First, the U.S. economy slowed and inflation skyrocketed in the face of a global increase in the price of oil, a further sign to business that the position of the dollar remained precarious and that monetary policy had to be adjusted to give the financial sector confidence in the value of the nation's currency. Second, the rising global oil prices were interconnected to the U.S. foreign policy crisis in Iran, where a revolution ushered to power a self-proclaimed fundamentalist Islamic cleric, Ayatollah Ruhollah Khomeini. The new Iranian regime provided a challenge to U.S. oil companies and financial institutions historically tied to pro-U.S. Middle Eastern regimes. Although U.S. multinational oil firms were no longer major owners of oil production facilities in the region, they had invested extensively in marketing and distribution contracts with all of the major Middle Eastern producers. Amoco, Chevron, Texaco, Conoco, and Shell viewed with trepidation the rise of a government that might threaten their distribution of oil throughout the vital Persian Gulf.[15]

Second, U.S. commercial banks located in the Eurodollar market had come to depend on financial deposits from Middle Eastern regimes, including Iran and, most important, Saudi Arabia and Kuwait. The flow of petrodollars from the Middle East to the Euromarkets of London and Paris was increasingly used to finance the expansion of U.S.-based multinational enterprises in Western Europe and throughout the less developed world. Most significantly, U.S.-based commercial banks recycled petrodollars to Latin American borrowers, especially Mexico and Brazil, during the competitive international banking climate of the 1970s.

Given the economic interests of U.S. oil firms and commercial banks in the regions, the Iranian revolution was a cataclysmic event. The emergence of an anti-U.S. regime in the Middle East threatened the interests of leading capital-intensive U.S.-based foreign investors that clamored for some type of U.S. military response. In addition, the revolution occurred in a wider context of the rise of left-wing and nationalist revolutionary movements throughout the less developed world. Most important for U.S. investors, the emergence of a successful revolutionary movement in Nicaragua and heightened class conflict in Central America raised warning flags regarding the need for an expanded U.S. military budget. By the last two years of the Carter administration capital-intensive U.S. firms with stakes in the Middle East and regionally based, often labor-intensive U.S. firms with investments in Central and South America had joined the chorus of business organizations that favored higher levels of military spending.[16] Often unable to agree on the amount and purposes of the military budget increases, this alliance of foreign investors nevertheless increased its contribution to right-wing organizations and think tanks committed to lobbying for increased military spending. The most important of these lobbying organizations was the Committee on the Present Danger, financed by a wide range of U.S. multinationals with a stake in foreign investments and, in the case of military contractors, domestic U.S. firms heavily dependent on military spending for profitability.[17]

The political economy of increased military spending formed the backdrop for the emergence of Ronald Reagan as a viable presidential candidate in the 1980 election as well as the right turn of multinational corporations previously committed to the embedded liberalism of the Bretton Woods financial regime. The changing structural conditions of the global economy provided the undercurrents for shifting business opinion as international firms looked for cost-cutting measures to better maintain global (or domestic) market share against increased competition. In addition, capital-intensive business firms such as multinational oil companies and investment and commercial banks joined traditional representatives of the military-industrial complex to lobby for dramatic increases in the U.S. military budget. However, the U.S. multinational community remained heavily divided regarding the policy prescriptions for promoting U.S. global competitiveness.

Domestic firms dependent on military spending advocated the most extreme increases in the military budget, whereas international investors sought to tailor the budget increases to specific weapons systems that could defend U.S. client states (especially in the Middle East and Central America) against instability and revolutionary movements hostile to private foreign investment. Furthermore, U.S. commercial banks urged a restrictive monetary policy that would protect the position of the dollar from further devaluation and strengthen the hand of bankers in recovering loans from the less developed world.

The Reagan administration consisted of a diverse array of ideologues who were stridently anticommunist and corporate factions committed to protecting their immediate interests. These political and economic interests did not always easily coexist, but each was dependent on the other in various ways. The first Reagan term was focused on a rapid military buildup, a substantial tax cut, especially for the wealthy, and some successful efforts to roll back the regulatory bureaucracy of the U.S. government. To curb the further weakening of the dollar that would be caused by higher military spending, the international banking establishment, with the cooperation of the Federal Reserve and the acquiescence of the Reagan White House, hiked interest rates and made the United States a more attractive site for financial speculation and foreign investment during the 1980s. During the decade, foreign investment continued to be concentrated around the large triad markets of the United States, Western Europe, and Asia, but the vast majority of new investment flows were going to the United States.[18] This trend, along with the political tendencies of Reaganomics, further accelerated the internationalization of the U.S. and global economies. The rapid flight of investment capital from Western Europe and Japan to the United States promoted the dissolution of capital controls and thereby signaled the end of effective national efforts to manage international finance.

The further internationalization of the U.S. economy generated considerable tensions among a diverse array of U.S. business groups, a conflict that cannot adequately be characterized as internationalist versus nationalist, although this division was part of the basis for the conflict. Instead, two distinctive sections of internationalist capital previously committed to free trade split into two groups: multilateralists and regionalists, each promoting an opposing vision of U.S. trade policy. Multilateralists were the most competitive U.S.-based global industries, centered on computers, pharmaceuticals, and telecommunications and highly dependent on foreign trade and investment throughout the world. They advocated a continuation of the GATT negotiations and pressed for a follow-up to the Tokyo Round negotiated during the Nixon and Ford administrations. Regionalist U.S. firms advocated bilateral and regional trade negotiations designed to improve the competitive position of U.S. firms within North America by institutionalizing discrimination against Western European and Japanese competitors. Despite their differences, regionalists and multilateralists often joined in supporting such diverse initiatives as the Caribbean Basin Initiative (CBI) and NAFTA, but each group competed over the political direction of these initiatives.[19]

Nationalists remained an important political force in U.S. politics, especially domestic business groups linked to increased military spending and declining sectors such as textiles, steel, glass, sheet, appliances, and agricultural interests such as sugar producers dependent on government price support schemes.[20] Various combinations of these interests opposed the expansion of regional trade initiatives such as CBI and NAFTA (although big sugar acquiesced to NAFTA after being provided with assurances that its domestic quota would be protected) and sought to restrict trade legislation that would increase competition between U.S.-based foreign investors and domestic firms within the U.S. domestic market. Thus, under Reagan, business conflict continued but became more complex because of the increased internationalization of the U.S. economy.

The following sections of the chapter develop the most important aspects of the rightward drift of business organizations during the late 1970s and early 1980s, focusing primarily on the dometic and foreign policy implications for the first Reagan term. The interconnectedness of domestic and foreign policy becomes strikingly obvious when we examine lobbying by multinational corporate firms to lower U.S. taxes on the wealthy and corporations and to tighten monetary policy to facilitate an international flow of capital to the United States. Business internationalists close to the Reagan administration viewed both strategies as essential for improving the international competitiveness of U.S.-based multinational corporations. Most important, a restrictive U.S. monetary policy would weaken capital controls in Western Europe, thereby encouraging a process of global restructuring that would become a euphemism for increased layoffs, reductions in social benefits, and liberalization of capital markets that U.S. finance capital had long been advocating.

THE POLITICAL ECONOMY OF REAGANOMICS

During the first Reagan term, the administration actively pursued two distinctive policies supported by an array of corporate think tanks and right-wing ideologues and acquiesced to a third policy tract pushed and implemented by the Federal Reserve. The first policy involved a commitment to a massive tax cut for wealthy Americans and U.S. businesses that would be justified ideologically and programmatically by the doctrine of supply-side economics. The second policy involved an effort to overhaul and drastically reduce social spending and government regulation of business. The third policy tract, disputed by some members of the Reagan administration and supported by others, involved following the lead of the Federal Reserve's move toward a restrictive monetary policy that would dramatically increase interest rates and attract substantial foreign capital investments to the United States. At each phase of policymaking, there was considerable cooperation and consultation among U.S.-based multinational corporations, their relevant lobbying organizations, and the Reagan White House.

Immediate foreign policy concerns advocated by the Defense Department, most notably Secretary of State Alexander Haig, initially took a backseat to efforts by the Reagan White House to promote the passage of a broad tax-cut measure championed by both ideological advocates of supply-side economics and business advocates of tax reduction. Reagan's core supporters, led by William Simon, then a leading portfolio manager for several large Arab business interests and a director of several U.S. multinational firms, and Charls Walker, a well-connected business lobbyist and chair of Reagan's tax policy proposals, advocated 3-year 10 percent personal income tax cuts and substantial depreciation allowances with projected revenue losses of approximately $750 billion over a five-year period. The supply-side justification for such an approach involved identifying the tax cuts as a primary stimulus to increased domestic investment, which supposedly had been deterred by the high rates of progressive taxation levied in the past few decades to pay for increases in government spending. Through the "Laffer Curve," developed by a California economist on the fringes of the economics profession, supply-side advocates within the Republican Party attempted to demonstrate that the existing U.S. taxation rates were so high that they discouraged significant investment and job creation. Lowering taxes would result in more investment, and the federal government would actually benefit from increased revenue. Most economists disputed the so-called Laffer Curve, arguing that the Reagan administration's estimates of overtaxation of businesses and the wealthy greatly exaggerated the progressive nature of the tax system. In fact, if viewed historically, taxation of U.S. corporations had long been dropping, thanks to a plethora of loopholes and tax breaks negotiated between business lobbies and Congress during the previous two decades. Still, bolstered by supply-side ideology and significant business support, the Reagan administration pushed ahead with the tax cut proposals.

Almost immediately there emerged divisions among various business sectors regarding the proposals emerging from the Reagan White House. The financial sector and capital-intensive high-tech firms, represented most aggressively by the Business Roundtable, worried that such an ambitious tax reduction plan would result in significant budget deficits and further weaken the value of the dollar.[21] The Business Roundtable lobbied the House Ways and Means Committee to lower the tax cuts and business depreciation allowances of the original White House plan. Concerned that it had gone too far and fearful that business opposition might derail the supply-side program, the White House responded by modifying its own plan; the modifications included lowering the tax breaks for businesses and wealthy individuals and trimming the business depreciation allowances outlined in the initial plan. In addition, the administration sought to attract southern Democrats to the tax reduction plan by adding special tax provisions for independent oilmen.[22]

Concerned about possible alterations in the bill that would make it less attractive for businesses, especially the elimination of significant depreciation allowances, business organizations descended on Washington in large numbers for what has been described as a "Lear Jet Weekend" to advocate for corporate tax relief. It was here that business conflict led to business compromise, as the financial sector, worried that the tax cuts were too heavy, cooperated with other business firms advocating decreases in the personal tax cuts and significant increases in the proposed corporate tax cuts. The compromise involved lowering the personal tax reductions to 5 percent for the first year of the tax cut. At the same time, business groups such as the Council on Capital Formation, the American Business Council, the U.S. Chamber of Commerce, and the National Association of Manufacturers successfully lobbied to increase the levels of corporate tax breaks and depreciation allowances included in the tax cut bill. The final dimensions of the bill were finely tailored to the lobbying efforts of the major corporate organizations, which succeeded in convincing both Democrats and Republicans to support massive tax breaks for businesses and corporations. In its final version, the Economic Recovery Tax Act cut tax rates for businesses in half, dropping them from 33 to 16 percent overall, and continued the twenty-year trend of reducing the corporate income tax share of federal tax revenues from 21.3 percent during the 1960s to 6.2 percent during the 1980s. The effective taxation rate for 275 major, profitable corporations was only 15 percent over the period 1981–1984, and 129 firms had managed to pay no income taxes in at least one of those four years.[23]

Much has been written and documented regarding the effects of the tax cuts on the increasing disparity of wealth in the United States. However, only recently has it been appreciated that the steady decline of real income for working-class Americans began as early as 1973 and that the overwhelming beneficiaries of the Reagan tax cuts were the wealthiest 1 percent of Americans. Although the top 20 percent saw dramatic improvements in their wealth and tax rates as well, the bottom 20 percent actually experienced a decline in their standard of living during the 1980s, exacerbated by significant cuts in social programs targeted to the low-income population. In 1983 the top 40 percent of the population received a larger share of income than at any other time since 1947, whereas the bottom 40 percent and the middle 20 percent received smaller shares than at any other time since then. Poverty increased dramatically, with some 33 million Americans—one in seven—living below the poverty line, 4.4 million more than in 1980, and 9 million more than in 1978. For children, the 1984 figures were staggering, with about one-fourth of all children under the age of six living below the poverty line and more than half of black children under the age of six living in poverty.[24]

Contrary to popular belief, there had already been significant erosion of real benefits (i.e., spending power) afforded by the various means-tested programs from the mid-1970s to the early 1980s. By 1981 Aid to Families With Dependent Children (AFDC) benefits for a family of four had already declined more than 33 percent from their 1970 levels, and food stamps and Low Income Energy Assistance had dropped by 21.7 and 19.2 percent, respectively. Seeking 60 percent cuts in discretionary grant programs and 30 percent cuts in low-income programs, the Reagan administration received some three-fourths of its budget cut requests for the first group of programs and approximately one-third of its requests for the second group. Overall, there was a 14 percent reduction in food stamps, 28 percent in child nutrition, 14 percent in AFDC, 11 percent in Supplemental Security Income, 11 percent in Low Income Energy Assistance, 16 percent in financial aid for needy students, 33 percent in health block grants and other health services, 20 percent in compensatory education, 24 percent in social services block grants, and 39 percent in general job-training programs.[25]

The Reagan cutbacks in social spending were accompanied by reductions in federal spending on regulation and oversight of business and a concerted effort to further weaken the position of organized labor in seeking institutional protection from the federal government. The Reagan administration moved immediately to begin a regulatory overhaul that resulted in diminishing resources for environmental, safety, consumer, civil rights, and antitrust agencies, whose monitoring of corporate health, safety, and hiring practices was reduced. Over the first Reagan term, the Environmental Protection Agency's overall budget was reduced by 35 percent, enforcement of strip-mining violations declined by 62 percent, and prosecution of hazardous waste violations declined 50 percent; the Food and Drug Administration's enforcement of its regulations declined 88 percent. Although the Office of Technology Assessment contended that there were over 300,000 waste sites that posed threats of groundwater contamination, as of 1985 the Reagan EPA had put only 850 of these on its priority list.[26] In addition, the administration moved to begin a massive privatization program that targeted as many as 35 million acres of federal land for sale at the low price of $17 billion, a boon to the western business constituency that had partially bankrolled his campaign for the presidency.[27] As many observers have noted, the administration also moved to reduce to virtual irrelevancy the antitrust division of the Justice Department, paving the way for one of the great merger manias in recent U.S. history.

The efforts to further dismantle the institutional protection given to organized labor by the federal government were perhaps the most important aspect of the Reagan domestic revolution, generating the broadest support throughout the multinational and domestic business constituency. Starting in 1983, the administration made major changes in basic labor law doctrine, all with the goal of favoring management over unions. The combined effect of the labor legislation was to restrict dramatically the number and type of cases that labor could appeal to the National Labor Relations Board (NLRB). Furthermore, employers could now legally engage in a wide range of behavior during union certification elections that had been previously prohibited by national labor law.

The new laws also freed employers from the constraints of collective bargaining decisions that had traditionally been imposed during work relocation decisions and simultaneously narrowed a broad range of labor-management issues previously subject to collective bargaining. The administration shifted a higher burden on unions in paying the costs of dispute resolution, reducing government obligations and oversight of union-management disputes. Exacerbated by the extent and duration of the 1981–1982 recession, by the end of 1984, for the third year in a row, "average first-year settlements in major bargaining contracts would lag substantially behind inflation, major strike incidence set a postwar low, and unions organized fewer than 100,000 new workers through NLRB representation elections."[28] Even during the recovery of 1983, "average weekly earnings were 12.5 percent below their 1972 peak, while real adjusted hourly earnings were still in decline."[29]

The Federal Reserve's tight monetary policy was one of the primary factors that increased the disparity between capital owners and workers by triggering increases in unemployment that undermined union bargaining and widened the gap between rich and poor. In analyzing the policy of the Federal Reserve, it's important to recognize the relationship between the largest U.S.-based multinational banks and the Federal Reserve's board of directors. Multinational banks have a good deal of influence on the direction of Fed policy, with representatives of the Bank of America, Citibank, Chase Manhattan, First National Bank, Morgan Guaranty Trust, Manufacturers Hanover Trust, and other prominent firms serving on an advisory board that is briefed and issues recommendations prior to major changes in Fed policy. Thus the primary corporate constituency that is closest to the Fed constitutes the apex of financial power in the United States.[30]

The relationship between the executive branch and the Federal Reserve is more complicated, and there were considerable divisions within the Reagan administration regarding the wisdom of the Fed's tight money policies of 1981 and 1982. Such a policy involved using traditional Federal Reserve tools such as the buying and selling of government bonds and securities to influence interest rates in the bond and money markets. By 1979 leading investment bankers and their corporate clients were panicked about the effects of spiraling inflation on the bond market, which continued to fall. The Carter administration, in an attempt to reassure international investment and commercial banks, committed itself to a tight money policy led by the newly appointed chairman of the Federal Reserve, Paul Volcker. By the time that Reagan took office, the tight money policy was already being implemented, and the incoming administration was confronted with the political decision of whether to verbally support or oppose the Fed's policies.

One bloc of Reagan officials in the National Security Council, led by Henry Nau, the senior member of the Reagan administration's staff responsible for international economic affairs over the period 1981–1983, advocated the continuation of a tight money policy in order to strengthen the value of the dollar internationally, restoring international confidence in the U.S. bond and securities markets.[31] Nau and other members of the national security bureaucracy were supported by representatives of the president's Economic Policy Board, led by Walter Wriston of Citibank. The long-term results of the tight money policy, which does not determine but does influence a range of interest rates, are reflected most glaringly in Fed policies during 1982, when the recession was at its height. During this period, the Federal Reserve allowed the federal funds rate and other short-term interest rates to climb as much as 300 basis points over a few weeks, rising from about 12.5 percent to a peak of 15.6 percent.[32] The cumulative effect was to exacerbate the recession of 1981 and 1982, in effect extending the recession through the second quarter of 1982.

Although some business officials, including the chief economist for the CED, and some Reagan officials, such as Secretary of the Treasury Donald Regan, criticized the Fed policies, most of the prominent Reagan administration officials supported the policy. The supporters included Reagan himself, who endorsed the policy in a February 1982 meeting with Paul Volcker, and Reagan's second chairman of the Council of Economic

Advisors, Martin Feldstein, who was publicly supportive of the tight money policy. In addition, David Stockman, head of the Office of Management and the Budget, reassured the Chamber of Commerce that the administration saw "a sustained period of unemployment as part of the cure, not the problem" of U.S. economic difficulties. Leading Chamber officials had endorsed a tight money policy during the early 1980s as a way of restraining wage demands and checking inflation by curbing the growth of the money supply. Those administration officials who objected to the tight money policy were typically adherents of the supply-side school of economics and feared that high interest rates would prevent the economy from benefiting from the tax breaks proposed by the administration and adopted by Congress in 1981. Some business organizations, including the leaders of the CED, were opposed to a restrictive monetary policy because they feared it would trigger "class warfare" in the U.S. and help destabilize the international economy.[33]

Still, international investors, especially the major corporate clients of U.S.-based investment and commercial banks, tended to support a tight money policy as a means to encourage capital flight from Europe. Their position, according to administration official Nau, was based on the connection between high U.S. interest rates and the revitalization of the dollar, whose strength would attract capital from Western Europe, putting further pressure on European governments to liberalize their capital markets.[34] Investment banks and their corporate clients were also increasingly dependent on the bond market for raising capital, especially in the competitive international environment of the late 1970s and early 1980s. The move to tighten interest rates would benefit these holders of liquid assets by raising the value of their investments.

Helleiner summarizes the reasons that the U.S. was able to attract substantial foreign capital during the decade of the 1980s, thereby exerting structural pressure on foreign governments to liberalize their capital markets:

> The basis of America's ability to attract the world's private capital in this period was its continuing structural power in global finance, a power that derived from the unique depth and liquidity of U.S. financial markets and the global importance of the dollar. Japanese investors, the largest single source of foreign financing in the 1980s, found U.S. financial markets to be the only ones deep enough to absorb their enormous pool of surplus savings. Latin American investors, another important source of capital, were attracted by the stability of the dollar and the security of U.S. financial markets compared with the instability and uncertainty of their own debt-plagued economies. The desirability of making U.S. investments was also reinforced by high U.S. interest rates, which emerged from the mix of loose fiscal and tight monetary policy that had facilitated the country's economic recovery.[35]

Although the U.S. state played an important role in liberalizing capital markets moving toward a tight monetary policy in the early 1980s, U.S.-based multinational banks were important in lobbying the U.S. government to adopt such a monetary policy. In addition, the most global and capital-intensive U.S. firms were increasingly joining with internationalist businesses from foreign countries to push for deregulation of capital markets. Business internationalists influential in the Group of Seven industrialized countries and such corporate bodies as the Trilateral Commission promoted deregulation efforts in Britain, Japan, and the European Community during the 1980s. Led by U.S. political and business officials, a diverse coalition of international firms, especially capital-intensive producers and financial interests, pushed for global deregulation.[36]

At the same time, the Reagan administration was committed to financial openness to finance the fiscal deficits caused by the tax cuts of 1981 and the hikes in military spending. If the United States had been a closed economy, its fiscal deficit would have further pushed up interest rates and induced a long-term recession whose effects would have been felt well beyond 1982. Instead, as much as one-half of the U.S. budget deficit was being financed with foreign capital by 1985, keeping interest rates as much as 5 percent lower than they otherwise would have been.[37] The administration, recognizing the crucial contribution of foreign investment to financing the growing U.S. budget deficit, became strong advocates of further moves to liberalize U.S. financial markets. In 1984 the Treasury Department persuaded Congress to abolish the 30 percent withholding tax on interest payments to foreign holders of U.S. bonds. In an effort to move the location of foreign capital investments from the Eurobond market to the United States, the Treasury Department issued a special set of treasury bonds directly into the Eurobond market in 1984. The department also allowed foreign investors to purchase treasury bonds anonymously, further encouraging capital flight from Latin America.[38]

During the early 1980s, a wide array of U.S.-based firms were starting to feel the negative effects of the tight money policies of the administration and the Federal Reserve, even multinational banking firms and capital-intensive investors that had initially supported those policies. After 1982 major U.S. private banks were faced with a mounting debt crisis in Latin America when Mexican officials announced they could not meet their debt obligations. In an effort to facilitate their collection of debts, these bankers relied on the administration, the Federal Reserve, and the International Monetary Fund, in consultation with U.S. and foreign-based commercial banks, to put together a bailout package and a rescheduling of the terms of the Mexican debt.[39]

Despite the debt crisis, Wall Street continued to endorse variations of a tight money policy through the first Reagan term and were joined by the Chamber of Commerce, the National Association of Manufacturers, the

Business Council, and the *Wall Street Journal* in endorsing Paul Volcker for a second term as chairman of the Federal Reserve.[40] However, several U.S. export interests were becoming concerned that the tight money policies were pricing them out of international markets on account of the steady increase in the value of the dollar. U.S. domestic industries, especially steel, autos, textiles, and electronics, were facing increased competition for the U.S. market as a result of relatively cheap foreign currencies, which provided opportunities for foreign firms to increase their exports to the United States. Imports to the United States had more than tripled from 1976 to 1984, fast eclipsing the growth in U.S. exports and foreign direct investment during this same period.[41]

However, the Reagan administration was not willing to abandon its tight monetary policy, which was increasingly viewed as necessary to attract foreign capital to the United States and finance the spiraling arms budget and tax cuts of the first Reagan term. Reagan moved to appease his diverse corporate constituency in several seemingly contradictory ways. First, the administration maintained a commitment to tight money policies by reappointing Volcker to a new four-year term beginning in 1983, a policy move designed to reassure Wall Street. The tight money policy was also seen as essential to attract foreign capital necessary to finance the growing U.S. budget deficit and to further encourage liberalization of capital markets in Western Europe and Japan, a policy that was supported by U.S. firms with considerable investments in Europe and Asia. Second, the administration and Congress moved to increase nontariff, and in some cases tariff, trade barriers in an attempt to protect U.S. domestic firms from the negative effects of the increased internationalization of the U.S. economy; steel, autos, and textiles sought and received protectionist measures from the government during the first Reagan term.[42] Third, the administration worked with U.S. banks, the IMF, and the World Bank to devise plans to facilitate the collection of debts owed by Latin American governments to the United States, with the most concerted effort directed toward the Mexican debt crisis. Finally, the administration also moved to satisfy a broad array of U.S. foreign investors and military contractors that had aggressively lobbied for hikes in the military budget. As we will show, a diverse array of U.S. business interests supported dramatic increases in military spending during the first term of the administration, though some business interests would become increasingly critical of the high costs of military spending by Reagan's second term, especially U.S. firms with considerable European investments.

THE POLITICAL ECONOMY OF MILITARY SPENDING

The Reagan administration initiated the biggest sustained peacetime military buildup in U.S. history. From 1980 to 1985, real military spending increased

39 percent, rising from 5.2 percent of GNP to 6.6 percent and increasing the share of the federal budget targeted for defense from 23 to 27 percent. The overwhelming majority of the spending hikes were for investment in new weapons systems, including weapons procurement, research and development, military construction, and warhead production. Such spending rose from over one-third (38 percent) of all military outlays to just under one-half (48 percent) during the first five fiscal years of the administration. The Reagan defense budget included the B-1 bomber, the neutron bomb, antiballistic missile systems, civil defense capabilities, and an 8 percent yearly increase in military spending. In effect, the Republican administration continued what had been started by Carter, who had already authorized funding for the MX missile, the Trident submarine, the Rapid Deployment Force, the "stealth" bomber, the cruise missile, and counterforce targeting leading to first-strike capability, while increasing the defense budget by 5 and 6 percent, respectively, during his last two years in office. Most striking is the enormous buildup of nuclear weapons under Reagan, which rose nearly three times the rate of the overall defense program. Over the 1980–1985 period, budget authority for strategic weapons grew from $9.4 to $35.3 billion, an increase of 276 percent, whereas authority for conventional and tactical weapons rose 111 percent. In the area of conventional weapons, the U.S. now had enough firepower to fight three wars on the scale of Vietnam at one time.[43]

Business support for a massive defense buildup was evident by 1979, when the political and fund-raising activities of the major pro-weapons business organization, the Committee on the Present Danger (CPD), increased dramatically. The organization, created in 1976, brought together a wide range of corporate sponsors that were committed to lobbying for military spending hikes. The membership of the committee was dominated by corporate elites from diverse sectors of the U.S. economy, including multinational financial institutions, multinational manufacturers, and defense contractors. Among firms tied to the founding board of directors, financial institutions dominated, holding 39 percent of the 110 positions on the CPD's board, and manufacturing industries held 33 percent of the board positions. What is most noteworthy is the leadership role played by U.S. commercial and investment banks with a heavy stake in overseas investments, including Citibank; Goldman, Sachs; and Dillon, Read. Industries such as Temple-Eastex, Ingersoll-Rand, Honeywell, and Hewlett-Packard were also represented on the board of directors, along with oil firms Mobil and Exxon.[44]

The committee's agenda, dating from its founding in 1976, included a commitment to reverse the spending trends of the first two years of the Carter administration, when the defense budget averaged a 3 percent increase per year.[45] During this period, Carter eliminated the B-1 bomber program on the grounds of cost effectiveness, cut funding for the proposed MX missile and Trident nuclear submarine, and deferred production and deployment of the neutron bomb in Western Europe. The committee used an extensive array of institutional connections to lobby for a reversal of these decisions, including numerous meetings with the Carter White House and the State and Defense Departments in which it advocated across-the-board increases in military spending. The CPD is widely recognized as being the most important and influential interest group in the defeat of the Strategic Arms Limitation Treat (SALT II), the major arms control treaty negotiated by the Carter administration. The committee spent $750,000 in its efforts to derail the agreement even before the treaty was announced and provided seventeen testimonies against the treaty before Senate committee.[46]

Working alongside numerous organizations commonly associated with the new right such as the American Security Council and the American Conservative Union, the CPD used the congressional debates over SALT II as a litmus test to criticize Carter's entire foreign policy record. In fact, the committee and other defense lobbies cared less about the specifics of the SALT II treaty than it did about the general defense policies of the administration. The committee advocated broad-based and across-the-board increases in the military budget that would have the advantage of satisfying the diverse members of its corporate constituency. Defense contractors had long lobbied for across-the-board spending increases but were now joined by a range of U.S. business internationalists that had not previously been active in debates over the military budget. We will now examine the reasons for the tremendous growth in CPD activities from 1979 through the first Reagan term, when the committee became most visible, as measured by its access to corporate contributions, public statements, and political lobbying efforts.[47]

Increased business support for the committee reflected a split among business internationalists previously committed to cooperation and trade with the Eastern bloc. In fact, the major political supporters of SALT II were U.S.-based business groups actively involved in East-West trade. U.S.-based multinational firms, led by Pepsico chairman Donald Kendall, provided one-third of the funding for the American Committee on the East-West Accord, the most important lobbying organization in favor of the treaty.[48] Such liberal internationalists continued to oppose the escalation of military spending during the early Reagan years, reflected by donations from business interests to peace groups (and the Democratic Party) during the first Reagan term. The distinction between firms that opposed the dramatic increases in military spending and those that supported such increases centered on several factors. The first was whether a firm was primarily or exclusively tied to investments in Western Europe or whether it had significantly diversified its investments toward the Middle East and the less developed world. The latter firms tended to support the Reagan administration's military buildup because of the perceived impact of the Iranian revolution and nationalist movements of the left on investments in the Third World. These firms included U.S.-based multinational oil companies Mobil, Exxon, Chevron, Amoco, and Texaco, all of which had considerable interest in the distribution and marketing of Middle Eastern oil and were threatened by instability in the region.[49] By the late 1970s and early 1980s, these firms had strong allies among commercial and investment banks that relied on long-term deposits from the region to finance loans.

The second factor that helped determine a firm's orientation was its dependence on military spending for profitability. Honeywell, General Electric, Lockheed, McDonnell-Douglas, and Motorola all bankrolled various lobbying organizations connected to the new right and the Reagan administration, including the American Security Council and the National Strategy Information Center. Buoyed by increased corporate contributions, these latter organizations increased in strength in the mid to late 1970s, alongside the Committee on the Present Danger. For example, the American Security Council received $1.7 million of corporate contributions by 1977, almost double its 1971 total of $910,000. The National Strategy Information Center received $1.1 million in contributions in 1976, almost double its 1971 contributions of $620,000.[50] These increased business contributions coincided with a surge in business support for the Committee on the Present Danger, which saw its influence escalate by the late 1970s and early 1980s. However, the committee's support base, as we have seen, was much more diversified—led by a range of financial, oil, and manufacturing interests with increasing investments in the less developed world.

Tracing the influence of the CPD on the Reagan military budget is a difficult challenge and includes the problem of disentangling the ideological tendencies of Reagan policymakers from the particular motivations of well-connected interest groups. We recognize that determining causality in foreign policy is also fraught with problems, given that many foreign policy decisions are undoubtedly overdetermined. Nevertheless, we can still appreciate the disproportionate influence wielded by the CPD by noting the abundance of former CPD officials who held high-level foreign policy positions within the administration. As Robert Scheer of the *Los Angeles Times* commented: "The personnel and perspectives of the Committee are represented amply on the Reagan foreign policy team. Reagan himself belonged to the 150 member committee, and 23 other members now hold top positions in his administration. The list reads like a Who's Who of the Reagan Administration."[51]

The committee's influence coincided with the split among the liberal internationalist elite previously committed to détente with the Soviets as a way to open the markets of Eastern Europe to U.S.-based trade and investment. By the late 1970s, however, U.S. firms were less enamored of the possibilities of the Eastern bloc market for several reasons. First, Western European governments had helped ensure that Western European manufacturing and financial interests had secured the vast majority of trade and investment opportunities in the East, leaving U.S.-based firms at a disadvantage. Second, U.S.-based investment and commercial banking firms—led by Dillon, Read; Goldman, Sachs; and Citibank—along with U.S. oil firms, had become increasingly dependent on business deals in the less developed world, the Middle East being the most important region. The instability in the Middle East led these firms to explicitly endorse increases in the military budget, especially conventional weapons and personnel that could effectively protect U.S. investments in the region.

The CPD lobbied aggressively for an expansion of military spending in conventional force deployment targeted for the Middle East. According to statistical data compiled by John Boies, there was a consistent correlation between CPD lobbying activities and increased expenditures on a wide range of conventional weapons, including ships, armored vehicles, guided missiles, and electronics and electrical equipment whose use was "necessary for effective force projection into the lesser developed world."[52] The CPD lobbied for a Rapid Deployment Force to help increase U.S. troop response to Middle Eastern crises, as well as ships and tanks later deployed in the region. As Boies notes: "Not only does the political action of the New Right increase aggregate expenditures on the military, but elite social movement political action and corporate income from assets abroad influence the allocation of weapons expenditures across categories of weapons. The data provides good support for the expected role of elite political activities and of economic interests abroad in the allocation of military expenditures."[53]

Several factors converged in the late 1970s to make the Middle East a more important location for U.S.-based multinationals. First, for U.S. investment and commercial banks, the Middle East generated a consistent surplus of capital investment that helped compensate for losses elsewhere—especially important with the emergence of the Latin American debt crisis of the early 1980s. Second, U.S. commercial banks were increasingly important sources of lending to U.S. oil firms, especially during the 1970s and early 1980s, when borrowing by twenty-four major oil companies increased 2.75 times.[54] The burgeoning debt was used to finance everything from the acquisition of oil companies, such as Chevron's 1984 takeover of Gulf Oil, to increased exploration and drilling during the late 1970s and early 1980s. Oil firms were increasingly dependent on lucrative marketing and distribution contracts from the Middle East to finance their debts, giving rise to increased political concerns about the stability of the region, from both commercial banks and their oil company clients.

However, despite this support for increased military spending from U.S.-based multinational corporations with investment stakes in the Middle East, other U.S. firms were much more preoccupied with the effects of the increased internationalization of the U.S. economy on their market share and profitability. The later Reagan presidency, as well as the presidencies of Bush and Clinton, would be preoccupied with enhancing the competitive position of U.S. export and foreign investment interest through regional and multilateral trade agreements.

THE POLITICAL ECONOMY OF TRADE

During its first term, the Reagan administration implemented far-reaching changes in the military and social welfare budgets that reflected particular concerns of a diverse corporate constituency, in addition to the ideological propensities of various White House and cabinet officials. Although there was broad agreement among U.S.-based multinational corporations regarding cuts in social programs and considerable business support for increased military spending, there were notable divisions on trade policy. These divisions intensified as the tight money policies of the Reagan administration increased the internationalization of the U.S. economy. Such internationalization is reflected in both the increased financial flows to the United States and the increased imports of goods and services that were, in part, by-products of the overvalued dollar. Multinational firms that were dependent on exports and had been steadily losing market share were weakened further by the rise of the dollar in the early 1980s, a trend that undercut their ability to export to foreign markets. In response, some multinationals increased their appeals for state protection and others pushed for regional trade agreements that would enhance their global competitiveness by discriminating against foreign rivals. Finally, for those multinationals that were dependent on both foreign direct investment and trade and able to maintain their international competitiveness, the preferred option was not protection but the further liberalization of trade through GATT.

Generally, then, U.S. firms split into three camps by the 1980s that reflected the different effects of globalization on firm profitability and market share. We define these three camps as multilateralists, regionalists, and protectionists.[55] The product life cycle remains a good gauge for understanding the extent to which various U.S.-based corporations have supported or opposed free trade during the 1980s, and it provides a useful analytic tool for separating various U.S.-based business interests into three political camps that illustrate the shifting nature of business conflict during the decade. Firms that exhibit a high degree of multinationality in the product life cycle—in other words, that are highly dependent on foreign trade (both exports and imports) and foreign direct investment across various regions of the world economy—tend to be leading proponents of a multilateral trading regime and opponents of protectionism or discriminatory regionalism. Leading Fortune 500 U.S.-based commercial and investment banks and telecommunications, computer, pharmaceutical, petrochemical, and retailing firms that are both highly competitive and exhibit a high dependence on foreign imports are likely to be the most ardent advocates of multilateralism in U.S. trade policy. We define these firms as multilateralists based on their support for extending the liberalization of trade throughout the globe through such institutions as GATT and their opposition to efforts to restrict movement of goods and services. We are aware that there are numerous distinctions among firms in the same sector, with less competitive and more nationally based firms in all sectors tending to support restrictive trade legislation.

The second group of firms are characterized by their relative dependence on regional foreign direct investment, with trade dependency focused on particular regional markets but with comparatively little global trade dependency. For these firms, production is concentrated on either the North American or European regional markets, and maintaining (or increasing) market share within these regional markets is the key to understanding their political behavior. These firms we identify as regionalists because of their political advocacy of regional trade agreements, especially the Caribbean Basin Initiative and NAFTA, that provided preferential access to the North American market and discriminated against Japanese and European competitors. By the 1980s, U.S.-based auto and electronics firms, faced with rising internationalization of the U.S. market and loss of market share, sought to promote regional trade agreements that would lower their costs of production by allowing for the increased production of component parts in low-wage locations in the Caribbean and Mexico. Regionalist firms in electronics and auto production joined with multilateral firms in supporting the CBI and NAFTA but for different reasons, suggesting the limitations of such coalitions in other trade contexts. Whereas multilateral interests supported these agreements for their liberal trade provisions, regionalist firms supported them for their restrictive investment provisions, as we will show in a detailed pair of case studies.

Other firms that have not entered the product life cycle (i.e., that still produce for the domestic market) and are import-competing industries that are labor-intensive tend to be political nationalists, opposed to both regional and multilateral trade agreements. These firms include producers of a wide range of manufactured products, including textiles, brooms, ceramics, footwear, glassware, luggage, and flat goods, in addition to agricultural producers of dairy goods, fruits, and vegetables, especially asparagus, avocados, canned tomatoes, citrus, sugar, and sugar beets. In the 1970s and 1980s these traditional protectionist industries were joined by other sectors such as steel, machine tools, and transport equipment manufacturers in lobbying for increased protection from foreign imports. Also, defense industries clamored for protection from foreign competition in the area of procurement policies and for retention of trade barriers invoked by special appeals to Congress that granted "national security" protection to select industries facing increased foreign competition. For the Reagan administration and the Republican Party, as well as southern Democrats close to the textile industry, these nationalists and labor-intensive industries were a consistent support base and were able to win significant trade concessions from both Congress and the administration throughout the 1980s.

In textiles, the precedence for protection was well established and, as we have shown, played a strong role in domestic U.S. trade politics throughout the post–World War II period. By the 1980s such protection had increased to the point where the United States had signed bilateral export restraint agreements with forty-six countries or territories. Even though steel producers resisted adopting protectionist policies during most of the 1960s and 1970s, the level of import competition grew dramatically by the late 1970s, when the import share of the U.S. market was 18 percent, up from 2 percent in the late 1950s. By 1982 U.S. steel producers filed more than 100 antidumping and countervailing duty complaints against steel suppliers from eleven countries. In October 1982 the cases against the European Community producers were settled by a voluntary restraint agreement that committed the European Community to limit its exports of steel pipe, tube, and carbon steel.[56] By December 1984 both Congress and the Reagan administration had cooperated to secure a total of fifteen export restraint agreements for the steel industry, lasting five years and covering 80 percent of U.S. imports of steel.[57]

Like the steel industry, leading U.S. firms within the machine tool industry reversed their earlier support for free trade legislation in the midst of increasing import penetration during the late 1970s and early 1980s. By 1983 the leading industrial lobby for the industry, the National Machine Tool Builders' Association (NMTBA), shifted toward a protectionist stance as its firms were faced with the "loss of major export markets, increasing competition in the world machine tool market and in the U.S. market in particular, a recession even more severe than those of the 1970s, and the loss of long-established domestic customers."[58] By 1986, with support from Congress and the Reagan administration, the NMTBA was able to secure voluntary export restraint agreements from Japan that limited exports to the United States of six types of tools to 1981 levels, followed by an agreement from Taiwan that limited standardized conventional tools to 1981 levels and verbal guarantees from Switzerland and West Germany that each would avoid taking advantage of the export restraint agreements signed with Asian countries. Part of the industry's lobbying strategy centered on the "national security" importance of the machine tool industry, with the NMTBA arguing that the machine tool industry deserved the same protection as that afforded to military producers Lockheed and Chrysler.[59]

Despite its free trade rhetoric, the Reagan administration often appeased protectionist interests close to the Republican Party, especially defense contractors and firms perceived to be important to national security interests, such as the machine tool industry. Traditional labor-intensive Republican Party firms in textiles and domestic manufacturing also received significant protectionist legislation from the administration. However, the administration also promised to support efforts to expand U.S. trade through regional trade agreements, endorsed by both regionalists and multilateralists within the business establishment. For multilateralists, in 1986 the administration also began negotiations on the Uruguay Round of GATT, which capital-intensive multinational firms hoped would open up more opportunities for global trade and investment.

By 1982 the Democratic Party was able to win significant business support from capital-intensive multinational firms critical of the Reagan administration's dramatic military buildup and lack of attention to improving trade and economic relations with Europe. Trade unions close to the Democrats criticized the Reagan administration for opposite reasons: that it had not protected U.S. jobs and that it had allowed labor legislation to be dismantled in favor of business interests. The Democratic Party was increasingly inclined to put business concerns first, however, as reflected in the disparity between the soft-money contributions given to the party by corporate firms versus labor organizations. Most notably in the Democratic camp were U.S. business interests with a strong stake in Western Europe, led by Bank of America, Chase Manhattan Bank, IBM, Xerox, and MCA, all of which extended corporate donations to the Democrats during the 1982 congressional elections and the 1984 presidential campaign.

In the case of European-oriented firms such as IBM, there was increased criticism of Reagan's defense policies, especially U.S. disputes with NATO allies over the construction of a pipeline to carry natural gas from the U.S.S.R., U.S. efforts to limit trade between Western and Eastern Europe (which a number of U.S. business groups continued to support), and the negative effect of high interest rates on European growth.[60] These capital-intensive multinationals were distinguished from the Reagan supporters by their lack of dependence on military spending for profitability and the high priority given to their European investments, as opposed to those in the less developed world. Between 1982 and 1984, these firms were joined by the Rockefeller Foundation and other business elites that channeled money to groups committed to arms control and nuclear issues.

A study of corporate funding for "international security and the prevention of nuclear war" found that over 70 percent of the financing for arms control organizations were provided by multinationally oriented foundations, including MacArthur, Carnegie, Ford, Rockefeller, and Alton Jones, all of which had considerable corporate backing.[61] A whole range of U.S.-based firms with considerable European investments began to criticize the Reagan Administration's military policies in Latin America. Meeting in Miami in 1984, these business interests, including Rockefeller Brothers Fund, Chemical Bank, IBM, Time, and Coca-Cola, issued a strong criticism of the administration's reliance on troop deployment and increased military aid to solve the region's problems.[62]

Other U.S. multinationals, a combination of multilateralists and regionalists, argued that the Reagan administration had not done enough to promote U.S. investment and trade opportunities. Regionalist and multilateral U.S. firms in electronics, pharmaceuticals, and commercial banking formed the Caribbean/Central American Action (CCAA) as early as 1979 and relied on close ties to the Reagan White House to promote the Caribbean Basin Initiative of 1983. Similarly, U.S. business interests, especially telecommunications, electronics, and autos, helped finance the U.S.-Mexico Business Council in 1986 to lobby for NAFTA. Since many of the structural and economic trends that led to corporate support for these agreements materialized in the late 1970s and 1980s, especially during the Reagan presidency, the remainder of the chapter will examine the origins of business support for such agreements and conclude with an examination of future patterns of business conflict in the wake of these regional agreements.

THE INTERNATIONALIZATION OF THE U.S. MARKET

U.S. auto and electronics firms faced vigorous competition from their Japanese counterparts in the 1980s, which provided the major impetus for industrial restructuring. Prior to 1982, Japanese auto firms did not have a single production plant outside Japan. Instead, led by Toyota, they relied on a "lean production" strategy that emphasized exports to the developed market economies as a method for increasing market share. Innovations in Japanese production provided formidable challenges to U.S. car manufacturers, which had been late in shifting from mass production methods to a more flexible production system. As Table 6.1 indicates, Japanese firms were able to increase their penetration of world markets through 1984.

The production strategy employed by Japanese firms involved a number of interrelated changes designed to increase output at considerably lower costs. They included the introduction of sophisticated computer technology to facilitate the designing and engineering phases of production, the

Table 6.1 Japanese Car Exports, 1974–1984

Importing Region	1974	1984	Rate of Increase
North America	796	1,990	2.5
European Community	235	790	3.4
Other Europe	109	240	2.2
Asia	177	450	2.5
Oceania	225	230	1.0
Latin America	84	210	2.5
Africa	101	90	0.9
Total	1,700	4,000	2.4

Source: Robert Gwynne, "The Third World Motor Vehicle Industry," in Christopher J. Law, ed., *Restructuring the Global Automobile Industry* (London: Routledge, 1991), p. 69.

relatively low parts inventory achieved by reliance on close functional relationships between customers and suppliers, the multiple tasks performed by Japanese auto workers to enhance productivity and inhibit the formation of independent unions, and protection from the Japanese government, which limits access to foreign firms and practices discriminatory intervention in favor of domestic producers. Prior to 1982, this productive system was combined with an emphasis on export promotion to penetrate successfully the developed market economies.[63]

Such import penetration posed a considerable challenge to U.S. auto firms, which saw their competitive advantage eroding in the U.S. market. In response, U.S. auto firms most severely affected by Japanese imports joined the United Auto Workers union to pressure the government to negotiate voluntary export restraints with Japan. U.S. manufacturers and labor union officials hoped these restraints would help create a level playing field in the U.S. market by encouraging Japanese companies to reduce exports in favor of foreign direct investment. In this regard, they hoped that Japanese direct investors would then have to operate under the same conditions as U.S. companies.

Japanese companies' newfound interest in foreign direct investment went well beyond the expectations of U.S. business and government elites, however. From 1982 to 1989, Japanese auto firms began establishing production plants in the U.S. market, a move that provided further challenges to U.S. companies. Table 6.2 indicates the extent of this investment.

Japanese firms in consumer electronics were also increasing their foreign direct investment in the United States, a trend that had begun in the 1970s with the television industry (where it had its greatest impact) and continued in the 1980s with the video recorder industry. The ability of Japanese producers to penetrate the consumer electronics market is based on the following five characteristics:

Table 6.2 Japanese-Owned or -Operated Assembly Plants in the United States

	Start-up	Production Capacity	Production Employees
Honda	1982	500,000	4,800
Nissan	1983	220,000	3,200
NUMMI (Toyota and GM)	1984	250,000	2,500
Mazda	1987	240,000	3,500
Toyota	1988	200,000	3,500
Diamond-Star Motors (Mitsubishi and Chrysler joint venture)	1988	240,000	2,900
Subaru/Isuzu	1989	120,000	1,700

Source: R. R. Rehder, "Japanese Transplants: A New Model for Detroit," *Business Horizons* 31, 1 (1995): 52–61.

1. labor costs one-half or one-third as high as those in Germany and the United Kingdom
2. designs requiring up to 30 percent fewer components than Western European or U.S. sets because of a greater use of integrated circuits
3. automation in the assembly of sets (for 65 to 80 percent of total components used, compared with 0 to 15 percent automation in German and UK plants), meaning that a Japanese company could produce a color television set in an average of 1.9 man-hours, compared with 3.9 in West Germany and 6.1 in Great Britain
4. large-scale plant operations
5. superior-quality components[64]

Historically, the Japanese consumer electronics companies, like their automobile counterparts, have relied on these advantages to export to European and U.S. markets. However, the proliferation of voluntary export restraints, coupled with the development of new technology, made it necessary and profitable to engage in foreign direct investments in the United States and Europe. The 1970s saw a wave of Japanese companies invest in television manufacturing plants in the United States, "totally changing the character of the American television industry, as Sony built a plant at San Diego in 1972; Matsushita and Sanyo bought out existing U.S.-owned TV plants by 1976; and Mitsubishi, Toshiba, Sharp and Hitachi have all launched U.S. factories."[65] As a result, only Zenith remained as an indigenous U.S. manufacturer by the end of the 1970s. By the 1980s, Japanese firms were repeating this wave of foreign investment in the area of video recorders.

To summarize, the primary factors causing this new trend of Japanese foreign direct investment in automobiles and electronics were threefold. First, Japanese companies relied on foreign direct investment to overcome the obstacles to import penetration of the United States. Second, new technologies allowed Japanese firms to tailor vehicles to consumer demand, making it more imperative and cost-efficient to locate in foreign markets. Third, especially by the mid-1980s, the value of the yen was high against the dollar, allowing for monetary opportunity to invest in production plants in the United States.

U.S. firms began to shift production strategies in an effort to withstand the Japanese competitive threat. In order to understand these strategies, one must remember that U.S. firms are fully internationalized themselves, with important stakes in the European and U.S. markets. The broad goals of U.S. firms have included three primary tasks, which are analytically distinct: (1) maintaining a competitive position in the European market, (2) maintaining a competitive postition in the U.S. market, and (3) eventually penetrating the relatively closed Japanese market. In the case of Western Europe, the strategies employed by U.S. firms were directed at rationalizing production and supply networks to lower cost and increase efficiency, the goal being to increase production and sales within Europe itself. In the case of the United States, U.S. producers sought to rely increasingly on supply and production networks in Canada and Mexico in an effort to gain a competitive advantage in the U.S. market.

Thus U.S. auto and electronics firms were solidly behind the free trade agreements with Mexico and Canada, which they saw as essential regional locations for improving their production system in the U.S. market. The recent investments by U.S. auto firms in Canada and Mexico represent an effort to integrate production for the U.S. market via the expansion of low-cost supply networks and production facilities. Thus regional trade agreements are preferred to GATT in meeting the competitive challenges of global competition. Meanwhile, electronics firms have lobbied heavily for both the CBI and NAFTA, reflecting their global production strategies in the face of the internationalization of the U.S. market in the 1980s.

The next sections of this chapter examine the economic and political strategies of U.S.-based auto firms in pursuing regional integration. These firms were part of a political coalition that began lobbying for NAFTA in 1986 as part of an effort to increase the regional economic integration already under way. At the same time, electronics firms pursued both the CBI and NAFTA as part of their regional integration strategy. In each case, the strategy pursued represented a significant departure from the framework of GATT, as we will explain in the final section of this chapter.

ELECTRONIC FIRMS AND THE CBI

Beginning in 1979, the Caribbean–Central American Action lobby, representing the interests of 90 percent of the Fortune 500 firms with investments in the Caribbean Basin, formed to lobby U.S. governmental officials to ease trade restrictions on products imported from Caribbean Basin countries. The formation of the CCAA anticipated and supported the efforts of the Reagan administration to promote the Caribbean Basin Initiative, which lowered tariffs on selected manufactured goods exported from qualified Caribbean Basin countries. The CCAA took an active role in drafting the CBI, with U.S.-based electronics and pharmaceutical firms realizing substantial tariff reduction on products produced and exported by affiliates or subcontractors in the region.[66]

U.S. electronics firms viewed the CBI as a means to discriminate against foreign competitors in the U.S. market. The agreement allowed producers of integrated circuits and metal oxide semiconductors to export partially produced products from the region duty free. These provisions complemented the duty-free provisions already established in Caribbean Basin free trade zones. In addition, the CBI implemented a low and flexible local content requirement that gave preferential treatment to U.S. firms. Eligibility for duty-free treatment was contingent on 35 percent of the product being produced in the Caribbean Basin, of which 15 percent could be accounted for by U.S. materials.

U.S.-based electronics firms joined with pharmaceutical firms and producers of baseball gloves, belts, fabricated metals, and food processors to lobby for the CBI. Electronics firms saw the agreement as a way to regionalize their operations by relying on low-cost, partial production in the Caribbean Basin to compete for the U.S. market. U.S.-controlled and/or operated firms accounted for five of the top ten imports from the region eligible for duty-free treatment.[67]

U.S. electronics firms, including Texas Instruments, Dataram, Kay Electronics, Beckman, and AVX Ceramics, were attracted to the Caribbean Basin in the mid-1970s as an export location for low-cost access to the U.S. market. From 1973 to 1978, for example, each of these firms abandoned previous low-wage havens for the more favorable economic conditions offered by Caribbean Basin countries. Dataram moved to El Salvador the year it closed down its Malaysian operation. Texas Instruments began production in El Salvador the same year it closed its Curacao plant. Finally, both Beckman and AVX moved their plants from Ireland to El Salvador to take advantage of cheap labor, proximity to the North American market, and numerous export incentives.

The move of U.S. multinationals into El Salvador was part of a broader trend of corporations subcontracting part of their operations to the Caribbean Basin for the U.S. market. In Haiti 150 U.S. and 40 other foreign-owned firms in electronics, computer parts, and clothing were producing for the U.S. market between 1975 and 1981, when the dollar value of international subcontracting in the Caribbean increased fourfold. In the Dominican Republic during the 1970s, over 50 percent of the products shipped to the United States were assembled by foreign contractors. By the late 1970s, foreign multinationals were increasingly viewing the Caribbean Basin as an important subcontracting area for enhancing international competitiveness and market position.[68]

The Business International Corporation, a consortium of business executives and advisors that offers publications and marketing seminars for corporate executives, has written extensively about the advantages of sourcing in the Caribbean Basin for multinationals competing for access to the U.S. market. In a publication titled *Improving International Competitiveness Through Sourcing in Latin America*, the authors argue that by the late 1970s and early 1980s, the Caribbean Basin had become an increasingly important region for U.S.-based multinationals faced with intensified global competition. The following advantages of the region were noted:

1. proximity to the world's largest and most sophisticated marketplace: North America
2. increased use of export processing zones which offer numerous tax incentives and investment options
3. inexpensive, stable, and skilled labor supply relative to other areas such as the Far East. This was especially true during the 1980s, as the Latin American countries realigned their exchange rates and the dollar itself depreciated relative to other hard currencies.[69]

In addition, U.S. multinationals turned toward sourcing arrangements in the Caribbean Basin to compensate for increased competition from Japanese firms in both the U.S. and the East Asian markets. In the 1950s and 1960s, U.S. foreign direct investment (FDI) dominated the East Asian region. By the early 1970s, Japan acquired what one analyst has termed a "hegemonic" position in FDI throughout East Asia.[70] Japanese corporations accounted for the majority of FDI in South Korea, Taiwan, Malaysia, Thailand, and Indonesia, whereas American FDI continued to lead only in the Philippines, China, and Hong Kong.

Some U.S. multinationals, especially electronics firms, responded by relocating operations closer to the U.S. market. The relocation strategy was especially attractive in the late 1970s and early 1980s. The most substantial benefits accrued to firms engaged in partial production for the U.S. market. As the Business International Corporation noted, by the late 1970s and early 1980s, the Caribbean region offered two distinct advantages for U.S. foreign investors: proximity to the U.S. market and lower wage costs.

These advantages were enhanced by the preferential local content requirements of the CBI, which discriminated against non-U.S. firms.

The battle over CBI reflected the diverse business interests involved in trade legislation. First, there were the regionalist firms represented by electronics companies that saw the agreement as leverage against foreign competition for the U.S. market. Spokespersons for AVX, Dataram, and other U.S. electronics firms testified before Congress that the CBI would give them a necessary competitive advantage against Japanese and European firms for access to the U.S. market. These firms saw CBI as further institutionalizing an ongoing trend of corporate relocation and restructuring necessary to reverse declining profitability and intensified global competition. As a result, U.S.-based electronics firms lobbied for local content laws that would give preferential treatment to U.S. firms.

The second group of firms in favor of CBI were the multilateralists in pharmaceuticals, services, and banking. These firms were more competitive in global markets and did not seek the restrictive local content laws preferred by electronics firms. Instead, they saw the regional trade agreement as complementary to broader efforts to revitalize the multilateralism of GATT on a global scale. They valued the agreement because it allowed for a greater reduction in U.S. tariff barriers, which furthered free trade goals.

Reagan administration officials supported the CBI mainly because it complemented broader security goals in the region. The administration insisted that the largest percentage of CBI money should go to El Salvador, where the administration was actively engaged in bolstering the military regime against rebel insurgents. Therefore, much of the aid attached to CBI reflected the Reagan administration's policy of bolstering a Salvadoran government that was facing an economic and political crisis.

Opponents of the regional trade agreement included domestic firms that stood to lose the most from reducing tariff barriers, especially the domestic textile and clothing industries tied to the national market. An examination of congressional debates over the content of CBI reveals that business nationalists also had some influence on the final legislation. The American Textile Manufacturers Institute and the American Apparel Manufacturers Association joined with the Amalgamated Clothing and Textile Workers Union and the International Ladies' Garment Workers' Union to lobby Congress, especially the Subcommittee on Trade of the House Ways and Means Committee, to maintain import restrictions. These business nationalists and their labor counterparts succeeded in excluding all textile and apparel products from the duty-free provisions of the CBI.[71]

By the late 1980s and early 1990s, many of the same coalitions that had been active in the battle over the CBI would again intervene in the NAFTA debates. An examination of regionalist, multilateral, and nationalist firms active in the NAFTA debate allows us to draw some important conclusions about the prospects for multilateralism in the coming decade.

Auto Firms and NAFTA

The U.S. automobile industry has developed a corporate production strategy that seeks to combat the effects of increased global competition. An important pillar of the strategy is regionalization of production along continental lines. This regionalization has proceeded along three general dimensions involving (1) moving phases of the production process, including the fabrication of engines and transmissions, from the United States to lower-wage sites in Mexico, Brazil, and Argentina (Mexico has become a preferred location since the late 1980s); (2) developing a North American production scheme characterized by knowledge-based or lean production in order to compete better with Japanese rivals for the U.S. market; (3) lobbying for a NAFTA agreement that extends preferential treatment to North American producers in Mexico.[72]

The strategies of U.S. auto firms cannot be separated from the arena of capital-labor relations. U.S. firms facing increased global competition have attempted to reduce labor and supply costs in order to prevent further erosion of market share in the United States. With this in mind, these firms have viewed the relocation of parts of the production process to cheap labor regions as an important strategy in competing with foreign firms for the U.S. market. Through relocation, U.S. firms have been able to take advantage of lower wages in Mexico, Brazil, and Argentina and force numerous concessions from U.S. workers.

From 1970 to 1984, U.S.-based transnationals dramatically increased their investments in plants and equipment in Latin America. According to Ross and Trachte, this trend was related to "a declining rate of profit and to rising price competition from foreign exports."[73] The result is illustrated by data comparing motor vehicle production in the United States to that in Latin America from the early 1970s to 1980. Between 1973 and 1980, the U.S.-to–Latin American ratio of General Motors declined from 28.8 to 1 to 14 to 1; for Ford, from 12.1 to 1 to 4.5 to 1; and for Chrysler, from 14.2 to 1 to 6.4 to 1. Overall, by 1980, "37.2 percent of the total motor vehicle production of the four leading U.S. automobile firms was located abroad."[74]

By the late 1980s, U.S. firms increasingly looked to Mexico as a preferred site for the relocation of motor vehicle production for the U.S. market, including the production of auto parts, engines and transmissions, and finished motor vehicles. A number of factors converged to make Mexico especially attractive to U.S. producers. First, the Mexican government implemented a series of trade liberalization measures that facilitated and encouraged U.S. transnationals to export more finished motor vehicles and auto parts. Second, the Mexican state implemented neoliberal reforms that have resulted in a devaluation of the peso and a reduction in wages in the auto industry and elsewhere, making Mexico more attractive to foreign investors. Finally, U.S.-based auto firms have been able to take advantage of Mexico's proximity to the United States, which has given them a cost edge over European and Japanese competitors in the production of parts and finished vehicles for the U.S. market.[75]

This combination of Mexican incentives and corporate interests has already resulted in dramatic increases in U.S. foreign direct investment in auto parts and assembly in Mexico. For example, during the late 1980s, U.S. auto firms had significantly increased their production and export of auto parts from Mexico to the United States, an increase that continued a trend established by the late 1970s and early 1980s. Hufbauer and Schott have provided statistics on the overall increase in the auto parts trade between the two countries:

> Mexican auto parts trade, almost all of which is with the United States, has grown dramatically. U.S. auto parts imports from Mexico grew from $2.1 billion in 1985 to $3.6 billion in 1989 and now represent 12 percent of total U.S. auto parts imports. U.S. exports of auto parts to Mexico likewise grew by 79 percent, from $1.9 billion to $3.4 billion, over the same period. Most of the recent growth can be attributed to original equipment parts manufactured by the big three and sold in both directions across the border.[76]

In addition to auto parts production, U.S.-based transnationals also have dramatically increased their production of finished vehicles in Mexico. Big Three vehicle production for the first half of 1992 jumped to almost 363,000—29 percent over the same period in 1991. Ford captured first place, followed closely by Chrysler, with GM third. About half of all production of finished vehicles is for export to the U.S. market, and the other half involves production for the Mexican market.[77]

The production of finished vehicles is increasingly being accomplished with the use of knowledge-based or lean sourcing techniques pioneered by the Japanese. This involves a shift to a workplace organization characterized by flexible work rules and job rotation, broadly defined job classifications, quality circles, work teams, and other measures designed to defuse labor-employer tensions and further motivate workers.

At the insitutional level, U.S. auto firms have worked with the Mexican state, especially the Confederation of Mexican Workers, the state's labor party organization, to consolidate the shift to a flexible labor system. This has meant shifting automotive production from Mexico City to northern and central Mexico to lower labor costs and facilitate an export-promotion strategy geared toward low-cost supply for the North American market. As other analysts have noted, U.S. auto companies have attempted to consolidate their control over Mexican labor in order to pursue this flexible production strategy.

At the same time, U.S. firms have asked for dual rules of origin requirements that extend preferential treatment to U.S. firms and discriminate against new entrants into the North American market. In free trade agreements, rules of origin requirements are used to determine what goods were actually produced in the member countries and therefore qualify for preferential treatment. In negotiations over NAFTA, U.S. auto firms insisted on 50 percent rules of origin agreements, which give preferential treatment to firms already established in North America.

The discriminatory measures embedded in regional trade agreements contrast with the multilateralism advocated by GATT. Although clearly allowing for regional trade agreements, GATT established criteria "designed to ensure that free trade arrangements lead, on balance, to growth in world trade and can thus be considered building blocks of a more open world trading system."[78] To the extent that NAFTA institutionalizes preferential treatment for U.S. firms and discriminates against foreign competitors, it can hardly be seen as compatible with the broad principles of GATT. As Preeg has noted,

> The U.S. intent for NAFTA was not directed at . . . tariff circumvention, which is likely to be small in any event, but to limit benefits to Japanese and other foreign direct investment in Mexico, in the automotive, computer and other high-technology sectors. A high level of North American value added, as the rule of origin test, and a narrowly drawn definition of value added constitute a form of performance requirements for foreign investment—ironically, just the kind of trade distorting investment measures the United States was trying to eliminate in the Uruguay Round negotiations.[79]

In fact, NAFTA brought together a coalition of corporate supporters advocating both discriminatory treatment against foreign investors and reduced tariff barriers. On the one hand, foreign direct investors in autos and electronics advocated tough rules of origin requirements that privileged existing market players and penalized late entrants, resulting in what Preeg has called a concept of "high-tech regionalism." On the other hand, multilateralists represented by banks, U.S. exporters, and retailers supported NAFTA for its liberalized trade provisions.

These corporate coalitions came together to lobby for NAFTA against import-competing industries that stood to lose market share if trade was liberalized. Opponents of NAFTA included labor-intensive industries producing footwear, glassware, luggage, brooms, and ceramics and agricultural producers of asparagus, avocados, canned tomatoes, citrus, sugar, and sugar beets. Other powerful critics of NAFTA included labor unions, religious organizations, and consumer and environmental interest groups that feared the consequences of liberalized trade and investment for U.S. labor, Mexican workers, and the environment.[80]

The battle over NAFTA suggested that multilateralists faced stiff opposition in securing a regional trade agreement that was compatible with the multilateralism of GATT. This was true for two reasons. First, corporate supporters of NAFTA included an uneasy alliance of foreign direct investors, multinational banks, and exporters, each of which supported the agreement for different reasons. These interests came together to lobby for NAFTA, but they have often been on opposing sides of the free trade debate in other, nonregional contexts. Second, NAFTA became a lightning rod for popular discontent, influenced by the legacy of corporate-labor battles of the 1980s that resulted in considerable union concessions in autos, steel, and textiles. The concessions were often won as a result of corporate flight or threats to close down plants in lieu of reduced wages and/or benefits.

MULTILATERALISM, REGIONALISM, AND PROTECTIONISM IN THE WAKE OF NAFTA

There are several noticeable trends that have affected trade politics from the late 1970s to the present. The first has been a defection of some multinational firms from the free trade coalition that previously dominated U.S. trade policy. Firms were more likely to defect if they faced the following conditions: increased import competition leading to a loss of market share in the United States and elsewhere, reliance on direct foreign investment geared toward regional markets, and low levels of trade relative to direct foreign investment. U.S.-based electronics and auto firms have geared production around regional markets via foreign direct investment in North America, the EEC, and Asia. The international character of these firms has not meant continued support for multilateralism but instead has resulted in support for regional trading blocs designed to increase protection against foreign competitors. In addition, electronics and auto firms supported nontariff barriers to trade, including voluntary export restraints, throughout the late 1970s and 1980s.

Does this mean an end to the multilateralism of GATT in favor of regional trading blocs? Not necessarily. Another trend in trade politics has been the emergence of antiprotectionist political organizations based among exporters, business and industrial import users, retailers and other trade-related services, and foreign governments of exporting countries. In general, the degree to which firms are dependent on exports as a percentage of overall production is a determining factor in their commitment to antiprotectionism. One well-documented trend in the late 1970s and 1980s was the fact that the U.S. economy as a whole saw substantial increases in trade dependence as a percentage of GNP. This trend meant that certain U.S. firms in selective industries developed a greater interest in antiprotectionist activity.

Since the late 1980s, groups with a high export dependence, including the National Association of Wheat Growers and the American Soybean Association, have increased their antiprotectionist lobbying efforts. However, these efforts tend to lobby selectively against trade restrictions involving particular foreign customers and do not usually involve a defense of multilateralism as a general principle. In addition, certain export-dependent groups, such as cotton growers, have joined the American Textile Manufacturers in lobbying for textile protection. Cotton growers identify their interests with domestic textile producers that would be hurt by free trade measures. The aircraft industry, which is also export dependent, opposed trade restrictions with steel-producing countries, since these countries constituted 21 percent of all aircraft exports and 8 percent of aircraft production. However, aircraft firms had less interest in opposing trade restrictions on countries producing shoes, since only 2 percent of industrial output went to these countries.[81]

The selective nature of antiprotection interests indicates significant limits in the development of an aggressive political coaltion advocating multilateralism. However, other political coalitions have developed over the past twenty years with a more widespread interest in antiprotectionist legislation. These groups tend to be concentrated in retailing and service firms that have a stake in importing automobiles, textiles, and footwear, all targets of protectionist efforts in the 1970s and 1980s. In fact, retailers formed several antiprotectionist coalitions in the 1980s designed to lobby against trade restrictions on textiles, automobiles, and footwear. According to Destler and Odell, retailers were most likely to lobby against trade restrictions under the following conditions:

1. if a particular group of retailers sold primarily to a market niche for which imports were a large share of current supply and domestic substitutes were available only in lesser quantity and at higher prices.
2. if the price elasticity of demand for a major product class was such that the higher prices caused by import restrictions would reduce sales volume substantially.
3. if import curbs were to be imposed quickly and without warning, disrupting the delivery of goods already contracted from overseas sources.[82]

These conditions are fairly narrow and do not imply a generalized coalition prepared to advance multilateralism. In addition, many of the antiprotectionist organizations established by retailers are burdened by "a younger and weaker tradition of collective political action on trade, and the uneasy coexistence of such action with the fierce commercial rivalries that characterize the retail business."[83] Furthermore, most of the lobbying organizations are established at the local level, "aimed at strengthening community ties (and bringing in customers) while avoiding controversial policy stands that might drive them away."[84]

With these limitations in mind, one has to search elsewhere to find stable political coalitions or interests that advocate a generalized commitment to multilateralism. The leading proponents of multilateralism are difficult to identify readily because they often eschew overt lobbying efforts used by earlier antiprotection groups. Instead, multilateralists often work with the executive branch in promoting multilateralism in specific institutional contexts, such as the GATT talks, U.S. bilateral negotiations with foreign governments, and multilateral organizations such as the World Bank and the IMF. The most notable multilateralists include banking and service firms that have numerous financial and trade interests connected to open markets.

The top Fortune 500 U.S.-based banks dramatically expanded their overseas lending throughout the 1970s and 1980s to both foreign governments and foreign firms. Bankers have been consistent proponents of multilateralist policies in negotiations with less developed countries over terms of debt repayment. In addition, bankers have promoted U.S. policies toward Europe designed to maximize trade and foreign investment. Bankers are not as subject to the limitations of sectoral politics as other firms because their capital is more fluid and their interests are tied to a wide range of investments in foreign governments and private firms. As a result, bankers have regularly advocated a commitment to multilateralism consistent with their varied interests in collecting government debts and reaping a return on investments in foreign and U.S.-based multinationals.[85]

With these general observations as a starting point, we must note that not all bankers are vigorous proponents of multilateralism. The following institutions, however, are more likely to support multilateralism: (1) commercial banks that are thoroughly multinational in character, dispersing loans around the world to both foreign governments and foreign firms; (2) investment banks linked to multinational firms heavily dependent on foreign trade relative to foreign investment; and (3) bank ideologically committed to multilateralism as a means to facilitate debt repayment from governments in the less developed world.

The fact that not all bankers will be committed to multilateralism weakens the potential free trade coalition. In fact, a striking development that may illuminate future trade patterns is the extent to which multilateralists in the banking community have been increasingly isolated from other multinational firms in recent decades as support for multilateralism has steadily eroded. The only trade agreement around which a wide range of multinational firms has been able to coalesce has been NAFTA, where such diffuse organizations as the Chambers of Commerce, the National Association of Manufacturers, and the Business Advisory Council have taken strong positions in favor of the agreement.

However, the extent of interest group agreement around NAFTA is a product of the regional nature of the agreement, which attracts different multinationals for different reasons. Whereas multilateralists see it as an important step for reinvigorating GATT, regionalists view it as additional leverage against foreign competition. The likelihood of such a powerful free trade coalition emerging in another, nonregional context is minimal at best. Equally interesting is that even with such a high degree of unity in the corporate community over NAFTA, the agreement is politically divisive, with nationalists being led by the unlikely bedfellows of organized labor and Ross Perot in opposing the accord. If, in fact, multilateralism is in part the product of interest group pressure, then the future of the global trading regime looks increasingly shaky in the 1990s.

NOTES

1. The Reagan campaign of 1979 borrowed from many of the same financial and corporate elites who had supported the Goldwater campaign in 1964. At its core was a group of western businessmen that included Jack Wrather, an independent oilman and director of several corporations, among them Continental Airlines, Capitol Records, and Muzak; Joseph Coors, the archreactionary head of Coors Brewery and a major donor to right-wing foundations, including the Hoover Institution; Earle Jorgenson, a director of the Jorgenson Steel Company, Northrup, Kerr-McGee Oil, and the American Iron and Steel Institute and a trustee of Cal Tech; William Simon, former treasury secretary under Nixon, and later served on the directorship of Dart Industries, Citibank, Xerox, and the Hoover Institution. By 1979 Simon was one of the ideological giants of the corporate right as president of the Olin Foundation, which aggressively financed conservative authors throughout the later part of the decade. Also important to Reagan was foreign policy adviser Richard Allen, whose support for dramatic increases in military spending can be traced to his close ties to pro-Israeli lobbies. Allen, like many other Reagan advisers and, later, policy officials, was a member of the Committee on the Present Danger's executive committee, a lobbying arm for multinational firms, domestic military contractors, and former Pentagon officials who championed dramatic increases in military spending. For useful background, see Philip Burch, "Reagan, Bush and Right-Wing Politics," in Paul Zarembka, ed., *Research in Political Economy* (Greenwich, CT: JAI Press, 1997).

2. For an account of the increasing internationalization of the U.S. economy and the corresponding growth of the political power of U.S.-based international finance, see Jeff Frieden, *Banking on the World: The Politics of American International Finance* (New York: Harper and Row, 1987), esp. pp. 196–246. For the growth of international political organizations linked to international finance and influential in promoting a neoliberal agenda, see Stephen Gill, *American Hegemony and The Trilateral Commission* (Cambridge: Cambridge University Press, 1990), esp. pp. 220–231. For a discussion of the increased structural position of

international finance in U.S. political economy, with details of the corporate inter-locks between manufacturing and financial firms, see Maurice Zeitlin, *The Large Corporation and Contemporary Classes* (New Brunswick, NJ: Rutgers University Press, 1989).

3. For details of increased corporate support for neoliberal think tanks dur-ing the 1970s and 1980s and their links to the Reagan and Bush administrations, see Amy Ansell, *Unraveling the Right: The New Conservatism in American Thought and Politics* (Boulder, CO: Westview Press, 1997).

4. For the political causes of corporate relocation strategies, see Robert Ross and Kent Trachte, *Global Capitalism: The New Leviathan* (Albany: State Univer-sity of New York Press, 1990), esp. pp. 62–114. For an extended discussion and ap-plication of the falling rate of profit and its implications for Fortune 500 firms, see Michael Webber and David Rigby, *The Golden Age Illusion: Rethinking Postwar Capitalism* (New York: Guilford Press, 1996), pp. 291–383.

5. For an overview of corporate strategies to reduce their costs, including re-location strategies and political mobilization against trade unions, see David Gor-don, *Fat and Mean: The Corporate Squeeze of Working Americans and the Myth of Managerial Downsizing* (New York: Free Press, 1996), pp. 204–237.

6. See Joyce Kolko, *Restructuring the World Economy* (New York: Pantheon, 1988), p. 226.

7. For a detailed history of the removal of capital controls in various Euro-pean countries, see Eric Helleiner, *States and the Reemergence of Global Finance: From Bretton Woods to the 1990s* (Ithaca, NY: Cornell University Press, 1994), pp. 169–191.

8. For a detailed account of renegotiating the terms of repaying the debt, see Howard Lehman, *Indebted Development: Strategic Bargaining and Economic Ad-justment in the Third World* (New York: St. Martin's Press, 1993).

9. For evidence of the influence and interest of international financial elites on the tight money policy of the Reagan administration, see Henry Nau, "Where Reaganomics Works," *Foreign Policy* 57 (Winter 1984–1985): 14–37.

10. Gordon, *Fat and Mean*.

11. On the regional mobility and its effects on the U.S. Northeast, see Barry Bluestone and Bennett Harrison, *The Deindustrialization of America: Plant Clos-ings, Community Abandonment and the Dismantling of Basic Industry* (New York: Basic Books, 1982).

12. For the best account of the tremendous shift in corporate donations from progressive to conservative foundations and think tanks, see John Saloma III, *Ominous Politics: The New Conservative Labyrinth* (New York: Hill and Wang, 1984).

13. Thomas Ferguson and Joel Rogers, *Right Turn: The Decline of the De-mocrats and the Future of American Politics* (New York: Hill and Wang, 1986), pp. 130–137.

14. Ibid., pp. 20–21.

15. For details of the marketing and distribution activities of U.S.-based oil firms in the Middle East, see Ronald W. Cox, "The Military-Industrial Complex and U.S. Foreign Policy," in Amy Ansell, ed., *Unraveling the Right* (Boulder, CO: Westview Press, 1997).

16. For details of labor-intensive firms in Central America supporting in-creases in U.S. spending in the region, see Ronald W. Cox, *Power and Profits: U.S. Policy in Central America* (Lexington: University Press of Kentucky, 1994); for the Middle East, see John L. Boies, *Buying for Armageddon: Business, Society and*

Military Spending Since the Cuban Missile Crisis (New Brunswick, NJ: Rutgers University Press, 1994), pp. 125–137.

17. The best account of the Committee on the Present Danger is Jerry Sanders, *Peddlers of Crisis: The Committee on the Present Danger and the Politics of Containment* (Boston: South End Press, 1983).

18. For an overview of investment trends, see Robert Wade, "Globalization and Its Limits," in Suzanne Berger and Ronald Dore, eds., *National Diversity and Global Capitalism* (Ithaca, NY: Cornell University Press, 1996), pp. 60–88.

19. A good case study of regionalist business firms supporting the CBI is Emilio Pantojas-Garcia, "The United States Caribbean Basin Initiative and the Puerto Rican Experience," *Latin American Perspectives* 12: 105–128. For NAFTA, see Margaret Commins, "From Security to Trade in U.S.–Latin American Relations: Explaining U.S. Support for a Regional Trade Agreement with Mexico," International Studies Association Annual Conference, unpubl. paper, University of North Carolina–Chapel Hill, 1992.

20. Commins, "From Security to Trade in U.S.–Latin American Relations."

21. On the politics behind the tax cut, see Robert S. McIntyre and Dean C. Tipps, *Inequity and Decline: How the Reagan Administration Tax Policies Are Affecting the American Taxpayer and Economy* (Washington, DC: Center on Budget Priorities, 1983), pp. 13–14.

22. Ferguson and Rogers, *Right Turn,* p. 121.

23. Citizens for Tax Justice, "Corporate Taxpayers and Corporate Freeloaders," (Washington, DC: August 1985), p. 2.

24. Kevin Phillips, *The Politics of Rich and Poor* (New York: Random House, 1990), pp. 82–83.

25. For the details of the spending cuts, see John Palmer and Isabel Sawhill, eds. *The Reagan Record* (Cambridge, MA: Bullinger, 1984), Table 6.1.

26. Ferguson and Rogers, *Right Turn,* p. 131.

27. Ibid.

28. See the U.S. House Committee on Government Operations, *Delay, Slowness in Decisionmaking, and the Case Backlog at the National Labor Relations Board,* 98th Congress, 2nd session, 1984, Report 98, pp. 17–22.

29. Ibid.

30. For a good account of the financial interests close to the Federal Reserve, see William Greider, *Secrets of the Temple: How the Federal Reserve Runs the Country* (New York: Simon and Schuster, 1987), pp. 11–47.

31. Nau, "Where Reaganomics Works."

32. Greider, *Secrets of the Temple,* p. 447.

33. For the administration's consultation with the Chamber of Commerce, see Paul C. Roberts, *The Supply-Side Revolution* (Cambridge: Cambridge University Press, 1984), p. 225.

34. For a discussion of the emergence of a transnational class committed to deregulation of capital markets, see Robert Pringle, "Financial Markets and Governments," Working Paper no. 57 (Helsinki: World Institute for Development Economics Research, 1987).

35. Helleiner, *States and the Reemergence of Global Finance,* p. 148.

36. For an account of the influence of a transnational class, led by the financial sector, on the policies of advanced industrial states during the late 1970s and 1980s, see Robert Cox, *Production, Power and World Order: Social Forces in the Making of History* (New York: Columbia University Press, 1987), pp. 359–368. See also William Robinson, *Promoting Polyarchy: Globalization, U.S. Intervention and Hegemony* (New York: Cambridge University Press, 1996), pp. 1–72.

37. Koichi Hamada and Hugh Patrick, "Japan and the International Monetary Regime," in Takashi Inogushi and Daniel Okimoto, eds., *The Political Economy of Japan*, Vol. 2, *The Changing International Context* (Stanford, CA: Stanford University Press, 1988). Also see Stephen Marris, *Deficits and the Dollar* (Washington, DC: Institute for International Economics, 1985), p. 44.

38. I. M. Destler and Randall Herring, *Dollar Politics: Exchange Rate Policymaking in the United States* (Washington, DC: Institute for International Economics, 1989), pp. 29–30.

39. A creditors advisory committee was formed immediately after Mexican officials announced their inability to service their debt. The committee consisted of the following U.S.-based banks: Citibank, Chase Manhattan, Chemical Bank, Morgan Guaranty Trust, Bank of America, Bankers Trust, and Manufacturers Hanover. See Greider, *Secrets of the Temple,* pp. 570–573.

40. As documented earlier in the chapter, Citibank had originally supported the tight money policy of the Fed, but it was now apparent that this policy greatly exacerbated the debt crisis. Still, Wall Street continued to support variations of the tight money policy, including another four-year term for the architect of that policy, Paul Volcker, who was the overwhelming favorite of Wall Street.

41. For complete data, see William Stant, "Business Conflict and U.S. Trade Policy," in Ronald W. Cox, ed., *Business and the State in International Relations* (Boulder, CO: Westview Press, 1996), p. 85.

42. For a discussion of these protectionist measures, see J. Michael Finger, "Trade Policies in the United States," in Dominick Salvatore, ed., *National Trade Policies* (New York: Greenwood Press, 1992), pp. 93–101.

43. All data here are from the Association of the U.S. Army, *FY 1986 Defense Budget* (Arlington, VA: AUSA, 1986), pp. 12, 22, and Tables 5 and 6. Also see William Kaufman, *The 1985 Defense Budget* (Washington, D.C.: The Brookings Institution, 1984).

44. The information about the Committee on the Present Danger is drawn from Boies, *Buying for Armageddon,* pp. 60–61.

45. For a good discussion of the Carter military budget, see David Skidmore, *Reversing Course* (Nashville: Vanderbilt University Press, 1996), p. 49.

46. Ibid., pp. 137–138.

47. Boies, *Buying for Armageddon,* p. 72.

48. Skidmore, *Reversing Course.*

49. For a good overview of oil firms in the Middle East, see Zuhayr Mikdashi, *Transnational Oil: Issues, Policies and Perspectives* (New York: St. Martin's Press, 1986).

50. Skidmore, *Reversing Course.*

51. Quoted in Committee on the Present Danger, *Can America Catch Up? The United States–Soviet Military Balance* (Washington, DC: Committee on the Present Danger, 1985), p. 11.

52. Boies, *Buying for Armageddon,* p. 119.

53. Ibid.

54. Mikdashi, *Transnational Oil.*

55. The following discussion draws from Ronald W. Cox, "Corporate Coalitions and Industrial Restructuring: Explaining Regional Trade Agreements," *Competition and Change* 1, 1 (1995): 13–30, reprinted by permission of Gordon and Breach Publishers.

56. Finger, "Trade Places in the United States," p. 95.

57. Gary Hufbauer, Diane T. Berliner, and Kimberly Elliott, *Trade Protection in the United States: 31 Case Studies* (Washington, DC: Institute for International Economics, 1986), p. 173.

58. Glenn Fong, "Export Dependence Versus the New Protectionism: Constraints on Trade Policy in the Industrial World" (Ph.D. dissertation, Cornell University, 1984), pp. 168–169.

59. Ronald Gutfleish, "Machine Tools," Chapter 7, in "Why Protectionism? U.S. Corporate and State Responses to a Changing World Economy" (Ph.D. dissertation, University of California–Berkeley, 1987), p. 315.

60. Ferguson and Rogers, *Right Turn,* p. 147.

61. This data comes from the Forum Institute, "Search for Security: A Guide to Grantmaking in International Security and the Prevention of Nuclear War" (Washington, DC: The Forum Institute, July 1985), Tables 1 and 4.

62. For details of the debates between capital-intensive and labor-intensive firms over U.S. policy in Central America, see Cox, *Power and Profits.*

63. For an overview of these trends, see James M. Rubenstein, "The Impact of Japanese Investment in the United States," in Christopher J. Law, ed., *Restructuring the Global Automobile Industry* (London: Routledge, 1991), Chapter 5.

64. Peter Dicken, *Global Shift* (New York: Guilford Press, 1992), p. 340.

65. Ibid.

66. Much of the following account is based on information contained in bimonthly newsletters published by the Caribbean/Central American Action organization (now the Caribbean/Latin American Action), in addition to material from Cox, *Power and Profits.*

67. See Pantojas Garcia, "The United States' Caribbean Basin Initiative and the Puerto Rican Experience."

68. For a summary of this trend, see Business International Corporation, *Improving International Competitiveness Through Sourcing in Latin America* (New York: BIC, 1989).

69. Ibid., pp. 2–4.

70. See William Nestor, *Japan's Growing Predominance over the World Economy* (New York: St. Martin's Press, 1990), especially Chapter 4.

71. For an account of these business conflicts, see the Caribbean/Central American Action report, "A Briefing on the CBI and Legislative History," August 7, 1989.

72. For a good discussion of these trends, see Lorraine Eden and Maureen Appel Molot, "Continentalizing the North American Auto Industry," in Ricardo Grinspun and Maxwell Cameron, eds., *The Political Economy of North American Free Trade* (New York: St. Martin's Press, 1993), pp. 297–313.

73. Ross and Trachte, *Global Capitalism,* p. 124.

74. Ibid.

75. For a detailed exposition of these trends, see Sidney Weintraub, Luis Rubio, and Alan Jones, eds., *U.S.-Mexican Industrial Integration* (Boulder, CO: Westview Press, 1991).

76. Gary Hufbauer and Jeffrey Schott, *The North American Free Trade Agreement* (Washington, DC: Institute for International Economics, 1992), p. 213.

77. Betsy Lordan, "Wheels of Fortune," *U.S./Latin Trade* 34, 1 (July 1993): 66.

78. Ernest Preeg, "The Compatibility of Regional Economic Blocs and GATT," in Sidney Weintraub, ed., *Free Trade in the Western Hemisphere* (London: Sage Periodicals Press, 1993), p. 165.

79. Ibid., p. 167.

80. For an overview of these divisions, see Margaret Commins, "Interest Group Competition and NAFTA" (unpublished manuscript, University of North Carolina–Chapel Hill, 1992).

81. I. M. Destler and John S. Odell, *Anti-Protection: Changing Forces in United States Trade Politics* (Washington, DC: Institute for International Economics, 1987), p. 40.

82. Ibid., pp. 50–51.

83. Ibid., p. 56.

84. Ibid.

85. For a general overview of the multilateralism of segments of the banking establishment, see Frieden, *Banking on the World.*

7

Conclusion:
The 1990s and Beyond

DEMOCRATIC DRIFT AND ELITE MASTERY

An observable pattern of twentieth-century U.S. electoral politics is that after the rigors of war, the voters have removed the party of war. Woodrow Wilson was exchanged for Warren Harding at the end of World War I. The New Deal lost its congressional majority in 1946. After Korea, Truman was ousted in favor of Eisenhower and a Republican Congress. Vietnam cost LBJ the possibility of a second full term. At the end of the Cold War, Democrats regained the presidency and Republicans, Congress, reversing the dominant Cold War–era polarity of divided government.

Walter Lippmann, from whose 1914 critical essay on the limitations of U.S. public opinion and domestic politics this section derives its title, saw the United States as an inward-oriented nation, unwilling to take its global position of leadership and exercise international power.[1] Lippmann, like John Dewey and many other prominent liberal and internationalist intellectuals supported the United States' entry into war in 1917. Lippmann later championed the U.S. cause in the Cold War as well. Yet the voters had re-elected Wilson in 1916 for the very reason that "he kept us out of war."

In U.S. history, only World War II and the Gulf War received consensual popular support. Perhaps in the 1990s public opinion favors a re-emphasis on domestic needs, for butter rather than guns. In a study of the "angry American," Tolchin notes rising insecurity, anxiety about the consequences of economic change, and popular antipathy to globalization.[2] Yet policy in both the Bush and Clinton administrations remained decisively internationalist in trade and military affairs even when it may have been politically costly for both to pursue such an agenda. At least one writer in the business press wonders if Clinton's trade and economic policies will lead to a serious breach between the administration and the rest of the Democratic Party.[3] McWilliams argues, with reference to Clinton's decision to support the Bush-developed NAFTA, that "Clinton allied himself, however wisely, with forces threatening the social world of middle America."[4]

The end of the Cold War brought no peace dividend, no "return to normalcy"; the military-security state built ostensibly to fight the war remains entirely intact. Victory in the Cold War for the United States witnessed no parades, no mass festival of celebration, nor initiation of any new day of civic observance. To the contrary, the end of the 1980s were, superficially at least, a period of what Lippmann viewed as drift, or, as today's less elegantly lettered pundits say, gridlock.

In 1987 the financial markets experienced their worst downturn since 1929 as the federal government absorbed the massive costs of deregulation, competition, and criminality in the savings and loan industry. Real wages continued to decline, profit margins continued to tighten, and foreign competition continued to erode the domestic industrial base. With the onset of recession in the new decade, a deficit-bound government could do little to encourage growth through the Keynesian fiscal techniques that had been employed, admittedly or not, from Roosevelt to Reagan.

In 1991 victory in the Persian Gulf did elicit nationalistic celebrations but left a lingering popular understanding that the war was a mercenary struggle for the oil interests, not democracy. For business elites, however, the Gulf War was a moment of mastery. Diverse interests in finance, oil, and military-industrial interests coalesced in support of U.S. intervention and the maintenance of Cold War levels of military spending.[5] For investment banking the Gulf region is a crucial area of global capital accumulation. U.S.-based petroleum firms have a strong stake in refining and shipping, and defense-related firms have an interest in demonstrating that their product has practical utility.

In the wake of the Gulf War, elites and policy planners have argued U.S. military spending must be predicated on the ability to fight two simultaneous regional wars on a scale similar to that with Iraq's Hussein regime. Military consumption spending in the Clinton administration has not been cut, as many conservatives feared, but instead has been flatlined.[6]

U.S. Defense Expenditures by Fiscal Year (billions of dollars)

1993	313.2
1994	305.7
1995	300.5
1996	298.1
1997	307.5.
1998	297.9 (est.)

It remains to be seen if Congress will stay within the reductions planned by the administration for fiscal year 1998. It is important to bear in mind, however, that these are nominal figures. Military spending is actually decreasing as a portion of the U.S. GDP and may suggest that Marxian analysts, such as Baran and Sweezy, have overemphasized the degree to which U.S. capitalism is dependent on military spending to absorb surplus capital. Nonetheless, by maintaining constant nominal spending, the federal government has also maintained its subsidy to the military-industrial complex through continued purchases of new, advanced military hardware that was designed and planned under Cold War conditions. In other words, the essential reality of military spending is that the U.S. economy is still on a war footing and will remain so for the foreseeable future. In fiscal year 1996 national defense expenditure was 3.5 percent of GDP. For fiscal year 1948, just prior to the Truman-supported Cold War turn in U.S. politics described earlier in this work, defense expenditure was 3.5 percent of GDP. In fiscal year 1997 defense accounted for 3.4 percent of GDP, a new low for the post–World War II period. By contrast, defense expenditure in 1940 was 1.7 percent of GDP.

Savings in the defense budget have been gained primarily by closing bases, forcing middle management (officers) into early retirement, and underpaying workers (enlisted). In other words, the downsizing techniques of the military establishment have been similar to those of contemporary private sector management. The long-term effects on unemployment and poverty rates, community and family systems, and public opinion remain to be seen.

The election of Bill Clinton in 1992 along with a Democratic Congress may have been the last hurrah of the old liberal internationalism.[7] In 1988, 1992, and 1996 the Democratic presidential candidates actually outspent their Republican rivals. First Michael Dukakis, then Clinton increased Democratic campaign financial support from business, especially in the high-technology, entertainment, and finance sectors.[8] In our analysis, this pattern of corporate liberalism illustrates a degree of business support for an activist federal role in such areas as health, vocational training, infrastructure, and public investment in new technologies. The inclusion of progressive economist Robert Reich in the Clinton cabinet also seemed to indicate the possibility after 1992 of an industrial policy that would go beyond military spending stimulus and capital export. However, Reich, the first Democratically appointed labor secretary who was not a product of the labor movement (indeed, Eisenhower had appointed a union president to this position as well), made a well-publicized remark to the effect that it remained an open question whether organized labor had a role to play in the emerging global economy. By the end of 1994, health care reform had failed, increased spending for both old and new infrastructure had been stymied, and the Republicans had captured both houses of Congress for the first time since the election of 1952.

In addition to high levels of military spending, the Clinton administration embraced other essentials of the conservative internationalism of the Reagan period, especially after the 1994 election. For the first time, a part of the New Deal Social Security system was repealed when the AFDC entitlement was removed in 1995 over Clinton's signature. The histrionics of the 1996 government shutdown were masterful re-election politics. With Nixonian panache, Clinton painted House Speaker Newt Gingrich and Republican senator Bob Dole into an extremist corner as the enemies of senior citizens, national parks, veterans, and other worthy beneficiaries of government spending.

The shutdown rejuvenated Clinton's standing in the polls among lower- to middle-income voters. Yet as some Republicans noted at the time, both the Clinton and the congressional Republican fiscal plans included future reductions in Medicaid and Medicare benefit levels, the difference being a matter of timing and degree. For the foreseeable future, the United States will continue to have the least comprehensive welfare state and lowest business taxes in the advanced capitalist societies. In a perverse yet politically expedient negation of John Rawls's theory of justice, attacks continue on the programs that assist the least well off.

After successful re-election, Clinton re-emphasized his internationalist commitments in trade policy. In the first term, regionalist and multilateralist interests triumphed over economic nationalism in Congress with the passage of NAFTA and a further round of GATT agreements that included enhancing the authority of the World Trade Organization. Clinton next sought renewal of the "fast track" trade negotiation authority that had been adopted as part of the 1974 Trade Act. Under this authority, Congress abnegated its right to amend bills that would implement future trade agreements; amendments likely to be added to protect domestic interests. Clinton sought fast track renewal as a prerequisite to further GATT talks as well as expansion of the North American Free Trade zone.

However, in late 1997 a tacit congressional coalition of conservative business nationalists and labor-oriented liberals rejected fast track authority despite Gingrich's support for the president's position. At the time the media depicted the vote as a victory for resurgent labor within the Democratic Party; however, the minority party alone could not have defeated the measure. A faction of Republican nationalists was necessary to the defeat of fast track negotiating authority. Both Clinton and Gingrich face tensions from subordinated nationalist elements within their coalitions.[9]

CONSERVATIVE HEGEMONY AND BUSINESS CONFLICT

The concept of hegemony suggests that power is based on the consent or acquiescence of subaltern groups and that the interests of these groups is given a lesser degree of consideration than those of elites. Conservative coalitions since Reagan have combined corporate interests in lower costs of capital (through lower wages, less public health and safety regulation, and lower taxes on profit) with middle income earners' preference for lower income tax rates. The contradictions within this coalition have been identified by Phillips as a corporate deregulation agenda that provides few if any solutions for declining real wages and middle- and working-class living standards.[10]

The Bush administration was caught in the tensions of its own electoral bloc. On the one hand, the capital market sectors demanded that the deficit be brought under control, even if that meant a tax increase (as long as this increase would fall, of course, on wage and salary earners or, better yet, consumers). On the other hand, the industrial sectors, especially those that were attracted to the supply-side ethos, and Bush's mass base among upper-middle-income voters required as the price of their support that he keep his pledge of no new taxes. The budget settlement of 1991 brought these tensions to the surface and fragmented the Reagan coalition in the run-up to the 1992 election. Fiscal conservative and nationalist resentments of Bush fueled the insurgency of Ross Perot and helped bring about the election of Bill Clinton, despite the many scandals beleaguering the Democrat's campaign.

Additionally, the issue of trade caused further stress in the Republican coalition as Patrick Buchanan's emergence and opposition to NAFTA brought to the fore a new version of old fault lines of the right: an old conservatism of isolationism and economic nationalism that had expressed itself from the 1930s to the beginning of the Cold War in the sharply anti–New Deal wing of the Republican party of which Senator Robert Taft was once the standard bearer. As we have seen, this tradition and those interests were represented by the strident anticommunism of Goldwater and Reagan, until the latter made a crucial internationalist turn in 1980.

Ideologically, this conservative nationalism is antipathetic to liberal multilateralism in both trade (GATT) and security issues (UN) and remains skeptical of the economic agenda of Cold War foreign aid and export promotion policies. After the 1994 elections, conservative nationalists in the Gingrich-led House sought to eliminate or sharply cut funds for such multilateralist-favored programs as USAID and the Export-Import Bank. To a significant extent, however, many industries that in the 1950s had a nationalist political economic interest have pursued export markets for both their products and new capital investment. Thus this sector has tended to move from isolationism to a position of conservative regionalism or even internationalism, favoring the use of U.S. power to repress anticapitalist political tendencies, as in Nicaragua and El Salvador, for example. In foreign economic policy, key national industries such as autos and electronics now increasingly take advantage of low wage markets in the Americas for new plant and equipment investment. They have evolved from nationalism to regionalism in their outlook, and a conservative ideology has, to a significant extent, followed suit.[11]

Patrick Buchanan's emergence as a presidential candidate in the 1990s gave the appearance of rejuvenating the old conservatism, yet this rejuvenation was ephemeral because of the underlying contradictions of the old right. One part of the old conservatism was strongly identified with the farms and industries of the Midwest and the Republican party, but another component was Southern and traditionally Democratic. Buchanan's hopes were based mainly in his supposed capacity to win crossover votes from socially conservative and strongly nationalistic white southerners who are nominally Democrats, yet this perception is out of sync with the times. Southern states typically do not have partisan voter registration on account of the historical repression of the Republican party and African American voting rights. There is therefore little institutional basis for regarding the South as even nominally majority Democrat as voters shift across party lines in open primaries to candidates who attract their interest.

After the 1996 elections, the continued Republican majority in Congress was completely dependent on the party's southern base. From 1992 to 1996, the Republicans gained thirty House seats and seven Senate seats in the South, without which they would still be the minority party in both chambers.[12] The Republican majority of 1994 was based to a great extent on an alignment of white male and affluent southerners, who had been voting Republican for president since 1964 (with the exception of Carter in 1976). In the midst of the rise of Gingrichian conservatism, there have been countervailing tendencies, based on a bare majority of the 39 percent of voters who turned out in 1994. Democrats retain a long-term advantage among the growing numbers of African American and Hispanic voters as well as among women. Of particular interest to students of voting behavior are younger voters who, facing daunting long-range economic prospects despite the positive aggregate statistics, have not been won over to the Republican coalition.[13] Further, the Republican embrace of cultural conservatism may help consolidate their position in the South but diminishes their prospects in other regions. The Democrats have actually gained ground in House seats from the Northeast during the 1992–1996 period.

With Bob Dole's departure from the Senate, the party leadership at the national level is now composed of Mississippi's Trent Lott and Haley Barbour and Georgia's Gingrich. This New South of Reagan-Gingrich Republicanism and the sunbelt more broadly is a region ideologically dominated by a global dream of free market capitalism that combines in an unacknowledged tension with social and cultural conservatism. Buchanan's financial base, such as it was, did derive in part from South Carolina textile interests that fit the parameters of economic nationalism. Topping the list of large donors to his campaign was the textile concern Leigh and Milliken; textile magnate Roger Milliken, who strenuously opposed NAFTA, also chaired the Buchanan for President committee.[14] However, even in the South Carolina textile industry a degree of regional trading interests has developed. On primary day 1996, the state's business and political establishment supported primary winner Bob Dole, who also scored a decisive victory in the Georgia primary.[15]

Perhaps closer to the spirit of the times, or at least the present trading patterns of U.S. industry, is the ideology of conservative internationalism. In the 1996 campaign Texas senator Phil Gramm called for a Western Hemisphere–wide free trade zone, from the Canadian arctic to Patagonia. Gramm's demiglobal plan is a dream of a former professor of orthodox free trade economics. Contributions to Gramm's campaign were over four times greater than those to the Buchanan campaign in the pre-primary corporate voting (19.2 million versus 4.4 million), and Gramm's largest supporters were in foreign-trade-oriented and antiregulatory industries such as insurance, securities marketing (Dean Witter), petroleum, computer software, and, intriguingly, funeral services.[16] However, given Gramm's performance in the primaries relative to Buchanan's, one wonders if trade liberalization has much mass appeal. As Fiske likes to point out, popular culture does not always buy what the power bloc is selling.[17] Indeed, even such a minor internationalist candidate as Senator Richard Lugar received nearly as much contributor support as Buchanan: $4,270,589 to Buchanan's $4,369,082 by the effective end of the primaries.[18]

Steve Forbes's largely self-financed campaign also expressed a free market ideology that even included a hint of low-wage-promoting social liberalism in opposition to Buchanan's xenophobic stand on immigration. The Forbes campaign suggested the possibility of an electoral bloc that would combine investor preferences with those of middle income voters in the form of the flat tax proposal. Yet as the campaign progressed, business conflict with the flat tax proposal became more evident as real estate and housing industry interests felt the potential threat to their privileged tax status. This business faction also organized a counter bloc to the incipient Forbes coalition by convincing some voters that the flat tax could hurt the value of their homes and depicted the Forbes tax proposal as a plan for tax shifting from the wealthy to the middle class. The Forbes campaign did acquire over $4 million in outside donations, including large sums from securities traders sensitive to capital gains tax.[19]

Globally oriented sectors of finance, manufacturing, and mining want fewer trade restrictions and lower taxes (Gramm) but are also concerned about improved public subsidy of worker training (education) combined with fiscal conservatism and devolution of federalism. The campaign of Lamar Alexander took this approach. The former Tennessee governor, secretary of education, and political outsider, by his own account, was able to raise close to $9 million, which included support from commercial bankers, a textile concern (Beaulieu, Inc.) and Vanderbilt University.[20]

As the front-runner, eventual nominee, and only Republican who could match Clinton's corporate fund raising, Bob Dole identified with supply-side ideology by including erstwhile Forbes supporter Jack Kemp on his ticket and endorsing a 15 percent cut across the board in income tax rates, a modest tax credit for dependent children, and a 50 percent reduction in the capital gains tax rate. Dole was well behind in the polls, and the effort was an unsuccessful design to reactivate the Reagan coalition and set the stage for a campaign that would, on the surface, oppose the middle class as taxpayer against the middle class as entitlement beneficiary. In terms of business conflict, the Dole effort was most strongly supported by manufacturing, retail, and securities marketing firms.[21]

Dole's tax plan had strong corporate support and won votes among the middle income to affluent strata. However, by contrast, the financial sector was also concerned about the possibility of renewed increases in the deficit, which benefited Clinton, who consistently referred to Dole's proposals as "schemes" that would ratchet up the deficit. The incumbent also retained strong business constituencies because of his successes with NAFTA, GATT, the deregulation of telecommunications, the guarantee of the continuation of the military-industrial state, and his acquiescence to a significant degree of sociofiscal conservatism in the repeal of the AFDC entitlement. The administration did successfully lobby Congress to retain the food stamp and Medicaid entitlements, but these social program are not without support among crucial business and professional constituents such as hospitals, medical colleges, agribusiness, and retail interests. It is worth noting that Dole claimed credit for the establishment of the food stamp program in his last Senate speech.

CORPORATE POWER AND CAMPAIGN FINANCE

By looking at campaign finance patterns we find indications of the dialectic of instrumentalism and autonomy that exists between business and government. The individual re-election funds of incumbent congressional representatives, who are in power, are supported by corporate and political action committees. This pattern obviously worked to the benefit of the Republicans in 1996. But for the out-of-power group, funds flow more readily as "soft money" to the party (i.e., the Democrats in 1996) arguably leaving a greater degree of latitude for individual opposition party lawmakers.

The campaign finance controversies since the 1994 election should be interpreted as a strategic Republican effort to gain and maintain the upper hand in the 1998 and 2000 elections. Any campaign finance reform the Democrats support will surely play to their areas of fund-raising advantage. Similarities in sectoral support helps further delineate the business dominance of the competing parties. The top Republican-supporting industries in 1995–1996 were, in descending order, tobacco, securities/investment, insurance, oil/gas, pharmaceutical/health products, telephone utilities, manufacturing/distributing, real estate, chemical and related manufacturing, and law firms. By contrast, lawyers top the Democrats' list, followed by media/entertainment, securities/investment, manufacturing/distributing, business services, telephone utilities, oil/gas, real estate, insurance, and beer/wine/liquor. Much overlap is indicated here, and as students of campaign finance well know, the contributor list reveals that many firms are playing both sides of the street. In 1995, for example, AT&T gave the Republicans $370,000 and the Democrats $313,684. Philip Morris gave to both parties, but clearly favored the Republicans ($992,149 to $199,000), and Seagram and Sons tilts Democratic ($285,000 to $175,000).

Comparison of campaign finance illustrates two parties oriented toward globalizing capitalism. The Democrats are resistant to tort reform and supportive of a combination of cultural liberalism and trade policy, which makes them the better friend of the cultural industry. Meanwhile, tobacco, insurance, health products, petroleum, and manufacturing support indicate the Republicans as an internationalist party of those who prefer their capitalism with less regulation on behalf of public safety, the environment, or labor. Yet neither party is likely to become populist in more than rhetoric with these underwriters. As far as countervailing power is concerned, in 1995 labor provided only 6 percent of the Democrats' soft money contributions (and less than 0.3 percent of the Republicans'), and ideological groups provided 1 percent of the Democrats' and 0.3 percent the Republicans' funds.[22]

Sectoral campaign finance analysis is somewhat limited as a method of business conflict research insofar as individual firms, or even different subsidiaries within the same conglomerate, may have different political and market orientations. For example, the securities industry contains both mass market retailers (Merrill Lynch, et al.) that could substantially increase sales in the event of a return of the capital gains exclusion and investment bankers whose foreign exposure implies a demand for currency stability that could be upset by significant changes in the current fiscal and monetary regime. In manufacturing and distribution there are those whose interest in low wages is at the forefront, exporters whose concerns will run to trade and foreign exchange rates, and large-scale retailers that are undercut by lower-wage competitors (some of the latter gave support to the

1996 increase in the minimum wage). Indeed, some interests have ideologically conflicted interests. For example, real estate could greatly boom with a cut in the capital gains tax, but it also benefits from tax expenditures and interest and housing subsidies that are a legacy of New Deal liberalism. In each of these cases, Clinton or Dole, Gingrich or Gephardt may provide the relative advantage at any particular point in time for any specific policy.

All of these issues must be considered in a context where the campaign investor should consider who is a plausible candidate, saleable to the public, and able to combine policy proposals in a politically feasible way. An example of political entrepreneurial success would be Reagan combining cuts in personal income tax rates with even sharper cuts in corporate income tax rates. An example of failure would be Clinton combining national health insurance with a regulatory structure for private sector health management organizations. As Martin points out, the majority of U.S. businesses did favor health care reform, but the Clinton efforts became convoluted by the tensions between the campaign for mass support and conflicting business interests.[23] The popular concern for health security without high taxes and business interests in regulatory and cost containment issues were ultimately too contradictory and complex for the administration-proffered solution.[24]

The Democrats' overwhelming campaign finance advantage among lawyers, organized labor, and liberal citizen groups provides relatively little of the total campaign funds. The only major business sectors that are primarily in the Democratic alignment are communications and electronics. The Republicans dominate in all other business sectors, in their ability to fund campaigns and pursue electoral success in the mass media age, but both parties are substantially corporate parties.

One might take from these campaign finance patterns a hint of what U.S. electoral politics might be like if our civil society were more substantially pluralist than a privatized terrain of corporate behemoths occasioned by rarer species of advocates for social causes, workers, and consumers. The Republican Party would have to be more responsive to the economic and cultural concerns of its mass base; the Democrats, to the progressive populism of labor and other new social movements. The kind of civic debate that Merelman deems is essential to democratic culture would be more attainable if public discourse were not the near monopoly of elite financial interests. Substantive deliberation could perhaps displace the spectacle of nondebate between the political facilitators of corporate interests.[25] But without organized systemic counters to business power, the ongoing decline of popular participation and the deepening of citizens' alienation will likely continue. The disparity between private affluence and public squalor grows as civic culture declines.

REPRISE: BUSINESS CONFLICT AND
THE DECLINE OF POSTWAR LIBERALISM

From our business conflict perspective, the New Deal coalition was also a corporate bloc favoring a global capitalist vision of capital-intensive, export-oriented opponents of old conservatism's protectionism and isolationism. Some national business interests were included in this bloc at various times, such as utilities, agriculture, and smaller lending banks especially in underdeveloped regions and rural areas with greater need for federal subsidy. Incorporated within this bloc were the moderate leadership of organized labor and the enfranchised array of social movements recognized by the McGovern Commission or otherwise included in the Democratic coalition: African Americans, feminists, Hispanics, Native Americans, antiwar students, environmentalists, and, later, lesbian/gay activists. In Barton Bernstein's well-known phrase, "the conservative achievements of liberal reform" from the 1930s on were to maintain a stable regime of corporate power even during periods of devastating economic depression or social upheaval with revolutionary undertones.

In our perspective, the New Deal coalition might also be called the Bretton Woods coalition for the global regime of managed currencies and liberal trade established for the postwar world. Within this framework, the advanced industrial nations practiced social Keynesianism to a certain degree without facing immediate balance-of-payments or inflationary crises while pursuing comparative advantage in world markets. Underpinning this system was the political economic hegemony of the United States and the dollar's value in relation to gold. Once the dollar could no longer be maintained as U.S. trade deficits increased, in part because of the pressures resulting from the successful neomercantilism of Japan and Germany, the Bretton Woods framework collapsed and with it the material bases of liberal hegemony in the United States. In the post–Bretton Woods world it has often seemed implausible to fund the welfare-warfare state, balance the budget, and maintain comparatively low tax rates in a context of low inflation and low unemployment and a stable currency, money market, and trade balance. The U.S. political economy was able to do so once, but those halcyon days have not been seen since the latter part of the Johnson administration.

The structural crises of the U.S. economy, post Bretton Woods, have helped to take liberalism out of power, but they have also undercut the ability of conservatism to maintain and consolidate power. A particular conjuncture of social and international tensions in 1968 fractured the Democratic electoral bloc, which had been dominant since the 1930s. Republican candidate Nixon was provided with an opening to electoral success, albeit with a minority of the popular vote (43.2 percent). Nixon, however, governed within the parameters of the New Deal system, supporting a national health scheme, a guaranteed income policy, worker safety, environmental protection, and affirmative action. Although he avowed Keynesianism, this was tempered by a desire to co-opt more progressive change and politically isolate new social movements.

With the election of Reagan in 1980, an important shift in the pattern of state support of business interests took hold. The Reagan approach emphasized lowering the costs of capital through tax cuts and deregulation while increasing the subsidy to the military-industrial sector. Yet Reagan, unlike Johnson, could not satisfy all major sectors in the global conditions of the 1980s, which appeared to threaten the economic hegemony of the United States and require the import of foreign capital. By lowering the costs of capital, increasing the defense budget, and avoiding a direct assault on the welfare state, the Reagan administration could accomplish short-term stimulus, extend U.S. military dominance in the twilight of the Cold War, and lead the political economy to fiscal and trade deficits that drew key financial sectors and firms back toward the Democrats. Declining real wages combined with higher educational and health care costs to provide the groundwork for middle-class unrest and increased corporate support for a centrist alternative.

Clinton, like Nixon, is a minority president who succeeded opportunistically when the opposing coalition cracked. Indeed, Clinton's campaign emphases—"balance the budget, reform welfare, cut taxes, protect medicare"[26]—are conservative compared with Nixon's rhetorical support of the full employment budget; an indication more of the secular and structural shift from liberal to conservative internationalism than of any individual predilections.[27] As a moderate internationalist, Clinton has stayed in power, governing within ideological parameters that keep trade, fiscal, and monetary policy within bounds that serve corporate globalists first and popular interests as an election-year afterthought.

As to the future possibilities of politics in the United States and other advanced capitalist nations, we can anticipate continued conflict among economic regionalism, nationalism, and internationalism as well as interrelated interests and ideologies of domestic state interventionism and laissez-faire. These basic dichotomies of modern ideology will continue to frame political debate but under conditions established by the post–Bretton Woods political economy. Global conditions will, in turn, structure the limits and possibilities of alternative nationalist, internationalist, liberal, and conservative politics.

A TYPOLOGY OF POSSIBLE FUTURES

In concluding our study, we suggest the political economic outlines of the possible future for the advanced capitalist states. These possibilities are combinations of the material (i.e., economic and ideological) factors that we have identified in this study as significant influences on the postwar trajectory of U.S. politics. Although a large part of our account has emphasized the global context of the decline of liberalism, we urge that the era has witnessed a *decline,* not a *demise,* of the liberal tradition. The Reagan-Gingrich right turns may someday appear to represent reactionary interludes between periods of liberal capitalist reform, as the 1920s were between the Progressive and New Deal eras. Perhaps we are in the early stages of a lasting conservative departure or maybe even a globalization-enhanced deconstruction and dealignment of the basic structures of the republic itself. We are only certain that the future is indeterminate and will be produced in the conflict and clash of interests.

Alternative 1: Conservative Internationalism. This approach entails a policy of curbing the welfare-regulatory state combined with a free trade disposition and a heavy emphasis on support for the military-industrial complex, including arms export. Free market economics within the context of a globalizing system can be characterized as a relatively less regulated exchange of commodities and capital across national boundaries. As Weiss points out, the U.S. predilection in recent years for this approach to global economic issues allows it to "exploit strong international leverage but at the expense of domestic adjustment capacity."[28] In policy terms, this bloc has nothing to offer those suffering from the declining social wage but lower taxes and fewer public services, a bidding-down process that structurally undermines governmental capacity to respond strategically to changes in the global economy. Tensions within this coalition are expressed in the reaction of the Republican mass base to the increasing multiculturalism of the United States. The continued presence of business nationalism and the regionalists' reluctance about future extensions of free trade zones in the Americas or the Pacific region also work against this tendency, which nonetheless appears to have the upper hand. Additionally, the antipathy of many multilateralists to an aggressive foreign policy and wasteful military spending continues to detract from the conservatives' ability to consolidate their hegemony.

Alternative 2: Liberal Internationalism. This approach would combine an emphasis on governmental investment in job training, new technological infrastructure, and other social services with a free trade disposition. Such a course would suggest a move toward the kind of corporatist structures utilized by Japan and Germany, which emphasize export promotion and support for emerging industries. We urge against underestimating the Democratic Party's ability to reinvent itself and construct a neoliberal bloc in the years ahead. However, given the political-economic strength of military-industrial interests and the national antipathy to increased taxation, it is easy to see the challenges this alternative confronts. Restoring the corporate tax as a substantial revenue source is politically unlikely insofar as liberal internationalism is a bloc dominated by capital-intensive business interests. Organized labor and other progressive social movements play critical roles as vote producers but are unlikely to be anything more than regional power brokers. The ongoing devolution of antipoverty programs also decreases the chances that a rejuvenated liberal internationalism would accomplish the historical promise of the New Deal/Great Society by implementing a comprehensive national welfare system, let alone even contemplate a universalistic social policy, as in the social democratic model.

Alternative 3: Conservative Nationalism. If this tendency were to gain power, it would seek to cut back the New Deal Social Security state and favor protecting domestic business interests from foreign competitors. Such a bloc would likely include a significant business regionalist component among investors in low-wage markets in Latin America and the Caribbean. It would also include the agricultural and industrial interests that sought side agreements to protect them from NAFTA. We seriously doubt if there is enough remaining of the strictly nationalist business sector to provide the necessary hegemonic leadership for a conservative nationalist bloc. Additionally, we hypothesize that the current cultural backlash associated with the religious right and angry white (southern) males is a manifestation of a sense of lost cultural hegemony, to some extent exacerbated by an understandable economic insecurity. But the United States is and was multilingual, multiracial, and multireligious, and will be increasingly so. The continued and even growing disaffection for the Republican Party among younger voters, women, and ethnic/racial minorities indicates that there already is a political price that has been paid by candidates Bush and Dole for their embrace of the cultural right. The precipitous drop in Perot's vote from 1992 to 1996 also hints at diminishing political returns for a populist version of fiscal conservatism and trade nationalism.

Alternative 4: Liberal Nationalism. Perhaps the weakest of all the possible political alternatives, this tendency practices a politics of maintaining and hoping to expand the welfare state while protecting national industry from low wage-cost imports. The primary organizational support for this tendency comes from organized labor and its coalition partners among environmentalists concerned about the threat to ecological standards posed by NAFTA and other public interest groups.[29] The Nader campaign of 1996 represents the nascent and limited organization of this tendency. Marginally plausible is the possible coalition of this tendency with business interests, in the agricultural and mining sectors, for example, that would aggressively favor export promotion with trade liberalization. These business interests, however, have a pronounced antipathy to liberal social programs as well as organized labor. It is very difficult to even imagine the political facilitator who could negotiate the contradictions of this bloc. Given the organizational conservatism of the U.S. labor movement and its regional and sectoral containment, the United States has notably failed to produce a labor-oriented political party.

Any future progressive politics in the United States necessarily requires the organization of working people. Contrary to the ruminations of former labor secretary Reich, we argue that there is no efficacious means to represent popular economic interests other than through independent organizations, that is, trade unions. Unfortunately, as we have seen, the AFL-CIO bureaucracy made a fundamental and historic mistake in embracing Cold War anticommunism and antisocialism to the extent of actually participating in the efforts of the U.S. government to disable militant labor groups in Latin America and Europe. Labor in the United States has a disastrous and not completely undeserved association with cultural nationalism, xenophobia, militarism, and racism. The unorganized and therefore politically unrepresented majority of the U.S. working class are multiracial and include disproportionate numbers of immigrants and women. An internationalism of the left could represent their interests. Labor organizations that promoted rather than downgraded the interests of foreign workers would be required.

To consider the possibility of a left internationalism in the post-Reagan age of Gingrich and Clinton seems quixotic indeed. Nonetheless, public support for family leave, child care, secure jobs, pensions, education, and health insurance and disaffection with corporate profligacy remain widespread if disarticulate. In 1995, the *Chicago Tribune* political cartoonist MacNelly published a visual commentary on the developing underdevelopment of the times. In the cartoon, an unspecified member of the business-political elite declares that "the current economic recovery has created over 7.8 million jobs." Meanwhile, a twenty- to thirty-something waiter thinks to himself, "And I have three of them."[30] In summer 1997 the UPS strike witnessed a surprising success for some of those who hold multiple jobs and indicated their potential power. Perhaps even more encouraging was the broad public sympathy for the strike, despite the fact that it was led by one of the most corrupt and conservative of U.S. unions. Further, the strike was not an isolated case; as Moody notes, the number of strikes of 1,000 or more workers rose in 1996 for the first time in many years.[31] It remains to be seen, of course, if a renewed union movement develops in the coming years. Our sense is that although this is plausible, it is less likely to be initiated by established union structures than by a shift to a broader economic justice agenda promoted by newly mobilized union activists, groups of working women, subordinated racial and ethnic groups including immigrants, and the environmental justice movement. The manifold tensions among these groups, however, is a formidable barrier to any serious internationalism-of-the-left alternative in U.S. politics.

This work may be criticized for depicting globalization primarily in the conceptual framework of political economy.[32] Although we have emphasized the role of ideology, the growth of a global consumer culture and the role of national identities have perhaps not been given their due as shaping forces in contemporary world and U.S. politics. There is a growing body of scholarly literature that re-emphasizes the role of culture and identity in international relations. However, we do note that two significant contributors to this literature also make the admission that the end of the Cold War has led to a "primacy of economic issues" in the globalization process. Mansbach and Ferguson also urge that this economic primacy "opens up a broad field of polities that, until recently, political scientists have been pleased to leave to analysts in management schools."[33] It is in that broad field that our version of conflict theory operates, treating the market and labor orientations of firms and business sectors as key variables in the political process.

On a more theoretical note, we argue that the abstract dichotomy between culture and economy is largely false. A more valid distinction in the understanding of political action may be between analyses based on rational choice assumptions and those based on reconstruction of historical contexts and conjunctures. To illustrate, Katzenstein recently noted that many international relations theorists have urged a more "sociological" approach that would emphasize the role played by norms and identities in politics. Yet Katzenstein writes that international relations "work has continued to draw almost exclusively on economic imagery and follow a rationalist path."[34] Our take on this debate is that economic rationality is cultural or, better yet, that norms, identities, and economic rationalities are mutually intertwined and embedded in particular histories. In other words, in the post–World War II era of U.S. politics, the rational interests of particular economic interests are inseparable from these same groups' norms and values. The Business Roundtable, for example, may urge fiscal conservatism because of their rational interest in the stability of the financial markets as well as their sense of what is good for free enterprise as a system.

In the real world there is not necessarily any contradiction between norms and interests. As the human sense of identity is conditioned by material circumstance, so, too, is the perception of economic interest influenced by values. The distinction being made is more academic than practical. Utility maximization and rational choice are artifacts of textbooks and conceptual models. Politics, by contrast, arises from human interests in status, power, and recognition and conflicts among these interests. In the period of U.S. political history that we have studied, business internationalist interests have maintained the upper hand through struggle and crisis while shifting from a relatively liberal to a more conservative globalism in terms of social, fiscal, and national defense policy preferences. The current trend of globalization of the economy is to a significant extent the historical product of the political success of these internationalist corporate interests and U.S. monetary, trade, and other policies that have adjusted and readjusted to the global economy by promoting and supporting the export and import of financial capital with little regulation of the effect of these flows on society.

No corners have been turned, no inevitable patterns established. If the reader takes nothing else from this work or disdains our political engagement, there is still the important lesson that globalization is a process *constructed* by government policy. The global economy is not some inevitable by-product of unfathomable economic laws, but something that is being made, and can be unmade or remade, through human agency. The ways in which globalization is pursued will determine whether or not human communities can sustain decent livelihoods and benefit from their own labor. As a final note, it is well worth considering that foreign trade and capital flows in 1913 for the present-day OECD countries stood at 16 percent of their collective GDPs. It was well into the postwar period, and following a notable dip after 1973, that a comparable level of internationalization was again attained (17.9 percent by 1991).[35] We are, in other words, living in this century's second wave of globalization. The first one crashed against the breakers of nationalism, imperialism, war, and revolution. There is no rational reason to adopt a dogmatic belief that the current pattern of globalization is permanent. Current academic fashion overemphasizes, callously celebrates, or unduly doomsays the reality of globalization. It is a comprehendible and alterable historical process that requires more comparative and theoretical study as well as practical engagement to which we hope we have in a modest yet provocative and intellectually productive way contributed.

NOTES

1. Walter Lippmann, *Drift and Mastery* (Englewood Cliffs, NJ: Prentice-Hall, 1961).

2. Susan Tolchin, *The Angry American* (Boulder, CO: Westview Press, 1996).

3. For corporate internationalist attitudes on Clinton, see Alain Enthoven and Sara Singer, "Give Clinton Some Credit," *Fortune*, November 1, 1993, p. 50; Ann Dowd, "Clinton Agenda for Business," *Fortune*, January 24, 1994, pp. 48–51; and David Shribman, "Can Clinton Make Peace with His Party?" *Fortune*, January 12, 1998, p. 48.

4. Wilson Carey McWilliams, *The Politics of Disappointment* (Chatham, NJ: Chatham House, 1995), p. 199. See also M. Levinson, "Regarding Clinton Economic Package," *Dissent* 40, 2 (Spring 1993): 142–5 on the limitations of Clinton's economic liberalism.

5. Ronald W. Cox, "The Military-Industrial Complex and U.S. Foreign Policy: Institutionalizing the New Right Agenda in the Post-Cold War Period," in Amy Ansell, ed., *Unraveling the Right* (Boulder, CO: Westview Press, 1998).

6. *Economic Report of the President* (Washington, DC: USGPO, 1998), pp. 377, 374, and *Budget of the United States: Analytical Perspectives* (Washington, DC: USGPO, 1997).

7. An example of multilateralist optimism after the election of Clinton is in J. C. Clad and R. D. Stone, "New Mission for Foreign Aid," *Foreign Affairs* 72, 1 (1993): 196–205.

8. Herbert Alexander and Anthony Corrado, *Financing the 1992 Election* (Armonk, NY: M. E. Sharpe, 1993), pp. 119–120, 155–156, 295. There was also substantial increase in support for Clinton in 1992 from Archer Daniels Midland and through 1996 the liquor industry, especially Anheuser-Busch and Seagram and Sons.

9. Paul Krugman, "Competitiveness: A Dangerous Obsession," *Foreign Affairs* 73, 2 (March/April, 1994): 28–44, suggests that the perspectives of Reich, Magaziner, and Tyson lend themselves toward trade nationalism. A. C. Holden, "The Repositioning of Ex-Im Bank," *Columbia Journal of World Business* 31, 1 (Spring 1996): 82–93, covers congressional efforts to cut export subsidy programs after the 1994 elections.

10. Kevin Phillips, *Arrogant Capital* (Boston: Little, Brown, 1994).

11. Ronald W. Cox, "Explaining Business Support for Regional Trade Agreements," Ronald W. Cox, ed., *Business and the State in International Relations* (Boulder, CO: Westview Press, 1996).

12. Richard E. Cohen, "Campaigning for Congress: The Echo of '94," in Larry Sabato, ed., *Toward the Millennium: The Election of 1996* (Boston: Allyn and Bacon, 1997) pp. 187–188.

13. McWilliams, *The Politics of Disappointment,* p. 198.

14. Center for Responsive Politics/Federal Election Commission, 1996. http://www.vote-smart.org/congress/finance/softmoney.html and http://www2.pbs.org/wgbh/pages/frontline/president/tindex.html.

15. Ronald Cox and Daniel Skidmore-Hess, "The Politics of the 1993 NAFTA Vote," *Current Politics and Economics of the United States* 1, 2/3 (1995).

16. Federal Election Commission.

17. John Fiske, *Understanding Popular Culture* (Boston: Unwin Hyman, 1989).

18. Federal Election Commission.

19. Ibid.

20. Ibid.

21. Ibid.

22. Ibid.

23. C. J. Martin, "Mandating Social Change: The Business Struggle over National Health Reform," *Governance: An International Journal of Policy and Administration*, 10, 4 October 1997: 397–428.

24. M. A. Peterson, "Political Influence in the 1990s: From Iron Triangles to Policy Networks," *Journal of Health Politics, Policy, and Law* 18, 2 (Summer 1993): 395–438, suggests that power is too atomized to make coalition-building for reform likely. This argument appears to suggest that a pluralist perspective is more valid than our elite approach. However, we point out that it also implies the hegemony of the status quo by default.

25. Richard Merelman, *Making Something of Ourselves* (Berkeley: University of California Press, 1984). See also Murray Edelman, *Constructing the Political Spectacle* (Chicago: University of Chicago Press, 1988).

26. Brooks Jackson, "Financing the 1996 Campaign: The Law of the Jungle," in Sabato, *Toward the Millennium*, p. 237.

27. F. C. Fowler, "The Neoliberal Value Shift and Its Implications for Federal Education Policy under Clinton," *Educational Administration Quarterly* 31, 1 (February 1995): 38–60, emphasizes the differences between the Clintonian value of "growth and community" versus the 1960s–1970s liberal goal of "equality."

28. Linda Weiss, "Globalization and the Myth of the Powerless State," *New Left Review* 225: 25.

29. A study that in contrast to ours argues that labor and environmental interests have a significant impact on congressional decisionmaking is L. Kahane, "Congressional Voting Patterns on NAFTA: An Empirical Analysis," *American Journal of Economics and Sociology* 55, 4 (October 1996): 395–409.

30. Tolchin, *The Angry American*, p. 51.

31. Kim Moody, "Towards an International Social-Movement Unionism," *New Left Review* 225: 53.

32. A work that covers other aspects of globalization is Malcolm Waters, *Globalization* (London: Routledge, 1995).

33. Yale Ferguson and Richard Mansbach, "The Past as Prelude to the Future? Identities and Loyalties in Global Politics," in Yosef Lapid and Friedrich Kratchowil, eds., *The Return of Culture and Identity in IR Theory* (Boulder, CO: Lynne Rienner Publishers, 1996), p. 42.

34. Peter J. Katzenstein, "Introduction," in Peter J. Katzenstein, ed., *The Culture of National Security* (New York: Columbia University Press, 1996), p. 15ff.

35. Weiss, "Globalization and the Myth of Powerless State," p. 7.

Acronyms

AFDC	Aid to Families with Dependent Children
AFL	American Federation of Labor
AFL-CIO	American Federation of Labor and Congress of Industrial Organizations
BAC	Business Advisory Council
BCIU	Business Council for International Understanding
BOP	balance of payments
CBI	Caribbean Basin Initiative
CCAA	Caribbean/Central American Action
CEA	Council of Economic Advisors
CED	Committee for Economic Development
CFR	Council on Foreign Relations
CNTP	Committee for a National Trade Policy
COC	Chamber of Commerce
CPD	Committee on the Present Danger
ECA	European Cooperation Administration
ECAT	Emergency Committee for American Trade
ECSC	European Coal and Steel Community
EDC	European Defense Community
EEC	European Economic Community
EPA	Environmental Protection Agency
EPU	European Payments Union
FDI	Foreign Direct Investment
FY	fiscal year
GATT	General Agreement on Tariffs and Trade
GDP	gross domestic product
GNP	gross national product
IEPA	International Economic Policy Association
IET	interest equalization tax

223

IMF	International Monetary Fund
IPAC	Industrial Policy Advisory Committee
IRC	Industrial Relations Counselors, Inc.
LDC	less developed country
MNC	multinational corporation
NAFTA	North American Free Trade Agreement
NAM	National Association of Manufacturers
NEP	New Economic Policy
NFIB	National Federation of Independent Business
NIRA	National Industry Recovery Act
NMBTA	National Machine Tool Builders' Association
NRA	National Recovery Administration
NSC	National Security Council
OCDM	Office of Civil and Defense Mobilization
OECD	Organization for Economic Cooperation and Development
OEEC	Organization for European Economic Cooperation
OFDI	Office of Foreign Direct Investment
OMB	Office of Management and Budget
OPEC	Organization of Petroleum Exporting Countries
RTA	Reciprocal Trade Act
SALT II	Strategic Arms Limitation Treaty
SSA	Social Security Administration
TEA	Trade Expansion Act
WEU	Western European Union

Selected Bibliography

BOOKS AND ARTICLES

Adamson, Walter L. *Hegemony and Revolution*. Berkeley: University of California Press, 1980.

Aglietta, Michel. *A Theory of Capitalist Regulation: The U.S. Experience*. London: New Left Books, 1979.

Alexander, Herbert. *Financing the 1968 Election*. Lexington, MA: D. C. Heath, 1971.

———. *Financing the 1964 Election*. Princeton, NJ: Citizens' Research Foundation, 1965.

Alexander, Herbert, and Anthony Corrado. *Financing the 1992 Election*. Armonk, NY: M. E. Sharpe, 1993.

Ambrose, Stephen. *Eisenhower: The President*. New York: Simon and Schuster, 1984.

———. *Nixon,* Vol. 2. New York: Simon and Shuster, 1989.

American Bankers Association. *Appendix to the Congressional Record*. 79th Congress, 1st Session, January 3–March 22, 1945, Vol. 91, Part 10.

Anderson, Robert B. "The Balance of Payments Problem." *Foreign Affairs* 38 (April 1990): 419–433.

Ansell, Amy. "Business Mobilization and the New Right," in Ronald W. Cox, ed., *Business and the State in International Relations*. Boulder, CO: Westview Press, 1996.

——— ed. *Unraveling the Right: The New Conservatism in American Thought and Politics*. Boulder, CO: Westview Press, 1998.

Armstrong, Philip, Andrew Glyn, and John Harrison. *Capitalism Since World War II: The Making and the Breakup of the Great Boom*. London: Fontana Press, 1984.

Aronowitz, Stanley. *False Promises*. New York: McGraw-Hill, 1974.

Aronson, Jonathan. *Money and Power: Banks and the World Monetary System*. Beverly Hills, CA: Sage Publications, 1977.

Bain, Joe S. *International Differences in Industrial Structure*. New Haven, CT: Yale University Press, 1966.

Baran, Paul, and Paul Sweezy. *Monopoly Capital*. New York: Monthly Review Press, 1966.

Bell, Coral. *The Diplomacy of Détente*. New York: St. Martin's Press, 1977.

Berger, Suzanne, and Ronald Dore. *National Diversity and Global Capitalism*. Ithaca, NY: Cornell University Press, 1996.

Berkowitz, Edward, and Kim McQuaid. *Creating the Welfare State*. New York: Praeger, 1980.

Bernstein, Barton, J. "The New Deal: The Conservative Achievement of Liberal Reform," in Barton Bernstein, ed., *Towards a New Past: Dissenting Essays in American History*. New York: Pantheon Books, 1968.

Block, Fred. *The Origins of International Economic Disorder*. Berkeley: University of California Press, 1977.

―――. "The Ruling Class Does Not Rule," in Margaret Levi, ed. *Marxism*, vol. 2. Aldershot, UK: Edward Elgar Publishing, 1991.

Bluestone, Barry, and Bennett Harrison. *The Deindustrialization of America: Plant Closings, Community Abandonment and the Dismantling of Basic Industry*. New York: Basic Books, 1982.

Bluestone, Barry, and Bennett Harrison. *The Great U-Turn*. New York: Basic Books, 1988.

Boies, John L. *Buying for Armageddon: Business, Society and Military Spending Since the Cuban Missile Crisis*. New Brunswick, NJ: Rutgers University Press, 1994.

Boylan, James. *The New Deal Coalition and the Election of 1946*. New York: Garland Press, 1981.

Brecher, Jeremy. *Strike!* San Francisco: Straight Arrow Books, 1972.

Brenda, Piers. *Ike: The Life and Times of Dwight D. Eisenhower*. London: Martin Secker and Warburg, 1987.

Brents, Barbara. "Class Power and the Control of Knowledge: Policy Reform Groups and the Social Security Act." Paper presented to the meeting of the American Sociological Association, San Francisco, 1989.

Brody, David. *Workers in Industrial America*. New York: Oxford University Press, 1980.

Burch, Philip H. *Elites in American History,* Vols. 1–3. New York: Holmes and Meier, 1981.

―――. "The NAM as Interest Group," *Politics and Society* 4, 1 (Fall 1973): 97–130.

―――. "Reagan, Bush and the Right-Wing Politics," in Paul Zarembka, ed., *Research in Political Economy*. Greenwich, CT: JAI Press, 1997.

Burnham, Walter Dean. *Critical Elections and the Mainspring of American Electoral Politics*. New York: W. W. Norton, 1970.

Business and Industry Committee for Bretton Woods. *Appendix to the Congressional Record*. 79th Congress, 1st Session, March 23–June 8, 1945, Vol. 91, Part 11.

Business International Corporation. *Improving International Competitiveness Through Sourcing in Latin America*. New York: BIC, 1989.

Campagna, Anthony. *U.S. National Economic Policy, 1917–1985*. New York: Praeger, 1987.

Carter, Dan. *From George Wallace to Newt Gingrich*. Baton Rouge: Louisiana State University Press, 1996.

Castells, Manuel. *The Economic Crisis and American Society*. Berkeley: University of California Press, 1979.

Citizens for Tax Justice. "Corporate Taxpayers and Corporate Freeloaders." Washington, DC: Citizens for Tax Justice, August 1985.

Clad, J. C., and R. D. Stone. "New Mission for Foreign Aid." *Foreign Affairs* 72, 1 (1993): 196–205.

Cohen, Richard. "Campaigning for Congress: The Echo of '94," in Larry Sabato, ed., *Toward the Millennium: The Election of 1996*. Boston: Allyn and Bacon, 1997.

Collins, Robert M. *The Business Response to Keynes*. New York: Columbia University Press, 1981.

Commins, Margaret. "From Security to Trade in U.S.–Latin American Relations: Explaining U.S. Support for a Regional Trade Agreement with Mexico," International Studies Association Annual Conference, unpublished paper, University of North Carolina–Chapel Hill, 1992.

———. "Interest Group Competition and NAFTA." Unpublished manuscript, University of North Carolina–Chapel Hill, 1992.

Committee for Economic Development. *The Dollar and the World Monetary System*. New York: CED, 1966.

———. *The European Common Market and Its Meaning to the United States*. New York: CED, 1959.

———. *National Objectives and the Balance of Payments Problem*. New York: CED, 1960.

Committee on the Present Danger. *Can America Catch Up? The United States–Soviet Military Balance*. Washington, DC: CPD, 1985.

Conybeare, John. *U.S. Foreign Economic Policy and the International Capital Markets: The Case of Capital Export Controls, 1963–1974*. New York: Garland, 1988.

Council on Foreign Relations. *Studies of American Interests in the War and the Peace*. Economic and Financial Series. New York: CFR, 1940–1945.

Cox, Robert. *Production, Power and World Order: Social Forces in the Making of History*. New York: Columbia University Press, 1987.

Cox, Ronald W. "Corporate Coalitions and Industrial Restructuring: Explaining Regional Trade Agreements," *Competition and Change* 1 (1995): 13–30.

———. "Explaining Business Support for Regional Trade Agreements," in Ronald W. Cox, ed., *Business and the State in International Relations*. Boulder, CO: Westview Press, 1996.

———. "The Military-Industrial Complex and U.S. Foreign Policy:" Institutionalizing the New Right Agenda in the Post–Cold War Period," in Amy Ansell, ed., *Unraveling the Right: The New Conservatism in American Thought and Politics*. Boulder, CO: Westview Press, 1998.

———. *Power and Profits: U.S. Policy in Central America*. Lexington: University Press of Kentucky, 1994.

Cox, Ronald W., and Daniel Skidmore-Hess. "The Politics of the 1993 NAFTA Vote," *Current Politics and Economics of the United States* 1, 2/3 (1995): 131–144.

Cumings, Bruce. *The Origins of the Korean War*. Vol. 2, *The Roaring of the Cataract*. Princeton, NJ: Princeton University Press, 1992.

———, ed. *Child of Conflict*. Seattle: University of Washington Press, 1983.

Destler, I. M., and Randall Herring. *Dollar Politics: Exchange Rate Policymaking in the United States*. Washington, DC: Institute for International Economics, 1989.

Destler, I. M., and John S. Odell. *Anti-Protection: Changing Forces in United States Trade Politics*. Washington, DC: Institute for International Economics, 1987.

Devereux, Eric. "Industrial Structure, Internationalism and the Collapse of the Cold War Consensus: Business, the Media, and Vietnam" in Ronald W. Cox, ed., *Business and the State in International Relations*. Boulder, CO: Westview Press, 1996.

Dicken, Peter. *Global Shift*. New York: Guilford Press, 1992.

Divine, Robert A. *Eisenhower and the Cold War*. New York: Oxford University Press, 1981.

Domhoff, William. *The Power Elite and the State: How Policy Is Made in America*. New York: Aldine de Gruyter, 1990.

Dowd, A. "Clinton Agenda for Business." *Fortune*, January 24, 1994, pp. 48–51.

Dryden, Steve. *Trade Warriors: USTR and the American Crusade for Free Trade*. Oxford: Oxford University Press, 1995.

Dumbrell, John. *The Carter Presidency*. Manchester, UK: Manchester University Press, 1993.

Eckes, Alfred. *A Search for Solvency*. Austin: University of Texas Press, 1975.

Edelman, Murray. *Constructing the Political Spectacle*. Chicago: University of Chicago Press, 1988.

Eden, Lorraine, and Maureen Appel Molot. "Continentalizing the North American Auto Industry," in Ricardo Grinspun and Maxwell Cameron, eds., *The Political Economy of North American Free Trade*. New York: St. Martin's Press, 1993.

Eden, Lynn. "Capitalist Conflict and the State: The Making of United States Military Policy in 1948," in Charles Bright and Susan Harding, eds., *Statemaking and Social Movements: Essays in Theory and History*. Ann Arbor: University of Michigan Press, 1984.

"Editorial: The Rockefeller Report." *Fortune*, June 1958, pp. 97–98.

Edsall, Thomas. *The New Politics of Inequality*. New York: W. W. Norton, 1984.

Enthoven, Alain, and Sara Singer. "Give Clinton Some Credit." *Fortune*, November 1, 1993, p. 52.

Epstein, Leon. *Political Parties in the American Mold*. Madison: University of Wisconsin Press, 1987.

European Recovery Program. *Hearings Before the Senate Committee on Foreign Relations*. 80th Congress, 2nd Session, 1951–1952.

Ferguson, Thomas. "From Normalcy to New Deal: Industrial Structure, Party Competition, and American Public Policy in the Great Depression," *International Organization* 38 (Winter 1984): 41–94.

―――. *Golden Rule: The Investment Theory of Party Competition and the Logic of Money Driven Political Systems*. Chicago: University of Chicago Press, 1995.

―――. "Industrial Conflict and the Coming of the New Deal: The Triumph of Multinational Liberalism in America," in Steve Fraser and Gary Gerstle, eds., *The Rise and Fall of the New Deal Order*. Princeton, NJ: Princeton University Press, 1989.

Ferguson, Thomas, and Joel Rogers. *Right Turn: The Decline of the Democrats and the Future of American Politics*. New York: Hill and Wang, 1986.

Ferguson, Yale, and Richard Mansbach. "The Past as Prelude to the Future? Identities and Loyalties in Global Politics," in Yosef Lapid and Friedrich Kratchowil, eds., *The Return of Culture and Identity in IR Theory*. Boulder, CO: Lynne Rienner, 1996.

Finegold, Kenneth, and Theda Skocpol. *State and Party in America's New Deal*. Madison: University of Wisconsin Press, 1995.

Finger, J. Michael. "Trade Policies in the United States," in Dominick Salvatore, ed., *National Trade Policies*. New York: Greenwood Press, 1992.

Fiske, John. *Understanding Popular Culture*. Boston: Unwin Hyman, 1989.

Fong, Glenn. "Export Dependence Versus the New Protectionism: Constraints on Trade Policy in the Industrial World." Ph.D. dissertation, Cornell University, 1984.

Fordham, Benjamin. *Building the Cold War Consensus: The Political Economy of U.S. National Security Policy, 1949–1951*. Ann Arbor: University of Michigan Press, 1998.

Forum Institute. "Search for Security: A Guide to Grantmaking in International Security and the Prevention of Nuclear War." Washington, DC: Forum Institute, July 1985.

Foster, John Bellamy. *The Theory of Monopoly Capitalism*. New York: Monthly Review Press, 1986.

Fowler, F. C. "The Neoliberal Value Shift and Its Implications for Federal Education Policy Under Clinton." *Educational Administration Quarterly* 31, 1 (February 1995): 38–60.

Franklin, John Hope, and Alfred A. Moss, Jr. *From Slavery to Freedom*. New York: Alfred A. Knopf Press, 1994.

Frieden, Jeffrey. *Banking on the World: The Politics of American International Finance*. New York: Harper and Row, 1987.

———. "International Investment and Colonial Control: A New Interpretation." *International Organization* 48, 4 (1994): 559–594.

———. "Sectoral Conflict and U.S. Foreign Economic Policy," in John Ikenberry, David Lake, and Michael Mastanduno, eds., *The State and American Foreign Economic Policy*. Ithaca, NY: Cornell University Press, 1989.

General Agreement on Tariffs and Trade. *Textiles and Clothing in the World Economy*. Geneva: GATT, July 1984.

Gibbs, David. *The Political Economy of Third World Intervention*. Chicago: University of Chicago Press, 1991.

———. "Taking the State Back Out: Reflections on a Tautology." *Contention* 3, 3 (1994): 115–137.

Giddens, Anthony. *A Contemporary Critique of Historical Materialism*. Stanford, CA: Stanford University Press, 1995.

Gill, Stephen. *American Hegemony and the Trilateral Commission*. New York: Cambridge University Press, 1990.

———, ed. *Historical Materialism and International Relations*. New York: Cambridge University Press, 1993.

Gilpin, Robert. *The Political Economy of International Relations*. Princeton, NJ: Princeton University Press, 1987.

Ginsberg, Benjamin, and Martin Shefter. *Politics by Other Means*. New York: Basic Books, 1990.

Gordon, Colin. "New Deal, Old Deck: Business and the Origins of Social Security, 1920–1935," *Politics and Society* 19, 2 (1991): 165–207.

Gordon, David. "Chickens Home to Roost: From Prosperity to Stagnation in the Postwar U.S. Economy," in Michael Bernstein and David Adler, eds., *Understanding American Economic Decline*. New York: Cambridge University Press, 1994.

———. *Fat and Mean: The Corporate Squeeze of Working Americans and the Myth of Managerial Downsizing*. New York: Free Press, 1996.

Gourevitch, Peter. *Politics in Hard Times*. Ithaca, NY: Cornell University Press, 1991.

Gowa, Joanne. *Closing the Gold Window: Domestic Politics and the End of Bretton Woods*. Ithaca, NY: Cornell University Press, 1983.

Gramsci, Antonio. *Selections from the Prison Notebooks*. New York: International Publishers, 1971.

Greenberg, Edward S., and Richard P. Young. *American Politics Reconsidered*. North Scituate, MA: Duxbury Press, 1973.

Greenstein, Fred. *The Hidden Hand Presidency*. New York: Basic Books, 1982.

Greider, William. *Secrets of the Temple: How the Federal Reserve Runs the Country*. New York: Simon and Schuster, 1987.

Gutfleish, Ronald. "Why Protectionism? U.S. Corporate and State Responses to a Changing World Economy." Ph.D. dissertation, University of California–Berkeley, 1987.

Gwynne, Robert. "The World Motor Vehicle Industry," in Christopher J. Law, ed., *Restructuring the Global Automobile Industry*. London: Routledge, 1991.

Hamada, Koichi, and Hugh Patrick. "Japan and the International Monetary Regime," in Takashi Inogushi and Daniel Okimoto, eds., *The Political Economy of Japan*. Vol. 2, *The Changing International Context*. Stanford, CA: Stanford University Press, 1988.

Hamby, Alonzo. *Beyond the New Deal: Harry S. Truman and American Liberalism*. New York: Columbia University Press, 1973.

Harris, Nigel. *Of Bread and Guns*. New York: Pantheon, 1977.

Hawley, James. *Dollars and Borders: U.S. Government Attempts to Restrict Capital Flows*. Armonk, NY: M. E. Sharpe, 1987.

Hearden, Patrick. *Roosevelt Confronts Hitler*. DeKalb: Northern Illinois University Press, 1987.

Helleiner, Eric. *States and the Reemergence of Global Finance: From Bretton Woods to the 1990s*. Ithaca, NY: Cornell University Press, 1994.

Hobsbawm, Eric. *The Age of Extremes*. New York: Pantheon, 1995.

Hogan, Michael. "American Marshall Planners and the Search for a European Neocapitalism," *American Historical Review* 90 (February 1985): 44–72.

———. *Informal Entente: The Private Structure of Cooperation in Anglo-American Economic Diplomacy, 1918–1928*. Columbia: University of Missouri Press, 1977.

———. *The Marshall Plan: America, Britain, and the Reconstruction of Western Europe, 1947–52*. Cambridge: Cambridge University Press, 1987.

Holden, A. C. "The Repositioning of Ex-Im Bank." *Columbia Journal of World Business*, 31, 1 (Spring 1996): 82–93.

Hudson, Michael. *Global Fracture*. New York: Harper and Row, 1977.

Hufbauer, Gary, and Jeffrey Schott. *The North American Free Trade Agreement*. Washington, DC: Institute for International Economics, 1992.

Hufbauer, Gary, Diane T. Berliner, and Kimberly Elliott. *Trade Protection in the United States: 31 Case Studies*. Washington, DC: Institute for International Economics, 1986.

Hughes, Emmit J. *The Ordeal of Power*. New York: Atheneum, 1963.

Hunt, Michael. *Ideology and U.S. Foreign Policy*. New Haven, CT: Yale University Press, 1987.

Jackson, Brooks. "Financing the 1996 Campaign: The Law of the Jungle," in Larry Sabato, ed., *Toward the Millennium: The Elections of 1996*. Boston: Allyn and Bacon, 1997.

Joseph, Paul. *Cracks in the Empire*. New York: Columbia University Press, 1987.

Kahane, L. "Congressional Voting Patterns on NAFTA: An Empirical Analysis." *American Journal of Economics and Sociology* 55, 4 (October 1996): 395–409.

Katzenstein, Peter J., ed. *The Culture of National Security*. New York: Columbia University Press, 1996.

Kaufman, William. *The 1985 Defense Budget*. Washington, DC: The Brookings Institution, 1984.

Keohane, Robert. "State Power and Industry Influence: American Foreign Oil Policy in the 1940s." *International Organization* 36, 1 (Winter 1982): 165–183.

Kcttl, Donald F. *Leadership at the Fed*. Washington, DC: The Brookings Institution, 1986.

Kidron, Michael. *Western Capitalism Since the War*. Baltimore: Penguin Books, 1968.

Kolko, Gabriel. *Main Currents in Modern American History*. New York: Pantheon Books, 1984.

————. *The Roots of American Foreign Policy*. Boston: Little, Brown, 1969.

Kolko, Gabriel, and Joyce Kolko. *The Limits of Power*. New York: Harper and Row, 1972.

Kolko, Joyce. *Restructuring the World Economy*. New York: Pantheon Press, 1988.

Krugman, Paul. "Competitiveness: A Dangerous Obsession." *Foreign Affairs* 73, 2 (March/April 1994): 28–44.

Kurth, James. "The Political Consequences of the Product Life Cycle: Industrial History and Political Outcomes." *International Organization* 33, 1 (Winter 1979): 1–34.

LaFeber, Walter. *The American Age: U.S. Foreign Policy at Home and Abroad*, Vol. 2. New York: Norton, 1994.

Lee, R. Alton. *Truman and Taft-Hartley*. Lexington: University of Kentucky Press, 1966.

Lehman, Howard. *Indebted Development: Strategic Bargaining and Economic Adjustment in the Third World*. New York: St. Martin's Press, 1993.

Levin, N. Gordon, Jr. *Woodrow Wilson and World Politics*. New York: Columbia University Press, 1968.

Levine, Rhonda. *Class Struggle and the New Deal: Industrial Labor, Capital and the State*. Lawrence: University Press of Kansas, 1988.

Levinson, M. "Regarding Clinton Economic Package." *Dissent* 40, 2 (Spring 1993): 142–145.

Lippmann, Walter. *Drift and Mastery*. Englewood Cliffs, NJ: Prentice-Hall, 1961.

Lordan, Betsy. "Wheels of Fortune." *U.S./Latin Trade* 34, 1 (July 1993): 66.

Maier, Charles, ed. *In Search of Stability: Explorations in Historical Political Economy*. Cambridge: Cambridge University Press, 1987.

Mandel, Ernest. *Decline of the Dollar*. New York: Monad Press, 1972.

————. *Europe vs. America*. New York: New Left Books, 1970.

Marris, Stephen. *Deficits and the Dollar*. Washington, DC: Institute for International Economics, 1985.

Martin, C. J. "Mandating Social Change: The Business Struggle over National Health Reform." *Governance: An International Journal of Policy and Administration* 10, 4 (October 1997): 397–428.

Matusow, Allen. *The Unraveling of America: A History of Liberalism in the 1960s*. New York: Harper and Row, 1984.

Maytag, Fred, II. *Taxes and America's Future*. New York: National Association of Manufacturers, 1954.

McCormick, Thomas. *America's Half Century*. Baltimore: Johns Hopkins University Press, 1994.

McIntyre, Robert S., and Dean C. Tipps. "Inequity and Decline: How the Reagan Administration Tax Policies Are Affecting the American Taxpayer and Economy." Washington, DC: Center on Budget Priorities, 1983.

McKeowan, Timothy. "A Liberal Trade Order? The Long-Run Pattern of Imports to the Advanced Capitalist States." *International Studies Quarterly* 35 (1991): 151–172.

McQuaid, Kim. *Uneasy Partners: Big Business in American Politics, 1945–1990.* Baltimore: Johns Hopkins University Press, 1994.

McWilliams, Wilson Carey. *The Politics of Disappointment.* Chatham, NJ: Chatham House, 1995.

Melman, Seymour. *The Permanent War Economy.* New York: Simon and Schuster, 1985.

Merelman, Richard. *Making Something of Ourselves.* Berkeley: University of California Press, 1984.

Mikdashi, Zuhayr. *Transnational Oil: Issues, Policies and Perspectives.* New York: St. Martin's Press, 1986.

Miliband, Ralph. *The State in Capitalist Society.* New York: Basic Books, 1969.

Milner, Helen. *Resisting Protectionism.* Princeton, NJ: Princeton University Press, 1988.

Miroff, Bruce. *Pragmatic Illusions.* New York: David McKay Company, 1976.

Moody, Kim. "Towards an International Social-Movement Unionism." *New Left Review* 225 (September/October 1997): 52–73.

Morgan, Iwan. *Eisenhower Versus the Spenders.* New York: St. Martin's Press, 1990.

National Association of Manufacturers. *Tax Rule Reforms Mean Faster Economic Growth.* New York: NAM, 1960.

Nau, Henry. "Where Reaganomics Works," *Foreign Policy* 57 (Winter 1984–1985): 14–37.

Nestor, William. *Japan's Growing Predominance over the World Economy.* New York: St. Martin's Press, 1990.

Nixon, Richard. *RN: The Memoirs of Richard Nixon.* New York: Grosset and Dunlap, 1978.

Nolt, James H. "Business Conflict and the Origins of the Pacific War." Ph.D. dissertation, University of Chicago, 1994.

Nowell, Gregory P. "International Relations Theories: Approaches to Business and the State," in Ronald W. Cox, ed., *Business and the State in International Relations.* Boulder, CO: Westview Press, 1996.

———. *Mercantile States and the World Oil Cartel, 1900–1939.* Ithaca, NY: Cornell University Press, 1994.

O'Connor, James. *The Fiscal Crisis of the State.* New York: St. Martin's Press, 1973.

Odell, John. *U.S. International Monetary Policy: Markets, Power and Ideas as Sources of Change.* Princeton, NJ: Princeton University Press, 1982.

Oliver, Robert. *International Economic Cooperation and the World Bank.* London: Macmillan Press, 1975.

Organization for Economic Cooperation and Development. "OECD's Code for Liberalization of Capital Movements." *OECD Observer* 55 (December 1971): 38–43.

Painter, David. *Oil and the American Century.* Baltimore: Johns Hopkins University Press, 1986.

Palmer, John, and Isabel Sawhill, eds. *The Reagan Record.* Cambridge, MA: Bullinger, 1984.

Pantojas-Garcia, Emilio. "The United States' Caribbean Basin Initiative and the Puerto Rican Experience," *Latin American Perspectives* 12: 105–128.

Parrini, Carl. *Heir to Empire: United States Economic Diplomacy*. Pittsburgh: University of Pittsburgh Press, 1969.

Peterson, M. A. "Political Influence in the 1990s: From Iron Triangles to Policy Networks." *Journal of Health Politics, Policy and Law* 18, 2 (Summer 1993): 395–438.

Phillips, Kevin. *Arrogant Capital*. Boston: Little, Brown, 1994.

———. *The Politics of Rich and Poor*. New York: Random House, 1990.

Preeg, Ernest. "The Compatibility of Regional Economic Blocs and GATT," in Sidney Weintraub, ed., *Free Trade in the Western Hemisphere*. London: Sage Periodicals Press, 1993.

Pringle, Robert. "Financial Markets and Governments." Working Paper No. 57. Helsinki: World Institute for Development Economics Research, 1987.

Quadango, Jill. *The Transformation of Old Age Security*. Chicago: University of Chicago Press, 1988.

———. "Welfare Capitalism and the Social Security Act of 1935." *American Sociological Review* 49 (1984): 640.

Rehder, R. R. "Japanese Transplants: A New Model for Detroit." *Business Horizons* 31, 1 (1995): 52–61.

Reich, Robert. *Work of Nations*. New York. Vintage Press, 1992.

Reichard, Gary. *The Reaffirmation of Republicanism*. Knoxville: University of Tennessee Press, 1975.

Reichley, James. *Conservatives in an Age of Change: The Nixon and Ford Administrations*. Washington, DC: Brookings Institution, 1982.

Roberts, Paul C. *The Supply-Side Revolution*. Cambridge: Cambridge University Press, 1984.

Robinson, William. *Promoting Polyarchy: Globalization, U.S. Intervention and Hegemony*. New York: Cambridge University Press, 1996.

Rogers, Joel, and Thomas Ferguson, eds. *The Hidden Election*. New York: Pantheon Press, 1981.

Rosecrance, Richard. *The Rise of the Trading State: Commerce and Conquest in the Modern World*. New York: Basic Books, 1986.

Rosenbaum, Herbert, and Alexej Ugrinsky. *The Presidency and Domestic Politics of Jimmy Carter*. Westport, CT: Greenwood Press, 1994.

Ross, Robert, and Kent Trachte. *Global Capitalism: The New Leviathan*. Albany: State University of New York Press, 1990.

Rubenstein, James M. "The Impact of Japanese Investment in the United States," in Christopher J. Law, ed., *Restructuring the Global Automobile Industry*. London: Routledge, 1991.

Ruggie, John. "International Regimes, Transactions and Change: Embedded Liberalism in the Postwar Economic Order." *International Organization* 36, 2 (Spring 1982): 379–416.

Saloma, John, III. *Ominous Politics: The New Conservative Labyrinth*. New York: Hill and Wang, 1984.

Sanders, Jerry. *Peddlers of Crisis: The Committee on the Present Danger and the Politics of Containment*. Boston: South End Press, 1983.

Schriftgeisser, Karl. *Business and Public Policy*. Englewood Cliffs, NJ: Prentice Hall, 1967.

Scofield, Jerri-Lynn. "The Business of Strategy: The Political Economy of U.S. Trade Policy Toward the U.S.S.R., 1945–1975," in Ronald W. Cox, ed.,

Business and the State in International Relations. Boulder, CO: Westview Press, 1996.

————. "Foreign Policy as Domestic Politics: The Political Economy of U.S. Trade Policy, 1960–1975." Ph.D. dissertation, Oxford University, 1997.

Shepherd, William G. "Causes of Increased Competition in the U.S. Economy, 1939–1980." *Review of Economics and Statistics* (November 1984): 624.

Shoup, Lawrence, and William Minter. *Imperial Brain Trust*. New York: Monthly Review Press, 1977.

Skidmore, David. *Reversing Course*. Nashville, TN: Vanderbilt University Press, 1996.

Sloan, John W. *Eisenhower and the Management of Prosperity*. Lawrence: University Press of Kansas, 1991.

Sloan, John W. "President Eisenhower, Professor Burns, and the 1953–1954 Recession," in Melvin J. Dubnick and Alan R. Gitelson, eds., *Public Policy and Economic Institutions*. Greenwich, CT: JAI Press, 1991.

Sobel, Robert. *The Age of Giant Corporations: A Microeconomic History of American Business, 1914–1970*. Westport, CT: Greenwood Press, 1972.

Solomon, Robert. *The International Monetary System, 1945–1976*. New York: Harper and Row, 1977.

Sorauf, Frank. *Inside Campaign Finance: Myth and Realities*. New Haven, CT: Yale University Press, 1992.

Stallings, Barbara. *Banker to the Third World*. Berkeley: University of California Press, 1987.

Stant, William. "Business Conflict and U.S. Trade Policy," in Ronald W. Cox, ed., *Business and the State in International Relations*. Boulder, CO: Westview Press, 1996.

Stein, Herbert. *Presidential Economics*. Washington, DC: American Enterprise Institute, 1988.

Theoharis, Athan. "The Rhetoric of Politics: Foreign Policy, Internal Security, and Domestic Politics in the Truman Era, 1945–1950" in Barton Bernstein, ed., *The Politics and Policies of the Truman Administration*. Chicago: Quadrangle Press, 1970.

Tolchin, Susan. *The Angry American*. Boulder, CO: Westview Press, 1996.

Trubowitz, Peter. *Defining the National Interest*. Chicago: University of Chicago Press, 1998.

U.S. Congress. *Congress and the Nation, 1945–1964*. 3 vols. Washington, DC: Congressional Quarterly, 1965.

U.S. Congress. House Committee on Government Operations. *Delay, Slowness in Decisionmaking and the Backlog at the National Labor Relations Board*. 98th Congress, 2nd Session, 1984, Report 98.

Van Der Pijl, Kees. *The Making of an Atlantic Ruling Class*. London: Verso, 1984.

Vatter, Harold. *The U.S. Economy in the 1950s*. Chicago: University of Chicago Press, 1984.

Vogel, David. *Kindred Strangers: The Uneasy Relationship Between Business and Politics in America*. Princeton, NJ: Princeton University Press, 1996.

Wade, Robert. "Globalization and Its Limits," in Suzanne Berger and Ronald Dore, eds., *National Diversity and Global Capitalism*. Ithaca, NY: Cornell University Press, 1996.

Wala, Michael. *The Council on Foreign Relations and American Foreign Policy in the Early Cold War Era*. Providence, RI: Berghahn Books, 1994.

Walters, Robert, and David Blake. *The Politics of Global Economic Relations*. Englewood Cliffs, NJ: Prentice Hall, 1972.

Waters, Malcolm. *Globalization*. London: Routledge, 1995.

Walton, Richard. *Henry Wallace, Harry Truman, and the Cold War*. New York: Viking Press, 1976.

Webber, Michael, and David Rigby. *The Golden Age Illusion: Rethinking Postwar Capitalism*. New York: Guilford Press, 1996.

Weintraub, Sidney, Luis Rubio, and Alan Jones, eds. *U.S.-Mexican Industrial Integration*. Boulder, CO: Westview Press, 1991.

Weiss, Linda. "Globalization and the Myth of the Powerless State." *New Left Review* 225 (September/October 1997): 3–27.

Wexler, Immanuel. *The Marshall Plan Revisited*. Westport, CT: Greenwood Press, 1983.

Wilkins, Mira. *The Maturing of Multinational Enterprise*. Cambridge: Harvard University Press, 1974.

Wood, Robert. *From Marshall Plan to Debt Crisis*. Berkeley: University of California Press, 1986.

"World Finance Survey." *Economist,* December 14, 1974.

Zeitlin, Maurice. *The Large Corporation and Contemporary Classes*. New Brunswick, NJ: Rutgers University Press, 1989.

Zieger, Robert. *The CIO, 1935–1955*. Chapel Hill: University of North Carolina Press, 1995.

PRESIDENTIAL LIBRARIES AND ARCHIVES

Jimmy Carter Presidential Library, Athens, Georgia.

Dwight D. Eisenhower Presidential Library, Abilene, Kansas.

Gerald R. Ford Presidential Library, Ann Arbor, Michigan.

Herbert Hoover Presidential Library, West Branch, Iowa.

Lyndon B. Johnson Presidential Library, Austin, Texas.

John F. Kennedy Presidential Library, Boston, Massachusetts.

National Archives, College Park, Maryland.

Harry S. Truman Presidential Library, Independence, Missouri.

Index

Acheson, Dean, 51
Acts of Congress: Economic Recovery Tax
   Act, 169; Employment Act, *1946,* 75;
   Export Control Act, *1949,* 93; Fordney-
   McCumber tariff, *1922,* 18; Full
   Employment Act, *1946,* 96, 154;
   Humphrey-Hawkins Act, *1978,* 154;
   Jackson-Vanik amendment, 153;
   Landrum-Griffin Act, 95; Lundeen bill,
   25–26; Mutual Security Assistance Act,
   76, 77; National Industrial Recovery Act
   (NIRA), 23, 35n21; National Labor
   Relations Act, 11; Reciprocal Trade
   Agreements Act, *1934,* 19, 29, 90–91,
   106, 108–109; Revenue Act, *1964,* 115,
   118; Smoot-Hawley tariff, *1930,* 18;
   Social Security Act, *1935,* 19, 24–26;
   Taft-Hartley Act, 30, 60, 71, 95; Trade
   Act, *1974,* 131, 136n88, 150, 152, 157;
   Trade Act, *1979* 136n88, 150, 154–155,
   157; Trade Expansion Act (TEA), *1962,*
   106, 107, 108–110, 119–120, 131;
   Wagner Act, *1935,* 19, 23–24, 25
Affirmative action, 4
Africa, 54
African Americans, 10; as Democrats, 208;
   lower wages of, 24, 24n21; in the
   post–World War II era, 30; social welfare
   programs and, 4, 118
Agency for International Development
   (USAID), 207
Agricultural Adjustment Administration, 24
Aid to Families with Dependent Children
   (AFDC), 4, 119, 170, 206
Alcoa, 156
Aldrich, Winston, 32
Alexander, Lamar, 209–210
Allen, Richard, 197n1

Alton Jones Foundation, 184
Ambrose, Stephen, 143
American Apparel Manufacturers
   Association, 190
American Bankers Association, 47, 48–49,
   50, 53
American Business Council, 169, 174–175
American Committee on the East-West
   Accord, 177
American Conservative Union, 177
American Federation of Labor (AFL), 24,
   26
American Federation of Labor–Congress of
   Industrial Organizations (AFL-CIO), 46,
   95–96, 112–113, 217
American Labor Party, 100n12
American Plan, 22
American President Lines, 47
American Security Council, 177, 178
American Soybean Association, 195
American Telephone and Telegraph
   (AT&T), 211
American Textile Manufacturers Institute,
   190, 195
Americans for Democratic Action (ADA),
   100n12
Amoco, 164, 177
Anderson, Robert B., 80, 98, 117
Angry white males, 4, 15n11, 216
Ansell, Amy, 146, 150, 153
Anticommunism, 54, 62, 166; in the
   McCarthy era, 58, 68, 71
Antidumping, 155, 182
Antilabor organizations, 163–164
Antitrust laws, 23, 120
Argentina, 28, 191
Armco, 78, 156
Arms control, 9

Asia: communist expansion in, 58, 67; European recovery and, 54; parts production in, 121, 162; U.S. direct investment in, 46; U.S. military involvement in, 39, 72. *See also individual countries*
Aski marks, 28
Atlantic Alliance. *See* North Atlantic Treaty Organization
Australia, 125, 130
Auto industry, 184–187, 191–194
AVX Ceramics, 188, 190
Ayres, Leonard, 49

B-1 bomber, 176–177
Balance-of-payments: deficits in, 68, 80, 127–128, 129, 130; in the Kennedy era, 98, 114; in the Nixon era, 131, 132, 137; as restraint on U.S. foreign economic policy, 97; surpluses in, 53, 56, 71–72
Balanced budgets, 151
Ball, George, 91
Bank of America, 26; band exchange rates, 126; capital controls, 125; Democratic Party, 183; Fed policy, 172; Mexican debt crisis, 200n39
Bank of England, 143
Bank of International Settlements (BIS), 32
Bankers Trust, 200n39
Banking: capital controls, 31, 32, 44; deregulation of, 149; Eurodollar market, 121–124; inflation, 163; international loans, 88; International Monetary Fund, 49; Marshall Plan, 53; Middle Eastern deposits, 165; multilateralism in, 196; New Deal provisions for, 81; Vietnam war opposition of, 131
Barbour, Haley, 208
Basel Agreement, 125
Beaulieu, Inc., 210
Beckman, 188
Belgium, 77
Bell, Coral, 151
Bentsen, Lloyd, 156
Bernstein, Barton, 213
Bernstein, Carl, 144
Bilateral assistance, 45–46, 77. *See also* Marshall Plan
Block, Fred, 48, 141, 145
Blough, Roger, 112
Boies, John, 179
Brazil, 28, 165, 191
Bretton Woods system: balance-of-payments, 98; business conflict and, 47–51; capital controls under, 2–3; class conflict and, 30–33; development of, 18, 26, 27–30; end of, 125–126, 128, 142,

143–144; Eurodollar market, 122; interest bloc role in, 37–38; in the Kennedy-Johnson era, 99; Keynesian economics in the, 154; liberalization of, 2; nationalist opposition to, 39; Nixon support of, 142–143; political economy of, 42–47; purpose of, 2; as transfer from British to U.S. world hegemony, 27
Bristol-Myers, 47
British Carborundum, 94
British loan, 20
Brussels Treaty Organization, 77
Bryan, William Jennings, 101n25
Buchanan, Pat, 4, 13, 152, 207, 208–209
Budget, Bureau of the, 110
Buffett, Howard, 49
Bullis, Harry, 91
Bundesbank, 127
Bureau of Labor Statistics, 30
Burgess, W. Randolph, 49, 77
Burns, Arthur F., 75, 94–95, 98, 99; capital controls, 138, 139, 140, 141, 142, 145; dollar devaluation, 144; exchange rates, 147
Bush, George H. W., 13, 216
Bush administration, 13, 203, 207
Business Advisory Council (BAC), 99n3; conflict over appointments to, 112; employment, 75; internationalism in, 18, 46, 68; Nixon's enemies list, 145; North American Free Trade Agreement, 197; role in Eisenhower administration, 90; Social Security, 24–25, 73, 74; Trade Department proposal, 156; wage and price controls, 144
Business Committee for Tax Reduction, 116
Business conflict, 5–6, 15n4; approach in political science, 15n4; Bretton Woods and, 47–51; decline of postwar liberalism and, 9, 213–214; long-term political planning, 40; Marshall Plan and, 51–56; in the Nixon era, 144–147; in the Reagan era, 166–167, 214; U.S. foreign policy and, 17–20, 37
Business Council for International Understanding (BCIU), 149, 150
Business and Defense Services Administration, 90
Business and Industry Committee for Bretton Woods, 50
Business International Corporation, 189
Business International Washington Roundtable (Business Roundtable), 129, 148–149, 156, 163, 169, 218
Business internationalists: Cold War role of, 7, 62; conflict with nationalists, 18, 79, 81–89; continued dominance of,

218–219; General Agreement on Tariffs and Trade, 12, 20; the Great Society and, 117–119; interventionism in the economy, 61–62; in the Kennedy era, 111–117; without liberalism, 153–157, 215; long-term political planning by, 40–42; the New Deal and, 20–26; trade expansion, 107–108; Western Europe and, 7, 42–43, 46, 76–81, 93–95, 97

Business nationalists: in the Clinton era, 207–208; Cold War, 57; conflict with internationalists, 79, 81–89; conservatism of, 216; effect of Goldwater defeat on, 117–118; in the McCarthy era, 59; Marshall Plan and, 39, 55–56; military aid to Western Europe, 45; *Business Week*, 63n13

Byrd, Harry, 115

Calder, Curtis, 54
California Spray and Chemical, 94
Caltex, 94
Campaign finance, 210–212
Canada, 110, 125, 130, 187
Capital controls: elimination of, 128, 129, 131–132, 137–142, 145–146; the International Monetary Fund and, 44, 45, 46, 50; under Bretton Woods, 2–3; U.S. opinion shift on, 122–126; in Western Europe, 31–32, 44, 130, 162
Capital-intensive business: appeasement of Hitler by, 28–29; attitude toward Western Europe, of 43; in the Democratic Party, 24, 26, 183; New Deal support by, 6–7; and the product life cycle, 40; Vietnam war opposition, 130–131
Capital market deregulation, 12, 174
Capital Markets Working Group, 148
Capital shortfall theory, 148–149
Caribbean Basin Initiative (CBI), 12, 167, 181, 184, 187–190
Caribbean/Central American Action (CCAA), 184, 187–188
Carnegie Foundation, 184
Carter, Jimmy, 11, 150, 151, 154
Carter administration: economic downturn during, 164; economic policies, 150; labor-backed program defeat during, 154; military spending, 165–166, 176; rightward shift in, 161; tight-money policy of, 172; trade reorganization, 155, 156, 157
Castells, Manuel, 151
Caterpillar, 107
Central America, 108, 165, 166
Chambers of Commerce, 22, 25, 46, 134n31

Chase Manhattan (Chase National Bank): Bretton Woods, 47; capital controls, 137, 142; Democratic Party, 183; German recovery, 78; Mexican debt crisis, 200n39; U.S.–Western Europe tariff reduction, 107
Chemical Bank, 184, 200n39
Chevron, 164, 177, 178
Chiang Kai-shek, 57
Chile, 28
China: communist victory in, 57, 67; U.S. investment in, 145, 189; U.S. recognition of, 146
Chrysler, 183, 192
Citibank. *See* First National City Bank of New York
Citizenship rights, 96
Civic culture, 212
Civil rights: Kennedy downplaying of, 114; in the post–World War II era, 30, 62; in the Reagan era, 170; southern opposition to, 60
Class conflict, 14. *See also* Labor unions
Clayton, William, 51
Clinton, Bill, 217; on big government, 4; business constituencies of, 205, 210, 212; election of, 207, 214; North American Free Trade Agreement, 203–204; social welfare programs, 206
Clinton administration, 203
Coca-Cola, 184
Cold War: consensus internationalism of, 7, 62; cost of, 145; end of, 203, 204; Jackson-Vanik amendment, 153; long-term nature of, 69; nationalist support of, 57
Coleman, John, 91
Colson, Charles, 138, 139, 140, 141, 145
Commerce, U.S. Department of, 46, 63n13; antidumping, 155; capital controls, 139, 140; foreign direct investment, 137; foreign market access, 90; protection for textile industry, 109; tariffs, 155
Committee for Economic Development (CED): Bretton Woods, 26; capital controls, 123; Commission on Money and Credit, 115; employment, 75, 154; inflation, 154; International Monetary Fund, 49; internationalist interest bloc, 18, 46, 68, 112; political role of, 113–114, 134n29; tax-exempt status of, 91; tight-money policy, 173; trade expansion, 106; wage and price controls, 144
Committee for a National Trade Policy (CNTP), 91, 107, 131
Committee on the Present Danger, 9, 165, 176–179, 197n1

Common Market. *See* European Economic Community (EEC)
Communism, 58, 61, 67, 71
Competitiveness, 151
Congress of Industrial Organizations (CIO), 61, 71
Connally, John, 141
Connecticut Manufacturing Association, 25
Conoco, 164
Conservatism, 67; in the *1990*s, 207–208; among Democrats, 4, 208; cultural, 11, 216; in the Eisenhower era, 76; emergence of, 147–153; hegemony of, 206–210; internationalist, 215; military spending, 58, 130; multinationalist, 153, 157; nationalist, 216
Cooley, Harold, 109
Cooper, John, 146
Coors, Joseph, 197*n*1
Cordon, Guy, 88
Corporate commonwealth, 72–76
Corporate political blocs, 18
Council of Economic Advisors (CEA), 75, 110
Council on Capital Formation, 169
Council on Foreign Economic Policy, 90
Council on Foreign Relations (CFR): Bretton Woods, 26, 47; business nationalists and, 45; internationalist interest bloc support from, 18, 42–43, 46
Cox, Ronald W., 108
Cumings, Bruce, 31, 58
Curacao, 188
Currencies: collapse of, 30; controls on, 31–32; convertibility of, 42, 79; devaluation of, 53, 127; exchange rate stabilization, 125; floating rates of exchange, 129, 147

Dataram, 188, 190
Dean Witter, 209
Declaration of Atlantic Unity, *1954*, 94
Defense, U.S. Department of, 177
Deficits: balance-of-payments, 68, 80, 127–128, 129, 130; budget, 12–13, 207; trade, 128, 132
Del Monte, 156
Democratic Party: African-Americans as members of, 208; capital-intensive investors in, 24, 26, 183; coalition, 213; conservatives in, 4, 208; labor influence in, 183; as neoliberal bloc, 215; Nixon appeal to members of, 151; North American Free Trade Agreement, 203–204
Denmark, 48
Dent, Harry, 152

Depreciation, 114
Depression, Great, 19–20, 57
Deregulation, 174, 207
Destler, I. M., 195
Détente, 9, 131, 145, 153
Deutchmark, 127
Devereux, Eric, 130, 145
Dewey, Charles, 49
Dillon, C. Douglas, 105; balance-of-payments, 114; taxation, 115, 116, 121
Dillon Read, 78, 176, 178
Divided government, 203
Dodge, Joseph M., 72
Dole, Robert, 206, 208–209; attack on big government, 4; cultural conservatives and, 216; supporters of, 212; tax cuts, 210; Trade Department proposal, 156
Dollar, U.S.: devaluation of, 128, 132, 144; floating of, 143; gap in Western Europe, 51, 55, 70; Japanese reserves, 51; overhang, 72; overvaluation of, 9; retention in U.S. of, 125; rise of, 180; stability of, 80, 99; strength of, 97, 124. *See also* Gold
Domestic Council, 148
Domhoff, William, 11
Dominican Republic, 189
Downey, Sheridan, 82
Du Bois, W. E. B., 71, 100*n*12
Du Pont, 26
Dukakis, Michael, 205
Dulles, John Foster, 59, 69, 77, 89
Dumbrell, John, 154
Durkin, Martin, 95

East-West trade, 131, 145, 152
Eastern Europe, 8, 131
Eastman Kodak, 29, 156
Economic Cooperation Administration, 44, 46
Economic Policy Board, 172
Ecton, Zayles, 88
Eden, Lynn, 58
Education, 68
Ehrlichman, John, 139
Eisenhower, Dwight D.: appointees of, 90; balance-of-payments, 98; business nationalist opposition to, 59, 83, 88; Cold War, 69; conservative influence on, 76; full employment, 154; inflation, 80, 97, 154; Korean War, 71; the military-industrial complex and, 68; organized labor, 100*n*15; welfare state programs, 72–73
Eisenhower administration: budget cuts, 67–68; internationalist policies, 76, 80, 89–90; tax policy, 115, 116; trade

politics, 90–93; U.S. aid to Europe, 79–80
El Salvador, 188, 207
Elections: of *1896*, 101n25; of *1936*, 26; of *1946*, 57, 59; of *1948*, 59, 60, 61, 73; of *1952*, 61, 100n12; of *1958*, 99; of *1960*, 99, 105; of *1964*, 83; of *1968*, 131; of *1994*, 15n11; of *1996*, 208–212, British, *1945*, 33
Electronics firms, 185–186, 187, 188, 189–190
Emergency Committee for American Trade (ECAT), 156–157
Employment, 75, 154
Entitlement reform, 12
Environmental Protection Agency (EPA), 170
Environmentalism, 216, 221n29
Ervin, Sam, 144
Esso, 94
Eurobonds, 174
Eurodollar market, 121–124, 125, 126–127, 128, 142
Europe. capital flight from, 173, competition with U.S. firms, 190; Fortune 500 companies in, 21; integration of, 78, 89, 93; macroeconomic growth rates of, 68. *See also* Western Europe
European Coal and Steel Community (ECSC), 78, 93
European Cooperation Administration (ECA), 79
European Defense Community (EDC), 77
European Economic Community (EEC): British membership, 79, 106; business internationalist support for, 7, 93–95; deregulation of capital markets, 174, large corporations in, 120; steel exports from, 182; tariff reduction, 107; U.S. investment in, 129
European Payments Union (EPU), 53, 78, 79, 94
European Recovery Administration, 52
European Recovery Program, 55
Evan, John K., 93
Export-dependent business: attitude toward Europe of, 43–44, 97; ECSC loan, 78; Marshall Plan, 53–54; tight money policies, 175
Export-Import Bank, 78, 90, 207
Exports: agricultural, 19; drop in, 56; state financing of, 162; to Europe, 124
Exxon, 176, 177

Fair Deal: internationalist-nationalist split, 82, 84–87; labor ineffectiveness toward, 30; military spending increases and, 39, 47; as victim of move to the right, 71

Farm workers, 19, 24
Fascism, 61
Fast-track legislation, 14, 206
Federal Reserve, 72; balance-of-payments, 98; capital controls, 139; Eurodollar market, 122; European recovery, 79; income gap, 171; tight-money policy, 81, 168, 171–172, 174
Federation of German Industries, 93
Feldstein, Martin, 173
Ferguson, Homer, 83, 88
Ferguson, Thomas, 26, 31
Ferguson, Yale, 218
Firestone Rubber, 78
First National City Bank of New York (Citibank), 77; Bretton Woods, 47; capital controls, 125, 142; Federal Reserve policy, 172; flexible exchange rates, 126; German recovery, 78; Mexican debt crisis, 200n39; military spending, 176, 178; tight money policy, 200n40
Fiske, John, 209
Flanigan, Peter, 139–140, 145
Floating rates of exchange, 9
Folsom, Marion B., 74, 117
Food and Drug Administration (FDA), 170–171
Food stamps, 170, 210
Forbes, Steve, 209
Ford, Gerald, 153
Ford, Henry, II, 116, 145–146
Ford administration, 144, 148, 150
Ford Foundation, 184
Ford Motor Company: European regionalism, 94; labor relations, 30; production in Mexico, 192; production of Nazi tanks by, 29
Fordham, Benjamin, 58, 82
Foreign aid, 17, 38, 95
Foreign direct investment, 63n13, 160n74; in Asia, 46, 145, 189; end or reduction of, 125, 130; European regionalism, 78, 94; Japanese, 184–187, 189; Marshall Plan and, 52; military aid as promoter of, 77; policy framework for promotion of, 40, 41; reduction of controls on, 137–138, 158n17; trade barriers and, 93; under Bretton Woods, 42; in the United States, 166, 173; in Western Europe, 42–44, 72
Foreign Operations Administration, 78
Foreign Policy Association, 77
Formosa. *See* Taiwan
Forrestal, James, 26
Fortune, 63n13
Franc, Swiss, 127

France: capital control programs, 123; Communist Party, 44, 50; German rearmament, 77; labor unions, 33, 61; state financing of exports, 162; World Bank loans to, 48
Fraser, Leon, 49
French-American Committee, 93–94
Frieden, Jeffrey, 58
Friedman, Milton, 126, 144

Galbraith, John K., 114
Galvin, Robert, 156
Gandhi, Indira, 146
General Agreement on Tariffs and Trade (GATT): export-dependent business support for, 43; Geneva Round, 133n11; internationalist business support for, 12, 20; Kennedy Round, 90, 131; nationalist opposition to, 207; regional trade agreements, 187, 193, 194; Tokyo Round, 136n88, 146, 152, 154–155, 167; trade liberalization, 180, 181; Uruguay Round, 183, 193; World Trade Organization, 206
General Electric: in the 1920s, 21; Bretton Woods, 47; German recovery, 78, 90; military spending, 178; Trade Department proposal, 156; U.S.–Western Europe tariff reduction, 107
General Mills, 47
General Motors: Bretton Woods, 47; labor relations, 30; production in Mexico, 192; production of Nazi tanks by, 29
Gephardt, Richard, 212
German-American Capital Commission, 78
German-American Economic Association, 78, 89, 93
Germany: Christian Democratic Party, 77; economic rise of, 124; growth rate, 99; labor unions in, 33; low military spending in, 69; productionist approach toward, 78; rearmament of, 77–78; reconstruction and recovery of, 29, 78, 90; U.S. competitiveness and, 151; U.S. exports to, 28–29; U.S. investment in, 28; voluntary export restraint agreements, 182–183; Weimar era, 19
Gibbs, David, 108
Gibbs-Hill France, 94
Giddens, Anthony, 96
Gillette, 107
Gingrich, Newt, 4, 206, 208, 212, 217
Global leadership, 27
Globalization perspectives, 1–2, 219
Gold: decrease in U.S. stock, 125; fixed-rate of, 4, 80, 97, 143; reserves, 51, 98; suspension of convertibility, 9, 128, 132. See also Dollar, U.S.

Gold Pool, 125
Goldman, Sachs, 176, 178
Goldwater, Barry M.: defeat of, 117–118; nationalist influence on, 83, 88, 130, 207; nomination of, 6; protectionism, 110, 120; Social Security, 73; social welfare programs, 119
Good Neighbor League, 26
Goodyear, 156
Gramm, Phil, 209
Great Society, 8, 117–119
Greenspan, Alan, 142
Group of Seven, 174
Guilder, Dutch, 127
Gulf Oil, 179
Gulf War, 203, 204

Hagedorn, George, 116
Haig, Alexander, 168
Haiti, 188–189
Hallinan, Vincent, 61, 100n12
Hamby, Alonzo, 58, 59
Hancock, John Milton, 26
Hanna, Mark, 101n25
Harriman, Averell, 26
Harriman, Henry, 24, 25
Health care, 30, 105, 205
Hecht, Rudolph, 26
Heinz, John, 156
Helleiner, Eric, 48, 173
Heller, Walter, 75, 116, 149
Heltzer, Harry, 138–139
Hemingway, W. L., 49
Herlong-Baker bills, 117
Hewlett-Packard, 156, 176
Hickenlooper, Bourke, 54
High volume production, 73, 100n16
Hight, John, 112
Hill, Richard D., 149, 150
Hilton Hotels, 47
Hispanics, 208
Hiss, Alger, 152
Hitachi, 186
Hitler, Adolf, 28–29
Hodges, Luther, 112, 133n11
Hoffman, Paul, 79
Honeywell, 94, 176, 177
Hong Kong, 189
Hoover, Herbert C., 83
House of Representatives, U.S.: Banking and Currency Committee, 49, 50; Ways and Means Committee, 114, 169; Ways and Means Subcommittee on Trade, 190
Housing, 60, 72
Hufbauer, Gary, 192
Humphrey, George, 69, 76, 80, 89, 96, 100n25

Humphrey, Hubert H., 100n12, 146

IBM. *See* International Business Machines (IBM)
Identity politics, 4, 216
Illinois Manufacturing Association, 25
Imperial Preference System, 28, 29
Import controls, 92, 110, 185
Imports, 120, 175
Income gap, 170, 171
India, 146
Indonesia, 189
Industrial Policy Advisory Committee (IPAC), 156
Industrial Relations Counselors, Inc. (IRC), 21
Inflation: banker concern with, 163; containment of, 16n25; currency controls and, 32; dollar-gold convertibility and, 80, 97; employment and, 154; military spending and, 71; in the Nixon era, 131, 137; wage hikes and, 10, 96; wage and price controls, 137, 144
Infrastructure development, 81
Ingersoll-Rand, 176
Institutional dynamics, 38–39
Intellectuals, 75
Interbusiness conflict. *See* Business conflict
Interest blocs, 37–38, 74–75
Interest Equalization Tax (IET), 121–122, 125, 137, 140
Interior, U.S. Department of, 92, 110
Internal Revenue Service (IRS), 146
International Business Machines (IBM), 107; capital controls, 139, 142, 143, cooperation with Nazis, 29; Democratic Party, 183, 184; European regionalism, 94; external borrowing by, 124
International Chamber of Commerce: capital controls, 125; European Economic Community, 93–94; Germany, 78; Trade Expansion Act, 107; U.S. Council of, 112
International Economic Policy Association (IEPA), 141, 158n17
International General Electric, 94
International Harvester, 156
International Monetary Fund (IMF): aid to Western Europe, 79; business internationalist support for, 7, 20; capital controls, 44, 45, 46; establishment of, 38, 39, 42; exchange rates, 127; guidelines for lending by, 49; increase of capital subscriptions, 125; loans to less developed countries, 149; Marshall Plan, 53; Mexican debt crisis, 174–175; monetarist approach to lending by, 50; as

multilateral trade arbiter, 144; Treasury Department role in planning for, 48
International Paper, 156
Internationalization, 184–187
Iran, 164–165, 178
Ireland, 188
Italy: Communist Party, 44, 50; labor unions in, 33; U.S. textile agreement with, 92; WEU membership for, 77

Japan: competition with U.S. firms, 184–186, 189–190, 191; depletion of dollar reserves, 51; deregulation of capital markets, 174; economic rise of, 124; foreign direct investment in the United States, 184–187, 189; growth rate, 99; low military spending in, 69; macroeconomic growth rates of, 68; reduction of investment in, 125, 130; state financing of exports, 162; U.S. competitiveness and, 151; U.S. textile agreement with, 92; voluntary export restraint agreements, 182, 185, 186
Job Guarantee Office, 154
Johnson, Louis, 58
Johnson, Lyndon B., 75; business supporters of, 117; election victory of, 83; Vietnam war, 130, 145
Johnson administration: capital controls, 131, 139; dollar stabilization, 124–125; Eurodollar market, 122, 126; military spending, 118; social welfare programs, 118
Johnson and Johnson, 94
Jorgenson, Earle, 197n1
Joseph, Paul, 149, 150
Justice, U.S. Department of, 120

Kaiser, Edgar, 145, 146
Katzenstein, Peter J., 218
Kay Electronics, 188
Kemp, Jack, 210
Kendall, Donald, 177
Kennedy, David, 139, 140, 141, 142
Kennedy, John F., 75; balance-of-payments, 98, 114; civil rights, 114; internationalist position of, 114; protection for textile industry, 109; tax policy, 114–115
Kennedy administration: dollar stabilization, 124; Eurodollar market, 122; trade expansion, 105–106; U.S.–Western Europe tariff reduction, 107
Kerr, Robert S., 109
Keynesian economics, 10, 68, 75, 99, 111; in the Bretton Woods framework, 154; criticism of, 148; Richard Nixon as supporter of, 132; taxation, 115–116

Khomeini, Ruhollah, 164
Kidder-Peabody, 142
Kissinger, Henry, 149, 150
Knowland, William F., 88
Kolko, Joyce, 148
Korean War, 39, 58, 61, 67, 71–72, 77, 100n12

Labor unions: Amalgamated Clothing and Textile Workers, 164, 190; antilabor activities, 163–164; auto industry struggles, 191; campaign funding by, 211; in the Clinton era, 14, 205; communists in, 61, 71; Confederation of Mexican Workers, 192; containment of, 62, 95–97, 217; corporate cooperation with, 19; decertification of, 61; decline of, 11, 153–154; future revitalization of, 217–218; International Association of Machinists and Aerospace Workers, 164; International Ladies Garment Workers Union, 190; moderation of, 10; NLRB appeals, 171; North American Free Trade Agreement, 193, 197; political influence of, 183, 221n29; in the post–World War I era, 21–22; in the post–World War II era, 30–31, 60–61, 71; Railway, Airline and Steamship Clerks, 164; restrictive monetary policy and, 163; self-limiting of, 153; threat to profit margins from, 5; United Auto Workers (UAW), 185; in Western Europe, 31, 33, 61
Labor-intensive manufacturing, 6, 22, 34n4
Laffer, Arthur, 142
Laffer Curve, 168
Landon, Alfred, 26, 110
Latin America: AFL-CIO union-busting in, 96, 217; capital flight from, 174; Fortune 500 companies in, 21; German exports to, 28, 29; market development in, 108; parts production in, 162; tariff barriers, 19; U.S. direct investment in, 46, 191
Leach, Paul, 148
League of Nations, 18
Leigh and Milliken, 209
Lend-lease, 28
Lending, 50, 88
Lessdeveloped world: East-West competition in, 57; IMF loans to, 149; market development in, 108; need for development in, 150; reduction of investment in, 130; strategic materials from, 54–55
Lewis, John L., 61
Libby, McNeil and Libby, 94
Liberal decline, 9, 153–157, 213–214

Liberal internationalism, 17–18, 74–75, 129–132, 161, 215–216
Liberal nationalism, 216–217
Liberty League, 20
Lippmann, Walter, 203, 204
Lockheed, 178, 183
Lodge, Henry Cabot, 59, 110
Lott, Trent, 208
Low Income Energy Assistance, 170
Loyalty tests, 71
Lugar, Richard, 209
Luxembourg, 77

MacArthur Foundation, 184
MacArthur, Gen. Douglas, 58, 67
McCann-Erickson, 94
McCarthy, Joseph, 58, 59, 88, 131
McCloy, John J., 91
McDonnell-Douglas, 178
McGovern Commission, 213
McKinley, William, 101n25
McNamara, Robert, 106
MacNelly, 217
McQuaid, Kim, 73, 95
McWilliams, Wilson Carey, 203–204
Malaysia, 188, 189
Mandel, Ernest, 129
Mansbach, Richard, 218
Manufacturers Hanover Trust, 142, 172, 200n39
Manufacturing Chemists Association, 111
Mao Tse-tung, 129
Marcantonio, Vito, 71, 100n12
Marshall, George, 51
Marshall, T. H., 96
Marshall Plan: business conflict and the, 51–56; business internationalist support for, 7, 20, 76; establishment of, 38, 42; guidelines for lending by, 52–53; nationalist opposition to, 39, 55–56
Martin, William McChesney, 49
Matsushita, 186
Mayo, Robert, 139
Maytag, Fred, II, 117
Meany, George, 95–96, 153
Medicaid, 4, 210
Merelman, Richard, 212
Mexico: Auto manufacturing in, 191–194; debt crisis, 174, 200n39; lending of petrodollars to, 165; parts manufacture in, 181; U.S. production facilities in, 12, 187
Middle East, 9, 12, 165–166, 179
Military contractors, 9
Military spending: balance-of-payments and, 129; in the Carter era, 165–166, 176; in the Clinton era, 13, 204–205; for the

Cold War, 71–72; economic benefits and liabilities of, 70–71; as economic waste, 69; in the Eisenhower era, 68, 88; in Germany, 69; impact on U.S. dollar of, 8; inflation from increases in, 71; in the Johnson era, 118–119; for the Korean War, 71; labor-intensive business support for, 31; military aid to Western Europe, 45, 76–77; NSC 68 and, 38, 39, 46, 47, 58, 69; in the Reagan era, 11–12, 166, 175–180; during recessions, 31; rise in, 150; southern support for, 59–60; for strategic materials, 83; in the Truman era, 39, 47, 57, 58, 68–69; for a two-war strategy, 204

Milliken, Roger, 152, 209

Mills, Wilbur, 109

Minnesota Mining & Manufacturing (3M), 94

Minsky, Herman, 121

Mitsubishi, 186

Mobil Oil, 176, 177

Monetarism, 50

Monetary policies, 75; tight money, 81, 168, 171–172, 174–175, 200n40

Moody, Kim, 217

Morgan, Iwan W., 76

Morgan, J. P., 21

Morgan Guaranty Trust, 142, 172, 200n39

Motorola, 178

Multilateralists, 166–167, 180–181, 183, 194–197

Multinational corporations: access to cheaper capital by, 128; in the Caribbean Basin, 187–190; conservative, 153, 157; financing of, 124, 125, 126–127; petrodollars for expansion of, 165; reliance on the nation-state of, 3; U.S.-based, 119

Muskie, Edmund, 145

Mutual Security Administration, 76

MX missile, 176, 177

Nader, Ralph, 216

Nasser, Gamal Abdul, 129

National Association of Manufacturers (NAM): aid programs for Europe, 46; Bretton Woods, 49; business nationalist orientation of, 68; Council for a Union Free Environment, 164; Marshall Plan, 54; New Deal opposition, 20, 22; North American Free Trade Agreement, 197; Social Security, 73; tariffs, 18, 111; taxation, 115–116, 117, 169; tight money policy, 174; trade reorganization, 156

National Association of Wheat Growers, 195

National Federation of Independent Business (NFIB), 134n31, 164

National Foreign Trade Council, 107

National Labor Relations Board (NLRB), 171

National Machine Tool Builders' Association (NMTBA), 182

National Metal Trades Association, 25

National Planning Association, 93, 149

National Recovery Administration (NRA), 23

National Right-to-Work Committee, 164

National Security Council: Document No. 68, 38, 39, 46, 47, 58, 69; Document No. 162/2, 69; import restrictions, 83; tight money policy, 172

National Strategy Information Center, 178

Nationalization, 33

Nau, Henry, 172

Nazis, 29

Nehru, Jawaharlal, 129

Neoliberalism, 11, 68, 128, 215

Netherlands, 77

New Deal: banking provisions, 81; business supporters and opponents of, 6, 19; coalition for the, 20–26; statist vs. societal approach to, 34n12; two periods of, 23, 27

New Economic Policy (NEP), 132, 133n22, 143–144

New York Times, 26, 91, 125

Nicaragua, 165, 207

Nixon, Richard: appeal to Democrats of, 151; attack on big government, 4; China, 145, 146; dollar stability, 99; economic policy contradictions of, 138, 213–214; Jackson-Vanik amendment, 153; move to the right of, 152; trade and fiscal policy, 105; Vietnam war, 131; Watergate, 144–147

Nixon administration: balance-of-payments, 127–128; Bretton Woods, 142–143; business conflict and, 144–147; capital controls, 131, 132, 137–141; détente, 131; foreign direct investment, 137; southern strategy, 152

Nkrumah, Kwame, 129

North American Free Trade Agreement (NAFTA): auto and electronic firms support for, 187, 191–194; environmental issues, 216; internationalist support for, 167, 184; multilateralism in the wake of, 194–197; nationalist opposition to, 167; passage of, 6, 206; protectionism, 194–197; regionalist support for, 181, 194–197; relocation of U.S. production under, 12; Republican opponents of, 13, 207

North Atlantic Treaty Organization
(NATO): European expenditures for, 124;
German membership in, 77; military aid
to, 38, 76, 91; Soviet gas pipeline, 183
Nuclear weapons, 176

O'Connor, James, 12
Odell, John S., 195
Offe, Claus, 96
Office of Civil and Defense Mobilization
(OCDM), 83
Office of Foreign Direct Investment, 140
Office of Price Administration (OPA), 60
Office of Technology Assessment, 171
Office of the U.S. Trade Representative,
155
Oil Import Administration, 92
Oil industry, 92, 109–110, 164, 179, 204
Oil shock, 11, 128, 132, 151
Olin Foundation, 197n1
Open shop laws, 61
Organic intellectuals, 75
Organization for Economic Cooperation and
Development (OECD), 141, 143, 219
Organization for European Economic
Cooperation (OEEC), 52, 55–56
Organization of Petroleum Exporting
Countries (OPEC), 128, 150

Pan American Airlines, 47
Parts production, 121, 162, 181
Peabody, George Foster, 26
Perkins, George, 76
Permanent arms economy, 68–71
Perón, Juan, 129
Perot, Ross, 4, 197, 207, 216
Peterson, Howard C., 106, 108, 111, 112
Petrodollars, 165
Petroleum Study Committee, 110
Philip Morris, 211
Philippines, 189
Phillips, Kevin, 207
Phoenix Rubber, 78
Plumley, Ladd, 116
Point Four, 57
Poland, 29
Political economy: of Bretton Woods,
42–47; of Congressional districts, 39, 46;
of internationalist-nationalist divide,
81–89; of the Kennedy-Johnson era, 105;
of macroeconomic management, 72; of
military spending, 175–180; the product
life cycle and, 40–42; of Reaganomics,
167–175; reconfiguration of, 148; of
trade, 180–184; war budget effect on, 62;
of Western Europe, 44–45
Post-Fordism, 12

Poverty, 170
Preeg, Ernest, 193
Price controls, 11, 23, 67, 71, 137, 144
Price supports, 81, 91
Privatization, 171
Product life cycle, 38–39, 40–42, 43
Production strategies, 184–185, 187, 191
Productionism, 50
Productivity, 148
Profit, 162
Progressive Party, 61, 100n12
Protectionism, 83, 92, 108–109, 131, 175,
194–197
Protectionist firms, 180, 181–183

Quadagno, Jill, 25

Racism, 151
Radford, Adm. Arthur, 69
Randall Commission, 90
Randolph, A. Philip, 96
Rapid Deployment Force, 179
Rashish, Myer, 114, 133n11
Rationing, 72
Rawls, John, 206
Rayburn, Sam, 75
Reagan, Ronald: challenge to Ford by, 149;
election of, 151, 197n1, 214
Reagan administration: business conflict
under, 166–167, 214; Caribbean Basin
Initiative, 188; military buildup, 166,
175–180; tight money policy, 172,
174–175; trade liberalization, 180
Reagan revolution, 11–12, 161–167
Reaganomics, 167–175
Recessions: in the Bush era, 204; Keynesian
tools against, 75; lower interest rates and,
72; Marshall Plan and, 56; military
spending and, 31; of 1974–1975, 144;
restrictive monetary policy and, 163
Regan, Donald, 172
Regionalists, 166–167, 180, 181, 194–197,
216
Regulation: in the Nixon era, 138; in the
Reagan era, 166, 170; standardization of,
19; threat to profit margins from, 5
Reich, Robert, 205, 217
Republican Party: angry white males in, 4,
15n11; conservative coalitions in, 4;
military spending, 58, 130; nationalist-
internationalist split in, 79, 81; North
American Free Trade Agreement, 13,
207; protectionist interests in, 183;
southern base of, 208; winning of 1946
election, 57
Ribicoff, Abraham, 156
Right-to-work laws, 95, 162, 163

Rockefeller, David, 108
Rockefeller, John D., 21
Rockefeller Brothers Fund, 99, 184
Rockefeller Foundation, 183, 184
Rockefeller Group, 78
Roosa, Robert, 122, 146–147
Roosevelt, Franklin D., 18, 90
Roosevelt Administration, 23, 27
Ross, Robert, 191
Roth, William, 156
Rural Electrification Administration, 24
Rusk, Dean, 105–106

St. Regis Paper, 156
Sanyo, 186
Saulnier, Raymond, 97
Saunders, Stuart, 116
Savings and loan bailout, 12
Scheer, Robert, 178
Schilling, Austrian, 127
Schlesinger, Arthur, 105
Schultze, Charles, 151
Scofield, Jerri-Lynn, 145, 153
Scott, Jeffrey, 192
Scripps-Howard papers, 26
Seagram and Sons, 211
Selig, Stephen, 155
Senate, U.S.: Appropriations Committee,
    83, 88; Bretton Woods, 50; Finance
    Committee, 148; trade barriers, 155
Sharp, 186
Shell Oil Co., 164
Shepherd, William, 120–121
Shultz, George, 128, 139
Simon, William, 148, 149, 168, 197n1
Sloan, John W., 69, 75, 97
Small business, 6
Small Business Administration, 109
Smithsonian Agreements, 1974–1975, 9
Social conservatism, 11, 216
Social Security, 72–74
Social Security Administration (SSA), 73
Social welfare programs: in the Clinton era,
    206, 210, 216; Kennedy downplaying of,
    114; labor-intensive business opposition
    to, 22; military spending as, 7; Reagan-
    era cuts in, 170; War on Poverty, 118–
    119
Sony, 186
South Carolina, 208–209
South Korea, 189
Soviet Union: gas pipeline, 183; growth
    rate, 99; Jewish emigration, 153;
    macroeconomic growth rates of, 68; trade
    with, 93, 131, 151; U.S. competition
    with, 77, 78; U.S. investment in, 145
Spang, Joseph, Jr., 91

Sputnik, 99
Stagflation, 147, 151
Standard Oil, 29, 47
Standard Oil of California, 94
Standard Oil of New Jersey, 78, 89, 94
Stans, Maurice, 139, 140
State Department, U.S., 44–45; bilateral
    economic aid, 50–51; European recovery,
    79; foreign market access, 90; German
    rearmament, 77; McCarthyite purge of,
    68; Marshall Plan, 52; military spending,
    177; productionist approach to lending,
    50
Stevens, Robert T., 89–90
Stevenson, Adlai, 106, 114
Stockman, David, 173
Strategic Arms Limitation Treaty (SALT II),
    177
Strategic materials, 54–55, 83
Strikes, 23, 30, 60–61, 71
"Studies of American Interests in War and
    the Peace," 27, 43
Subsidies, 81, 91
Sullivan and Cromwell, 89
Switzerland, 182–183
Swope, Gerard, 24, 25, 26

Taft, Robert, 30, 59, 67, 207
Taiwan, 57, 58, 182, 189
Tariffs: on carpets, 110; conflicts in the
    1930s over, 2, 19; countervailing duties,
    155, 182; with Eastern bloc countries, 93;
    in the Eisenhower era, 90–92; in Europe,
    43, 53; peril point procedure, 118;
    134n51; raising of, 18, 111; in the
    Reagan era, 175; on sheet glass, 110; on
    textiles and apparel, 190; on U.S.–
    Western European trade, 107
Taxation, 114–117, 134n38, 207; cuts in,
    166, 168–169, 210; Interest Equalization
    Tax (IET), 121–122, 125, 137, 140; of
    U.S. bond interest, 174
Temple-Eastex, 176
Tennessee Valley Authority (TVA), 24
Texaco, 164, 177
Texas Instruments, 188
Textile Advisory Committee, 109
Textiles, 92, 108–109, 131, 133n11, 155,
    182
Thailand, 189
Third world. See Less developed world
Thurmond, Strom, 152
Time, 184
Tolchin, Susan, 203
Toshiba, 186
Townsend-Greenspan, 142
Trachte, Kent, 191

Trade: deficits, 128, 132; in the Eisenhower era, 90–93; expansion, 105–111; liberalization, 149, 152, 180–184, 209; policy framework for promotion of, 41; regional agreements for, 187, 193; reorganization, 155, 156, 157

Trade barriers: Bretton Woods approach to, 28, 42, 43; erected by NAFTA, 193; intra-European, 76, 93; Marshall Plan approach to, 55–56

Trailor, 94

Treasury, U.S. Department of the: balance-of-payments, 98, 127; bond issues, 72; capital controls, 44, 45, 139; Eurodollar market, 122; European recovery, 79; International Monetary Fund, 48; loss of international trade decision-making, 155; Marshall Plan, 52, 53; monetarist approach to international lending, 50; protection for textile industry, 109; taxation, 174

Trilateral Commission, 174

Truman, Harry S, 58, 60

Truman administration: China, 57; European integration, 78, 89; European recovery, 79; internationalist policies of, 67, 76; internationalist-nationalist split, 81–82, 84–88; Korean War, 58, 100n12; Marshall Plan, 55, 56; military spending increases in, 39, 47, 57, 58, 68–69; problems of, 71–72

Underconsumption, 95

Underinvestment, 148

Unemployment, 56, 137

Union Carbide, 29, 156

United Kingdom (U.K.): capital control programs, 123; deregulation of capital markets, 174; EEC membership, 79, 106; German rearmament, 77; labor unions, 33, 61; loans to, 20, 32–33; monetary stabilization, 32–33; nationalization in, 33; reduction of investment in, 125, 130; state financing of exports, 162; trade barriers, 28; U.S. replacement as hegemon, 27; U.S. support for economy of, 29

United Nations (UN), 207; Council on Trade and Development (UNCTAD), 150

United Parcel Service (UPS), 14, 217

Urfer, Richard, 140

Uruguay, 28

Uruguay Round, 12

U.S. Chamber of Commerce: capital controls, 139, 141; foreign direct investment, 160n74; North American Free Trade Agreement, 197; taxation, 115, 117, 169; tight money policy, 174; Trade Department proposal, 156; trade liberalization, 78, 99n2, 112; union-busting by, 164

U.S. Steel, 26

U.S. Tariff Commission, 127

U.S.-Mexico Business Council, 184

Van Der Pijl, Kees, 147

Vandenberg, Arthur, 59

Vanderbilt University, 210

Vickerman, John, 149

Vietnam war: business opposition to, 8, 130–131, 145; escalation of, 124; public opposition to, 10

Vinson, Carl, 109

Vogel, David, 113

Volcker, Paul, 143, 172, 175

Voluntary export restraint agreements, 182–183, 185, 186

Voting scores, 84–87

W. T. Waggoner Estates, 81

Wage controls, 11, 71, 137, 144

Walker, Charls, 168

Wall Street Journal, 125, 149

Wallace, George, 10

Wallace, Henry, 61, 71, 100n12

War, 56–57

War on Poverty, 118–119, 147

Waste, economic, 69

Water resources, 72

Watergate, 144–147

Watson, Tom, 145

Weiss, Linda, 215

Welfare state: in the Carter era, 161; and decline of U.S. capitalism, 147; and the deficit, 12; dismantling of the, 4; in the Eisenhower era, 72–73; war budget instead of, 62; in Western Europe, 154

West Germany. *See* Germany

Western Europe: capital controls in, 31–32, 44, 130, 162; dollar gap, 51, 55, 70; ending of investment in, 125, 130; foreign direct investment in, 42–44, 72; German war debts, 19; internationalism and, 7, 42–43, 46, 76–81, 93–95, 97; labor unions in, 31, 33, 61; the Left in, 29; military aid to, 45, 76–77; nationalism in, 29; postwar revitalization of, 18, 79; regionalist institutions in, 43; tariffs in, 43, 53, 107; U.S.-owned production facilities in, 162; World Bank loans to, 48. *See also* Europe

Western European Union (WEU), 77

Westinghouse, 21, 47, 107

White, Harry Dexter, 48, 59

White, Ogden, 150
Wilkie, Wendell, 61
Wilkins, Mira, 63*n*11
Wilson, Arnold, 54
Wilson, Charles E., 89
Winchester, Lucy, 146
Women, 10, 208
Woodward, Bob, 144
World Bank: business internationalist support for, 7, 20; establishment of, 38, 39, 42; guidelines for lending by, 47–48; labor strength during, 30; Latin American debt, 175; loans to Western Europe, 48
World Trade Organization, 206

World War I, 18–19, 21
World War II: German trade restrictions as a motive for, 29; popular support for, 203; role of the Left in, 35*n*38; U.S. economy in, 6–7
Wrather, Jack, 197*n*1
Wrigley, 94
Wriston, Walter, 172
Wynne, Carl M., 49

Xerox, 183

Young, Milton, 88

Zenith, 186

About the Book

This thoughtful, highly original book investigates the influence of globalization on ideology and politics in the United States. Ronald Cox and Daniel Skidmore-Hess argue that U.S. policy has been motivated less by anxiety about the independence and stability of the domestic economy and more by worry about factors that might limit the participation of U.S. corporations in international markets. Connecting trends in domestic and foreign policy with the changing needs of industry, they associate increased globalization with the the breakup of the liberal, New Deal coalition; the collapse of the Bretton Woods Agreement in the 1970s; the neoconservative, antiregulatory movements of the 1980s; and the rightward drift of both the Republican and Democratic Parties.

Ronald W. Cox is associate professor of political science at Florida International University. His publications include *Power and Profits: U.S. Policy in Central America* and *Business and the State in International Politics*. **Daniel Skidmore-Hess** is assistant professor of political science at Armstrong Atlantic State University.